MEDIEVAL WEAPONS

Other Titles in ABC-CLIO's

WEAPONS AND WARFARE SERIES

MEDIEVAL WEAPONS

AN ILLUSTRATED HISTORY
OF THEIR IMPACT

Kelly DeVries

Robert D. Smith

A B C ☰ C L I O

Santa Barbara, California • Denver, Colorado • Oxford, England

Copyright 2007 by ABC-CLIO, Inc.

Library of Congress Cataloging-in-Publication Data
DeVries, Kelly, 1956–
Medieval weapons : an illustrated history of their impact /
Kelly DeVries and Robert D. Smith.
p. cm. — (Weapons and warfare series)
Includes bibliographical references and index.
ISBN-10: 1-85109-526-8 (hard copy : alk. paper)
ISBN-10: 1-85109-531-4 (ebook)
ISBN-13: 978-1-85109-526-1 (hard copy : alk. paper)
ISBN-13: 978-1-85109-531-5 (ebook)
1. Military weapons—Europe—History—To 1500.
2. Military art and science—Europe—History—Medieval, 500-1500.
I. Smith, Robert D. (Robert Douglas), 1954–   II. Title.

U810.D48 2007
623.4094'0902—dc22
2006102102

11   10   09   08   07   10   9   8   7   6   5   4   3   2   1

Production Editor: Vicki Moran
Editorial Assistant: Sara Springer
Production Manager: Don Schmidt
Media Editor: J. R. Withers
Media Resources Coordinator: Ellen Brenna Dougherty
Media Resources Manager: Caroline Price
File Management Coordinator: Paula Gerard

This book is also available on the World Wide Web as an eBook.
Visit abc-clio.com for details.
ABC-CLIO, Inc.
130 Cremona Drive, P.O. Box 1911
Santa Barbara, California 93116–1911
This book is printed on acid-free paper. ∞
Manufactured in the United States of America

CONTENTS

INTRODUCTION TO
WEAPONS AND WARFARE SERIES

WEAPONS BOTH FASCINATE AND REPEL. They are used to kill and maim individuals and to destroy states and societies, and occasionally whole civilizations, and with these the greatest of man's cultural and artistic accomplishments. Throughout history tools of war have been the instruments of conquest, invasion, and enslavement, but they have also been used to check evil and to maintain peace.

Weapons have evolved over time to become both more lethal and more complex. For the greater part of human existence, combat was fought at the length of an arm or at such short range as to represent no real difference; battle was fought within line of sight and seldom lasted more than the hours of daylight of a single day. Thus individual weapons that began with the rock and the club proceeded through the sling and boomerang, bow and arrow, sword and axe, to gunpowder weapons of the rifle and machine gun of the late nineteenth century. Study of the evolution of these weapons tells us much about human ingenuity, the technology of the time, and the societies that produced them. The greater part of technological development of weaponry has taken part in the last two centuries, especially the twentieth century. In this process, plowshares have been beaten into swords; the tank, for example, evolved from the agricultural caterpillar tractor. Occasionally, the process is reversed and military technology has impacted society in a positive way. Thus modern civilian medicine has greatly benefited from advances to save soldiers' lives, and weapons technology has impacted such areas as civilian transportation or atomic power.

Weapons can have a profound impact on society. Gunpowder weapons, for example, were an important factor in ending the era of the armed knight and the Feudal Age. They installed a kind of rough democracy on the battlefield, making "all men alike tall." We can only wonder what effect weapons of mass destruction (WMD) might have on our own time and civilization.

This series will trace the evolution of a variety of key weapons systems, describe the major changes that occurred in each, and illustrate and identify the key types. Each volume begins with a description of the particular weapons system and traces its evolution, while discussing its historical, social, and political contexts. This is followed by a heavily illustrated section that is arranged more or less along chronological lines that provides more precise information on at least eighty key variants of that particular weapons system. Each volume contains a glossary of terms, a bibliography of leading books on that particular subject, and an index.

Individual volumes in the series, each written by a specialist in that particular area of expertise, are as follows:

Aircraft Carriers
Ancient Weapons
Artillery
Ballistic Missiles
Battleships
Cruisers and Battle Cruisers
Destroyers
Helicopters
Machine Guns
Medieval Weapons
Military Aircraft, Origins to 1918
Military Aircraft, 1919–1945
Military Aircraft in the Jet Age
Pistols
Rifles
Submarines
Tanks

We hope that this series will be of wide interest to specialists, researchers, and even general readers.

Spencer C. Tucker
Series Editor

INTRODUCTION TO
MEDIEVAL WEAPONS

Whatever one's political or personal feelings, it is undeniable that warfare is endemic in the cultures of the world—people have always fought one another for power, prestige, property, and/or influence. Into the past, one can trace the development of warfare from individual combat, warrior to warrior, to conflicts fought at greater and greater distances. Flint arrowheads and knives became bronze spearheads and axes, which became iron swords and crossbow bolts, which became pikes and guns, which became today's advanced weapon systems designed to hit targets at long distance—attacking from tens of miles away or, with intercontinental missiles, from across the globe. This book will outline the weapons used from the fall of the Roman Empire to the Renaissance—from the spear and sword to the handgun and from the mail shirt to the fully armored knight.

It is sometimes said that warfare is the force that drives technology as man's desire to constantly improve weapons and protection from attack is the primary impetus for change. While this need to constantly find better forms of attacking one's enemy and protecting oneself has been a major spur to change, it would be wrong to believe there is a direct and deterministic link. Advances in technology were, of course, exploited by the military and used wherever possible, but it is incorrect to believe the two were inextricably linked. Only occasionally, for example the development of cast-iron cannon in England in the 1540s, are there explicit examples of the desire to develop technologies for warlike purposes, and here it is doubtful whether the change was an "improvement" or was driven by economic and monetary ends. It is true, however, to say that weapons and technology did, and still do, have many links and connections, which make a study of the two important.

Cave paintings, the earliest illustrations of man's behavior, show early man armed with a variety of weapons. While it is true that most of these are hunting scenes, showing man against beast, some depict men fighting men suggesting that warfare has been endemic since the dawn of time. In these illustrations the soldiers, to use the term that would later be applied to their occupation, are armed with spears, clubs, and rudimentary bows, a means of fighting wars that would remain unchanged until the large-scale adoption of gunpowder weapons after 1500. The weapons themselves improved and diversified, and some soldiers would become specialists, including those who fought on mounts—horses, camels, and elephants—but essentially the categories of weapons remained the same: handheld weapons and close-range and long-range missile weapons.

As warfare became more and more common, these earliest humans, who seem, like their descendants, to have been especially partial to hand-to-hand combat, the desire for increased defense developed. Protection of the vulnerable torso and head encouraged the development of armor. Although not often depicted, a few cave paintings show soldiers who are outfitted with thicker articles of clothing and headwear than others, which some have described as wicker or bark armor. A natural progression to portable defenses, or shields, seems to have followed shortly.

Emerging from the ancient world was the largest political entity before the modern era, the Roman Empire. Rome extended its boundaries beyond Italy throughout the Mediterranean, the Middle East, and Western Europe using armies of unparalleled size and strength to overwhelm previous inhabitants, and using weapons and armor hardly changed in purpose from those seen in the cave paintings. But these arms and armor, tied into a system of economic unity and prosperity and combined with a strong centralized political and military control, good leadership, and discipline, enabled the Romans to create military forces, both regular and irregular armies, that were able to conquer their opponents, even those using similar weapons. When breakdown did occur, the "fall" of the Roman Empire was similarly not tied to the superior use of military technology by those who defeated Rome, but to a collapse of that central Roman control and military unity, discipline, and leadership.

From the remnants of the Western Roman Empire—the Eastern became the Byzantine Empire—grew Western Europe's medieval kingdoms. These first appeared as tribal states named after their barbarian conquerors—Ostrogothic Italy, Visigothic Spain, Frankish Gaul—and later, after the division of Charlemagne's united kingdom by his grandsons, into the Holy Roman Empire (Germany), France, the Italian States, and the Low Countries, with bordering lands—England, Spain, and Scandinavia—militarily, diplomatically, and economically tied to them.

What the fall of the Roman Empire does mark is a transition in the population of Europe. For the next few centuries interactions between migrating peoples took the form of warfare, initially with the invasions of large barbarian forces and their families from over the Rhine and Danube Rivers and across the North Sea, and then with the settlement raids of Vikings, Hungarians, and Muslims. By the turn of the first millennium, the borders of Europe had been redrawn, and the earlier migrating peoples had become "Europeans." Confident in their civilization and religion, these Europeans convinced themselves to combine their militaries in purpose and leadership to attempt to retake the Holy Land and Spain from the Muslims who had occupied them for close to 500 years. In Spain, the crusades eventually removed Muslims from control, although not before 1492. But in the Middle East they were doomed to failure as local jealousies and national self-interests took their toll. There followed a period of intense internal strife and inter-European state conflict that marks the traditional division between the Middle Ages and the Early Modern period, even though it did not end in 1500 and, indeed, continued into the twentieth century.

ACKNOWLEDGMENTS

THIS BOOK COULD NOT HAVE BEEN written without the help and assistance of many colleagues and friends who, over the years, have been instrumental in the development of the knowledge of the authors and to all we owe a debt of gratitude and friendship. Similarly, we must thank the many libraries and museums that have enabled us to broaden and sharpen our knowledge.

Particular thanks are due to Ruth Rhynas Brown who served as both the picture researcher as well as the provider of the support network that enabled the authors to work together. The Midgely family of Menston, West Yorkshire, once again opened their home and their hearts. And, finally, to Barbara Middleton who has always indulged the frequent overseas trips of her husband, Kelly, a special thanks is owed. No doubt she has also enjoyed the solitude and quiet!

CHAPTER ONE

The Early Middle Ages, 376–750

HISTORY

The relationship between those living within the borders of the Roman Empire and those living without was never peaceful. Even when Roman political and military leaders did not send armies into these neighboring lands with the intent to extend the Empire, its borders were never entirely secure. The wealth of the Roman Empire was coveted by those unable to take direct advantage of it. This led to frequent border raids, forcing the Romans to build an extensive series of fortifications along much of their borders and station a large military presence along them. Even when natural hindrances to military activity were present, such as the Rhine and Danube rivers, the Saharan and Asia Minor deserts, and the North Sea, fortifications were built and garrisoned.

At the best of times, a fragile peace was maintained. Sometimes barbarian peoples were even allowed inside the borders of the Roman Empire, to settle in less populated areas or on less habitable terrain and to serve in the military as mercenaries. They were known as *foederati,* or confederates, but it seems that their presence was never entirely welcomed, and they were almost always treated with suspicion by the Romans themselves. As early as the first century, the respected writer Tacitus reported on those who lived across the Rhine and Danube. Germans, as he called them in his work *Germania,* were hard-working, family-oriented people whose lack of civilization was more than made up for by their loyalty and military capabilities. They were to be feared, he warned in an almost prophetic voice, because they would be a formidable foe should Rome continue to decline.

Tacitus did not identify these Germans by the names they would eventually become known to the Romans. Nor did he know of the existence of the non-German peoples who invaded their lands, pushing the Germans in a domino-like fashion, farther west and south. By the third century, however, most Romans knew about them as their raids became ever more frequent, and from 235 to 268 AD they penetrated deeper into once-secure Roman territory than ever before. With the death of Emperor Alexander Severus in 235 AD, stable government was replaced by military anarchy and administrative chaos. Emperors did not last long, meeting natural or unnatural deaths in quick succession. Frequently, one army and its candidate for emperor would march to Italy only to be opposed by another army with its contender candidate for emperor. The previously almost impervious defenses of the Empire were weakened and left open to raiding armies of barbarians determined to plunder the riches of the Empire. In 249, the Goths, a Germanic tribe from across the Danube, broke over the river and invaded the Balkans. In 256, the Franks, who lived across the Rhine, crossed it to attack Gaul, while at the same time the Saxons, also from the Germanic Rhineland, crossed the English Channel and raided the shores of Britain. The borders of the Empire were being challenged everywhere. In 256, the Borani, a tribe living in southern Russia, raided the eastern coast of the Black Sea, and in that same year the Sassanid Persians from Mesopotamia overran Armenia and Syria and in 260 even captured and imprisoned the inept Emperor Valerian. Sometimes the Romans were able to repulse these invasions, but their victories were too few to keep out the flood of barbarian tribes. By 262, the Goths had completely taken over northern Greece as far south as Athens, although they were not actually able to enter the town and were eventually driven back. In 268, another Germanic tribe, the Heruli, repeated the feat of the Goths, only this time capturing and sacking Athens.

Ultimately, such raids and invasions resulted in an examination of the Empire's defenses and military priorities. The province of Dacia (modern Romania), unprotected by natural boundaries, was abandoned. Fortifications along the borders were rebuilt and strengthened, and new walls were constructed to protect the larger, populated areas of the Roman Empire. This included building a fortified wall around Rome itself; the Aurelian wall, named after the emperor under whose initiative it was constructed, was 12 miles in circumference (20 kilometers), 12 feet thick (4 meters), and 20 feet high (6.5 meters). Designed not to withstand a lengthy siege, but to hold back a raid of barbarians, it included 31 fortified gates and towers, all equipped with artillery.

But the inexorable demise of Rome had begun. Despite what seemed like a sensible military reorganization and division of political power by Emperor Diocletian, the disagreements of his coemperors and successors led to years of civil war, which resulted in the removal of most Roman frontier troops. In 330, Constantine, the eventual winner of these conflicts, tried to bolster an Empire, that he in large part was to blame for weakening, by moving his capital away from Italy to the east, and rebuilding a small Asia Minor town, Byzantium, later to be called Constantinople. Did he believe the poorer, more vulnerable, western part of the Roman Empire could be allowed to fall to invaders while the richer, more defensible eastern part should be protected?

At Constantine's death in 337 the Empire still held together, though only tenuously. Forty years later, under Emperor Valens, the first group of barbarian tribes, the Visigoths, descendants of the third-century Goths who had invaded the Empire, successfully breached the Imperial defenses and remained, never to return or be forced back across the Danube River to their old lands. However, this breach was instigated in large part because of forces beyond the Visigoths or Romans. At some time during the middle of the fourth century, a new enemy of both emerged, the Huns. It is not known from where the Huns originated or why they chose to attack their neighbors at this time. It is usually thought that they originated in the steppe regions of Central Asia, and that they too were possibly being pushed out of their lands by the forces that would later be called the Mongols. The Huns not only attacked the Germanic tribes to their west and, eventually the Roman Empire, but they also went east and south, attacking China at about the same time. In the west, the attacks of the Huns pushed one tribe into another, eventually forcing the Visigoths into the Roman Empire.

In 376, the Visigoths found they had nowhere to go but into Roman lands. But they did not wish to do so by invasion. Instead, they petitioned Emperor Valens to allow them to cross over the Danube River and cultivate the wastelands of Thrace, and to become *foederati*. This request was not without precedent, nor could Valens easily turn it down, as refusal meant invasion rather than peaceful settlement. He agreed, but was unprepared for the large number who moved across the Danube as an estimated 200,000 Visigoths crossed into the Roman Empire. Perhaps as many as 50,000 settlers could have been fed from the Imperial stores, at least until their own crops came in, but 200,000 could not. Within two years the Visigoths were starving, becoming a military threat. In response, Valens collected his army from the east and marched against them without waiting for reinforcements from the west. At Adrianople (Hadrianople), on 9 August 378, the two armies clashed. The Romans were completely defeated, and Valens himself was killed. The Visigoths were free to settle wherever they wished.

Within twenty years other tribes, notably the Alans, Suevi, Vandals, and Ostrogoths, followed the lead of the Visigoths and crossed into the Empire. Others, such as the Burgundians, Alemanni, Franks, Angles, and Saxons, followed them. In 410, the Ostrogoths, led by Alaric, invaded and sacked Rome after a decade-long siege. Alaric set up his own Roman emperor, but in 476, after a series of weak and inept "puppet emperors" had quickly risen and just as quickly fallen, Romulus Augustulus, the last Western Roman emperor, was deposed by Odoacar the Ostrogoth.

Because the Huns were "not well suited to infantry battles, but . . . nearly always on horseback," according to the fourth-century writer Ammianus Marcellinus, it is often assumed that this was true of the other barbarian tribes, too. In addition, the infamy of the Huns, so often testified to by contemporary authors, has distorted the image of all barbarian tribes. However, although the Huns fought primarily on horseback, the Germanic tribes who overran the Rhine and Danube borders of the Empire from the fourth century on fought mainly on foot and had only small cavalry forces. In the Roman army the cavalry was filled mostly by non-Romans who served as auxiliaries, while the infantry, filled mostly by Roman citizens, undertook the primary battlefield fighting. In contrast, the mounted troops of barbarian armies performed the principal maneuvers on the battlefield.

It is evident that horses provided barbarian troops not only with their primary means of fighting, but they were also a mark of social distinction and class. For most barbarian tribes, those who could afford horses and were trained in using them provided the military and political leadership. In two of the earliest of their battles with the Romans, Visigothic cavalry, although few in number (How could the army have acquired a large number of horses when starvation was forcing the military conflict?) may even have been instrumental in deciding the outcome. In 378 at Dibaltum, a cavalry force delivered the decisive blow on a force of Romans who before then had been successful at withstanding infantry assaults. Even more impressive, in the midst of the battle of Adrianople, the Visigothic cavalry struck the rear of a weakened Roman left flank, crushing it and folding it onto the rest of the line, thereby greatly facilitating their victory.

However, before the end of the fifth century, the number of infantry in relation to cavalry had increased. Three theories for this are suggested. First, of course, cavalry required horses, and sometimes more than a single mount per soldier. These horses needed lots of pastures for grazing, lands that were readily available on the plains of the steppes, but not in Western Europe. Second, when not fighting against each other or against the Romans, barbarian soldiers often gained employment as mercenaries, in armies that were infantry-dominant, including those of the Empire. However, to make themselves more employable, they, too, had to learn to fight on foot. A final, perhaps more simple explanation of the transformation from cavalry to infantry may be that while the barbarians eventually conquered the Empire, it was a very lengthy campaign, with only a few military victories spaced out over more than two centuries of almost constant warfare. In truth, the Romans won more individual conflicts than they lost—although they lost the Western Empire, they held onto the Empire in the East—and these victories, which were brought about by infantry tactics, probably influenced barbarian military organization. All three of these explanations are probably correct in part, and all had the effect of decreasing the number of cavalry and increasing the number of infantry in early medieval barbarian armies.

There is also no doubt that Roman armies were influenced by those of the barbarians, and vice versa. This can be seen nowhere more clearly than in the generalship of the Roman army by Stilicho, himself a Vandal, or Aetius, who had spent his youth among the Ostrogoths and Huns. Both clearly prized their Roman military positions—and both also vied for political power in the Empire—but they also recognized the importance and, often, the superiority of barbarian strategy and tactics. The victory Aetius won over the Huns at the battle of Chalons in 451 is a good example. Realizing the need to stop the penetration of the Huns, led by Attila, further into Western Europe—they had most recently been besieging Orléans—Aetius used a personal bond of friendship and the fear of further incursions by the Huns in the west to make peace with the Visigoths in southeastern France and northern Spain. He then enticed them to join his army, an army composed of Alans, Ostrogoths, Visigoths,

Vandals, and even some Huns, although apparently few Romans. They were, however, supplied with Roman arms and armor. Aetius established a strong defensive position on terrain unfavorable to cavalry warfare and provoked his overly confident enemy to attack him. It became an infantry-on-infantry battle, much to the disadvantage of the cavalry-dominant Huns, who nevertheless fought with their customary spirit. In the end, the Romans and Visigoths prevailed, and Attila's conquest of Western Europe was halted. Had Aetius not used his own barbarian-filled forces, made an alliance with other barbarians, or known of his enemy barbarians' tactics, the battle of Chalons might have gone Attila's way, and the history of Europe would have been vastly changed.

What this means is that it is difficult to know exactly when the military of Western Europe ceased being "Roman" and became "barbarian." Certainly by the time of Chalons, the Roman army could no longer be called Roman, at least in ethnic makeup. On the other hand, as already noted, the barbarian armies adopted some Roman ways of fighting, as seen in their change to infantry-dominant tactics as used at Chalons and elsewhere. Over time, the number of barbarian invasions and migrations decreased, leading to further changes in strategy. By the end of the fifth century, the Ostrogoths had settled in Italy; the Visigoths had settled in Spain and southeastern Gaul; the Vandals controlled Egypt, northern Africa, and the islands of the central and western Mediterranean; the Alemanni and Burgundians had established themselves in eastern and Alpine Gaul and what would become Switzerland; the Franks had settled in Gaul, except for the part controlled by the Visigoths, Alemanni, and Burgundians; and the Angles and Saxons had settled in Britain. As barbarian peoples settled in new areas, they needed fewer horses for day-to-day life, and this had a consequent effect on the numbers of their cavalry troops.

The same question of the transformation from Roman to barbarian affects the political and economic history of the early Middle Ages as well. Historians often dwell on the weaknesses of Roman military power in the Western Empire, when in fact it may have been the erosion of political and economic power that was more decisive in the ultimate fall of Rome. As the Germanic invasions increased in intensity during the late fourth century and early fifth century, Roman politicians were unable to put their petty political squabbles behind them. This political infighting also affected military leaders and generals, who were frequently seen as a threat to their political masters. It was not uncommon for them to have to return to Rome or

Constantinople, often at the most inopportune time, to protect their positions. Even Aetius, fresh from his defeat of the Huns, did not escape Emperor Valentinian III's jealous wrath or dagger.

Of course, political instability had occurred in the earlier history of the Empire, although without the same dire consequences as later, due in large part to the strength of the Roman Imperial economy. It seems that as long as the wealth of the Empire and its citizens was preserved, it did not matter what the small minority of political leaders and officials did. Although invasions and raids naturally disrupted the economy, throughout the military problems of the third century, it remained strong. The Empire was even able to pay for the increased number of fortifications and troops employed at the end of the century.

This economic strength and stability changed in the wake of the constant invasions of the barbarians over the next two centuries. The sack of Rome in 410 produced an enormous quantity of booty, attesting to the wealth of the city's inhabitants. However, by the time the Vandals sacked Rome in 455, the chronicles report that only a silver bowl and a large menorah were taken. Elsewhere, invasions were also disrupting agriculture, industry, and trade. Armies trampled and burned farms and fields; pirates destroyed and robbed ships; miners abandoned mines; and merchants found it too risky to import goods, leaving shopkeepers with nothing to sell. Of all the disruptions brought about by the barbarian invasions, economic collapse clearly had the greatest impact on populations that had earlier been able to maintain themselves easily.

Barbarian occupation brought few immediate changes to Roman life, and most Romans seem to have simply accepted the new governments that were established. Part of this was undoubtedly because of the length of time it took for the barbarian kingdoms to take power from the fallen Empire. But part must also be attributed to the fact that few of the former inhabitants of the Empire had actually taken any role in its governance. There also seems to have been no great loss of population in either the rural or urban areas of Western Europe, with the exception of Rome itself, which saw a marked decline.

However, the barbarians brought two changes to Roman society that, while they did not initially alter the lives of the people they conquered, eventually changed the way they formed governments, recruited soldiers, and fought wars. Both were probably traditional to these Germanic tribes before they invaded the Empire, although there is no way of confirming this, and both differed considerably from what had been practiced in the Roman sphere of influence. The first was how leadership and property were passed down from father to son. In the Roman Empire the custom was primogeniture inheritance, with all property and titles passing from father to the eldest legitimate son, and, if no legitimate son was available, to an illegitimate or adopted son chosen by the father to succeed him. In contrast, the barbarian tradition was partible inheritance, which held that all property and leadership should be divided equally among all legitimate sons and, should the father choose, illegitimate sons as well. While seemingly more democratic and fair, this inheritance practice brought with it many problems. No matter how fathers tried to arrange the transfer of lands and titles—and the maps of some of these inheritances show some genuine attempts at equalizing wealth—it seems some sons always felt cheated by their brother or brothers. This often led to a volatile transfer of power, and sometimes outright civil war, and frequently to the assassination of one brother by another.

The second change introduced by the Germanic tribes who established the barbarian kingdoms of the early Middle Ages was in the recruitment and advancement of soldiers. No one in Germanic society was more respected than a warrior, nor was anyone deemed worth more in their legal codes. Generally, it was not difficult to find someone to serve in the military. But loyalty was a different matter. Once a soldier had distinguished himself in combat, the competence of his military abilities frequently brought offers from competing chiefs. How might a leader encourage that warrior to stay loyal to him? The answer lay in buying his services by rewarding him with land, titles, and awards, and thus creating an obligation to serve. In this way, a leader could ensure that a distinguished warrior and his personal retinue would be available to serve in his army whenever he was needed. Should that service not be provided, those lands and titles, all of which had originated from the leader's own holdings, would be forfeited back to him. In addition, because these lands came with laborers and peasants to work them, it was recognized that the landholder (or lord) would not be forced to do more than prepare for his required military service, in particular training himself and his retinue in the use of arms and in other military skills. Before the eighth century, variations of this tradition of military obligation could be found throughout the barbarian kingdoms of the Western Roman Empire, and, eventually, the families who held the lands and titles gained control of them, which led to the development of the medieval nobility.

During the invasion and occupation of the Western Roman Empire, the Eastern part, which later became known as the Byzantine Empire, remained militarily inactive. This came to an end, however, during the reign of Emperor Justinian, who ruled in Constantinople from 527 to 565. In 533, after securing his rise to and control of the Byzantine emperorship, Justinian decided to try to reacquire the lands of the Western Roman Empire. His first target was Vandal-controlled Egypt and North Africa. He sent an army of 10,000 infantry and 5,000 cavalry, mostly mercenaries, under the very capable generalship of Belisarius, and by March 534 Vandal power in North Africa had been destroyed, and the former provinces of Egypt and Africa had been restored to the Empire.

The following year Justinian sent his army, again under Belisarius, into Italy against the Ostrogoths. This reconquest took longer than it had in northern Africa; the Ostrogoths were then more united and were supported by the people. Rome held out against a Byzantine siege for more than a year before it fell in 538, and the Ostrogothic capital of Ravenna did not surrender until 540. A counterattack by the Ostrogoths regained Rome in 546, when Justinian was forced to pull out some of his army to respond to the Persians' attack and sack of Antioch in that year. But when they returned to Italy in 554, the kingdom was quickly restored to the Byzantines until Justinian's death in 565. This war destroyed Ostrogothic military and political power for good. However, Justinian's successors did not consider the occupation of Italy or of North Africa and Egypt to be important, and before long, Byzantine military numbers in those areas decreased as they became needed elsewhere. Italy fell to the Lombards and northern African and Egypt to the Arabs.

The Franks, one of the most northern of all the Germanic tribes, invaded the uppermost part of the Western Roman Empire in the fifth century. By that time the Romans had virtually abandoned that region; consequently, there was little resistance to their crossing of the Rhine River. In fact, this may have not been an invasion at all, at least not compared with the examples set by the Goths, Vandals, and Huns who had stormed across the Danube. Instead, the Franks seem to have lived side by side with the Romans in northern Gaul, fighting in their armies, living and working with them in their towns, and ultimately mixing with them in marriage and society. Within a very short time, they had colonized both sides of the middle Rhine River and were well on their way to acquiring the rest of Gaul. Yet, although initially peaceful in their crossing of the Rhine, they acquired Gaul by war and conquest.

These wars were fought principally by two of the most powerful Frankish military leaders. Childeric fought with the Romans against the Visigoths at Orléans in 463 and against the Saxons at Angers in 469. At the same time, he managed to carve out a fairly sizable territory, located around Tournai in what is now southern Belgium. The other was Childeric's son, Clovis, who in 486 conquered the Seine River valley by defeating his father's former allies, the Romans, at Soissons. In 491 he subjugated the Ripuarian Franks, in 496 he defeated the Alemanni at Tolbiac (modern Zülpich), and in 507 he crushed the Visigoths at Voulon. By then Clovis had conquered all of the lands of the old Roman province of Gaul and established the first Merovingian kingdom of the Franks. Perhaps even more importantly, in 496 he accepted baptism into Roman Christianity, becoming the first militarily powerful defender of Catholicism among the barbarians.

When Clovis died four years later, the Merovingian kingdom was the most powerful realm in Western Europe. But he had four sons, and, as barbarian tradition held, they divided their father's land among them. Immediately they began to fight each other, and thus a Merovingian tradition was born: the inheritance civil war. They fought one another for control of the whole kingdom—a common occurrence throughout the whole Merovingian period. Merovingian kings, and there were often many of them at the same time, were powerful and secure only when their army was strong and loyal. When it was not, an all-too-frequent situation, they did not last long, meeting untimely deaths as their lands were ravaged by warfare.

Had the Merovingian Franks had any significant outside enemies to face, their kingdoms may have fallen. In fact, the military security of the Merovingians was probably maintained by the nonroyal military lords, the majordomos (or mayor of the palace), who held subordinate positions to the king. The men who held these positions frequently wielded more power than did the kings. Three mayors were particularly important, those of Austrasia, Neustria, and Burgundy, and these positions were usually filled by three of the most prominent and powerful men of the kingdom. Of these the most important was the mayor of the palace of Austrasia, and in the second quarter of the seventh century this position was held by Pippin I. So powerful was he that at his death, in 640, he was easily able to pass his mayorship to his son, Grimoald, although there was no precedent for this. In 656 Grimoald, with equal ease, passed it on to his nephew, Pippin II. Pippin II was able to consolidate his power over the other two important mayoral positions by defeating them at the battle of Tertry in 687 before passing on all three mayorships to his illegitimate son, Charles Martel, in 714.

Charles Martel's biggest challenge came not from the Merovingian kings, whose power had been curtailed by their own rivalries and by Pippin I's union of the three most prominent mayoral positions, but from Muslim forces that had penetrated the Pyrenees from Spain and invaded southwestern Gaul. These armies succeeded in reaching as far north as Poitiers before they were soundly defeated in 732 by Charles Martel, who eventually drove them back into Spain. Historians also credit Charles Martel with the "modernization" of the Frankish army. He not only reorganized his troops and ensured that they were better armed, but he also formed a Frankish heavy cavalry.

By the time of Charles Martel's death in 741, the Merovingian throne had been vacant for four years. He had never seen fit to take over the empty throne; however, his son, Pippin III, did not hold such misgivings and in 751 assumed the throne, establishing a new dynasty, the Carolingians. Pippin III (known historically as Pippin the Short, from comparison with his son, Charlemagne, who was said to have been more than 6 feet tall, a height confirmed by the modern measurement of his bones) continued to strengthen the army and his kingdom until his death in 768, when his throne was inherited by one of the greatest military and political leaders of all time, Charlemagne.

During the early Middle Ages, Britain was as disunited politically and as frequently fought over as Merovingian Gaul, although this was not caused by the practice of partible inheritance. Roman military occupation, already declining throughout the fourth century, ceased entirely in the beginning of the fifth century, and the troops there were withdrawn to fight threats elsewhere in the Western Empire. For nearly a century after this, the Celtic inhabitants of what had been the province of Britannia were left to fend for themselves. There is little information about how well they fared, although invasions from north of Hadrian's Wall and across the North Sea are thought to have been frequent. The invasions of the Angles, Saxons, and Jutes were eventually successful, but not entirely and not immediately. Indeed, the tenacious defense by the people of Britain against these armies would later develop into the legends of King Arthur and his Knights of the Round Table.

The reason Britain was a target of raids from Saxony and the Jutland peninsula is not known. Some have suggested that Angle and

Saxon *foederati* on their own had been left behind to guard the province during the Roman withdrawal, and that they then turned on the people they were supposed to be protecting. Others follow more closely the story recounted by the seventh-century historian Bede of the Saxon brothers, Hengist and Horsa. Invited by one of the British leaders, Vortigern—described by Bede as a *tyrannus* or tyrant—to support his attempts at increasing his power, Hengist and Horsa landed with their forces in 449. Within six years they had turned against their host and defeated him—although Horsa was himself slain in the conflict. Hengist then turned against the other British chiefs who, unable to unite, were defeated one by one by the Saxons. By 488, when Hengist's son, Æsc, assumed the throne of Kent, it had become apparent that the Saxons were in Britain to stay, and were followed by the Angles and Jutes.

However, warfare did not end with the arrival of the barbarians in England. Until the invasion of Swein Forkbeard in 1014, his third invasion of England, the Anglo-Saxons were never united. However, it must be admitted, the paucity of sources means that many details of these wars are lost, including sometimes the most basic facts, such as who fought whom, where, as well as the result. The Viking raids, beginning at the end of the eighth century, were no doubt the worst of these wars, but even before these occurred, raids from the Scots and the Welsh were frequent and brutal, and conflict between the various British kingdoms was no less ruthless and cruel.

Because of the lack of sources for the period—one is forced to rely mostly on narrative histories and hagiographies written by churchmen—it is not known how armies in the former Roman Empire changed and became "medieval." One theory is that this transformation was slow and developmental, with barbarian military leaders and soldiers either serving in or influenced by Roman armies and slowly adopting their organization, strategy and tactics, and arms and armor. Eventually, as they had throughout their long history, Roman armies changed, taking on what historians would later see as an early medieval character. However, as with all armies throughout history, no aspect of these early medieval armies stayed static: their organization, strategy and tactics, and arms and armor all changed to face new threats and fit new fashions. Nor did any of these changes bring standardization to early medieval armies; such a concept was virtually unknown in preindustrial societies, although both the Roman and Carolingian empires set regulations as to how units must be organized; how campaigns, battles, and sieges must be carried out; and what must be worn and carried.

MILITARY ORGANIZATION

It has been usual to suggest that the military forces that made up barbarian armies were very different from those of Imperial Rome. The latter depended on the existence of large, standing, professional armies, maintained by state finances, and led by officers, many of whom had risen to those ranks through lengthy service, but who were themselves responsible to a central military and political bureaucracy. Barbarian kingdoms, it is argued, did not have standing armies. Although armies were frequently raised, they tended to be smaller and organized in smaller units than their Roman counterparts. They were also not paid out of state coffers, but by personal arrangement with or obligation to their leaders.

The system of obligation between leader and soldier is a disputed one. The sociological paradigm known as feudalism has lost favor among modern historians, largely because it was a general description for all of medieval society's obligations, military and nonmilitary, between all levels of the nobility and vassals of every rank. The justifiable rejection of this paradigm for early medieval society at large has resulted in its dismissal as an explanation for how armies at the time were raised and organized. While feudalism is probably not the correct definition for the recruitment commitments of early medieval soldiers, nonetheless there does seem to have been an obligation to serve between soldiers and their leaders, whether based on land holdings—which became the norm—or some other socioeconomic medium. This was a time, after all, when the warrior was deemed to be legally the top of the societal hierarchy, expressed in his extremely high wergild, literally man-price, meaning that it would cost the assailant of such a man an extremely large amount of money if he killed him. Being a warrior, or striving to become one, naturally drove a certain segment of the male population to military service.

When this failed to provide enough soldiers, others were called upon to fill the ranks. Many surviving legal codes indicate a general obligation of all "free" able-bodied men to be prepared for military service to their king, should he summon them, to provide their own arms and armor, and to serve him throughout the entirety of an expedition or campaign. Ignoring such service incurred severe punishments, and, in fact, it appears that most military leaders had no problem finding men to serve in time of conflict. Should a leader experience such difficulty, he was generally not a leader for long. In reality it was rare, if ever, that the lower classes or peasants were ever called upon to serve. They were, after all, needed to maintain agriculture and the economy on which it was based. As they had little chance to train, they did not make good warriors. So, most often they served as the militia, whose service was restricted to defending their homes and the lands of their lords.

The result of this was that, in essence, by the seventh century, the professional medieval soldier had come into existence—financially able to purchase arms and armor, if not also horses, and to have the time to train. A military hierarchy or nobility developed that was different from that of the Romans or even from that of the earlier barbarians. At least initially, ethnic designations still held sway, with soldiers fighting in the company of other tribal members, but as language, customs, and loyalties became more unified, even this distinction disappeared. Soon a wealthy elite class, trained to fight wars for their social betters, provided the bulk of the armies. With them came their retinues, men connected to them by similar obligations. More "professional," to use a modern term, they would campaign whenever their leaders required, and when they were not involved in offensive military operations they would defend their own and their leaders' lands. Although not knights by later medieval chivalric definitions—those required a ceremonial "dubbing," heraldry, and other traditions—their skill in arms and armor and their professionalism in tactics and strategy set them on a path toward that medieval historical reality.

The rise of a military nobility quickly led to the development of fortifications, especially along the oft-disputed and frequently changing borders and frontiers. Fortifications built in stone were far in the future, but an earth-and-wood *castrum* or *castellum* still provided protection to those who were or could get inside as well as an offensive impediment to any invading force not able to conquer it. Siege machines were available, although there is a question as to whether they were the same as those used by the Romans. More often, besiegers had to rely on forcing the inhabitants of such fortifications to surrender by starvation or treachery. Both required time, sometimes longer than a year, and often an invading army would decide that such an expenditure of time was not worth the effort.

Anglo-Saxon England in this, as in so many early medieval military matters, was different. Obligations to serve in the military differed from those of continental Europe, as did the number, experience, and prowess of professional military soldiers. No doubt part of the reason for this lies in the development of a different political and economic structure in Anglo-Saxon society. Some have also suggested that the peaceful conditions prevalent in England after the conquest by the Anglo-Saxons did not foster the rise of a military elite or the development of a class of society who had obligations to serve. Perhaps this, more than anything, explains why the namesake hero of *Beowulf,* the greatest Old English poetic epic, is a Geat, from southern Sweden, and not from Anglo-Saxon England. However, the idea that England was peaceful at that time may simply be attributable to our lack of contemporary sources.

Of course, there were military conflicts in Anglo-Saxon England. Before the Viking invasions at the very end of the eighth century and the attacks on its seacoasts and riverbanks, raids by Welsh and Scottish warriors seem to have been the biggest threat to England. But these were frequently small affairs, for the theft of cattle and other goods rather than any military expedition. Those who continued to live in the path of such raiders, similar to those who would later on face the Vikings, usually had to defend their lands without outside support; although, when such support was offered, it was gratefully received. Again the similarity to *Beowulf* should be noted: Beowulf and his army helped Hygelac and his people against their seemingly persistent, overpowering enemies. What formed was a militia, an army mustered solely for defensive warfare, one that had only a few outdated arms and armor, if any, and few experienced soldiers or leaders, if any. Soon those frontier areas that had been so well guarded by Roman soldiers and, in the case of the Anglo-Scottish border, by Hadrian's Wall, were denuded of population, inevitably forcing the raids that were its cause to extend farther and farther into the center and southern portions of the island.

There were also wars between the various Anglo-Saxon kingdoms, although their frequency may have been exaggerated in later narratives that wished to emphasize the Christianization of England. These conflicts involved more skilled and professional troops, including mercenaries from Europe and, especially, Scandinavia. But one gains the impression from written and archaeological sources that soldiers were never a large part of the population.

The early Middle Ages was a period of endemic warfare, and no region and few people escaped the violence of armed conflict or the constant recruiting, mustering, and moving of large forces throughout Europe. The effect of this on traditional agricultural societies and economies was, as expected, quite devastating. Indeed, warfare defined all aspects of life for all classes of people. Many ecclesiastics would even begin to find a justification of such conflicts within a Christianity that followed a leader who had preached peace. Warfare also continued to define the "hero," a definition that had changed lit-tle since the most ancient of times, and stories—epics, sagas, and narratives—all heralded the man who used his prowess and cunning to defeat his enemy on the battlefield and in individual martial con-tests.

STRATEGY AND TACTICS

Strategy and tactics in warfare after the barbarian invasions and up to the Carolingian age are difficult, if not impossible, to determine with any accuracy. The Ostrogoths in Italy and the Visigoths in southern France and Spain have the reputation that they were weak military powers in the centuries following their initial wars against the Romans and the Huns. Contemporaries have left the impression that the numbers of professional soldiers were small—only a few leaders and their mounted retinues—although these could be sup-plemented by levies taken from the general populace in times of struggle. However, these soldiers were rarely called up, seemingly both because of the lack of enemy threats and perhaps out of fear of arming and training individuals who might potentially turn those weapons and training against their leaders. Of course, this meant that, when there was a necessity for military action, the army that re-sponded to the levy was generally disorganized, disorderly, and undisciplined and had little desire to fight for people they did not know and causes they often saw no value in. This no doubt hastened the arrival of the professional medieval soldier, but by that time both the Ostrogoths and the Visigoths had been destroyed, the former by the Byzantines and the latter by Arab Muslims.

The Lombards ran into little opposition while filling the vacuum of political and military rule in Italy left when the Byzantines re-turned to the eastern Mediterranean in the sixth century. Still, they seem to have been effective warriors, although some modern com-mentators suggest that this effectiveness has been exaggerated by their use of violence and terror to pacify those whom they sought to control. Before occupying Italy, Lombardic cavalry had served with Roman and Byzantine armies. And their contemporary historian, a fan, Paul the Deacon, records that the Lombards remained largely a cavalry-dominant force throughout their conquest of Italy and later. However, it is clear that the Lombardic cavalry was supported by an equally large, or possibly larger, force of infantry, but these numbers seem not to have impressed contemporary narrative or hagiographical writers. At times, the cavalry also dismounted, but only when there was no other military alternative for their survival. The Lombards also had a provision for the general levy of troops, but, like their Gothic predecessors, they rarely used it.

Paul the Deacon also portrays the Lombards as having what one might describe as a permanent or standing army, better led, better equipped, and better trained than other early medieval forces. This would point to their being more unified and sure of their military goals. If this was the case, then it was the first such army in medieval Europe as the Franks did not acquire a standing army until the reign of Pippin III in the mid-eighth century. On the other hand, later Lombards suffered from political insurrections, most often because of disputed political inheritance, a situation that Charlemagne would use to his advantage when he advanced into Italy, attacked, and defeated them in 774.

The Ostrogoths, Visigoths, and Lombards were all, eventually, overrun by other military powers, and they left no lasting European realm. However, the Franks succeeded where their other barbarian counterparts failed, forming a medieval political entity out of which medieval (and even modern) Europe was created. Initially, the Franks fought solely as infantry, but by the beginning of the sixth century, they too had cavalry, although the cavalry was used almost wholly in support of their infantry. For example, most of the fighting done by Clovis's troops was on foot, against infantry enemies. The Frankish cavalry traveled to the battlefield on horses and then dismounted to fight with the infantry. But it is also clear from the evidence that the early Merovingian cavalry could make charges on horseback. Gregory of Tours, the chief historian of the early Franks, tells the story of two soldiers, Dragolen and Guntram, who fought against each other on horseback:

> [Dragolen] struck spurs to his horse and charged Guntrum at full speed. But his blow failed, for his spear broke, and his sword fell to the ground. Guntram . . . then, raising his lance struck Dragolen in the throat and unseated him. And as Dragolen was hanging from his horse, one of Guntram's friends thrust a lance into his side and gave him the finishing blow (Gregory of Tours, *The History of the Franks*, trans. Lewis Thorpe [Harmondsworth, England: Penguin Books, 1974], 290).

The most famous battle during this period was undoubtedly that fought somewhere between Tours and Poitiers (and called by both names) in 732. The Franks faced a determined and, before this date, a rarely defeated Muslim army, under the leadership of Abd ar Rahman al-Ghafiqi, that had crossed over the Pyrenees Mountains from the Iberian peninsula. Few original sources exist for this battle; those that do—from both the Muslim and Frankish sides—suggest that the Muslim army, containing Spanish, Berber, Moroccan, and Arab soldiers, fought on horseback and on foot as they were accustomed to, while the Merovingians, led by Charles Martel, fought solely on foot. Charles's Frankish soldiers were quite experienced, and this may have been the reason behind his victory. It appears that the Muslims charged repeatedly, both on horse and on foot, but the tightly packed Frankish lines remained solid. Eventually, the Muslim attacks petered out, possibly because of fatigue or the terrain, and the Franks were able to attack and defeat the Muslims. Abd ar Rahman al-Ghafiqi was killed and, as night fell, his army left the field, although a burial party is said to have returned later to bury their leader where he fell. The tactic of standing solidly in an infantry line while being attacked required an enormous amount of bravery, discipline, and leadership, and few armies possessed such qualities, although on this occasion it is clear that the Franks did. Charles Martel's leadership at Tours was a contributing factor in the assumption of the Merovingian throne by his son, Pippin, who then declared the beginning of a new dynasty, the Carolingian, fittingly named after the man who had ended the Muslim threat against the Franks.

LATE ROMAN ARMS AND ARMOR
Spears and Javelins

In discussing the arms and armor of the early Middle Ages, it is essential to look first at those of the Roman soldier. Throughout most of the history of the Empire, Roman infantry soldiers were characterized by the use of a single weapon, the *pilum*. The *pilum* was a heavy spear, used for thrusting or throwing. *Pila* had a leaf-shaped iron head, 2–3 feet (60–90 centimeters) long, embedded in or socketed onto a wooden shaft with a short iron spike at the rear. Sometimes, especially in the later Roman period, one or two weights would be attached to *pila*. These tended to increase their power but decrease their range, indicating perhaps a soldier's preference at those times for a thrusting rather than a throwing weapon. The length of *pila* seems to have been around 5 feet 4 inches (163 centimeters), although examples as long as 9 feet (274 centimeters) were found in the excavation of a bog site in Illerup, Denmark.

Roman armies were the only ones who used the *pilum*, which may mean there were strict regulations on its manufacture and trade, although there is no written evidence supporting this assumption. During the second century AD there was a decline in the use of the *pilum*, but in the third and fourth centuries it regained its popularity and was used against the early barbarian invaders. Only with the decline of Roman military power and the rise of the barbarians did the *pilum* finally die out. Javelins, shorter (approximately 40 inches or 103 centimeters) and lighter than the *pila* and with a smaller iron head, were also used by regular Roman soldiers during the late Empire, chiefly, it seems, by lightly armored skirmishing troops. No contemporary records document the range of these weapons, but modern experiments indicate a range of about 33 yards (30 meters) for *pila*, although they are only able to penetrate a wooden shield at 5 1/2 yards (5 meters), and 22 yards (20 meters) for javelins, which had a penetrating capability up to 11 yards (10 meters).

Javelins and *pila* could be used on horseback, but late Roman cavalry preferred lances. These were longer than *pila* and did not have long iron heads. Excavated lance heads show a variety of shapes, lengths, and weights. The total lengths of lances—head and shaft—can only be guessed at.

Swords

Roman soldiers also almost always carried an edged weapon to use as a secondary weapon to their *pila*. Most often these were worn on their right side and were drawn by and used in the right hand (to the Roman a left-handed person was *sinister*, the Latin word for left). From very early these were relatively short—no longer than 13 inches (35 centimeters), and most quite a bit shorter—and must be considered daggers. They had leaf-shaped blades and were sheathed in iron or leather scabbards with bronze edges, supports, and tips or chapes. Obviously, the dagger also had nonmilitary uses.

By at least the first century BC Roman soldiers had adopted the *gladius*. This was a short sword made with an iron blade to which a bronze-covered wood, bone, or ivory cross guard, pommel, and grip would be attached. They varied in length, and archaeological examples range between 22 and 30 inches (56 and 76 centimeters) overall with blades between 13 and 25 inches (34.5 and 64 centimeters). A *gladius* in the collections of the Royal Armouries in Leeds, England (IX.5583A) is 24 inches (63 centimeters) overall, with a blade length of 19 inches (49 centimeters), a width of 1.7 inches (4.3 centimeters), and a weight of 1 pound (444 grams), measurements not often recorded for similar excavated weapons.

Gladius scabbards were made of two thin pieces of wood, sometimes covered with a thin bronze sheet or leather, reinforced by bronze bands where the scabbard attached to the belt and at the chape; at times a third band was also attached further down the scabbard. Although ostensibly for adding strength to the scabbard, these bronze bands were also frequently tinned and decorated. On the bronze bands of the scabbard—the only pieces that remain—that carried the Royal Armouries *gladius* the upper band is engraved with a warrior moving to his right and wearing a crested helmet and a muscled cuirass; he carries a spear and a shield. The lower band is engraved with a partially clothed winged victory figure writing on a shield hanging from a palm tree. The chape is engraved with another winged victory figure holding a palm leaf. The symbolism here suggests that the soldier carrying this weapon was willing to fight, but hoped for peace through victory. Several other decorated *gladius* scabbards have been found. More complete scabbards show the tip of the chape to have been a cast bronze button. The blades of some extant *gladii* carry the names of owners or possibly manufacturers; the Royal Armouries *gladius* bears three apparently separate names: C. Valerius Primus, C. Valerius, and C. Ranius. The *gladius* continued to be used throughout the late Empire, although it steadily declined in popularity.

The *gladius* could only be used for thrusting and thus had limited effect when wielded from horseback. For this, it appears a longer sword was carried, called a *spatha*. The *spatha* appears at least by the end of the second century AD, primarily as a cavalry weapon, but it quickly found popularity among the infantry as well. Unlike the *gladius*, the *spatha* was usually worn on the left side and carried in a scabbard that was attached to a leather belt or baldric that was worn over the right shoulder across the body. The length of the baldric could be adjusted by a series of buttons. That the *spatha* was carried on the opposite hip from the *gladius* and from a baldric was probably because of the sword's relative length—extant examples are between 28–36 inches (71–92 centimeters) long overall, with a blade length of 23–27.5 inches (59–70 centimeters) and a width of 1.5–2.4 inches (4–6 centimeters). *Spathae* had similarly constructed wood, bone, or ivory cross guards, pommels, and grips as the *gladii*, and similarly decorated panels, although bronze was increasingly replaced by iron or sometimes silver. In the fourth and fifth centuries the *spatha* became more popular than the *gladius* for all Roman soldiers and may denote an increased desire to use the sword as a slashing rather than a thrusting weapon. According to the fourth-century Ammianus Marcellinus and seventh-century John of Antioch, the results of a *spatha* slash could be quite devastating, the former claiming one could split a human skull in two and the latter reporting a collarbone and torso penetrated by a *spatha*. In the late Roman Empire, daggers and swords would often be carried together.

Bows and Slings

Bows and slings were also used by Roman skirmishing troops. Unfortunately, there are no archaeological remains of these weapons, as they were made of wood and cloth, respectively, but they are often portrayed in art and are frequently mentioned in historical sources. Flavius Vegetius Renatus, perhaps the most famous late Roman military writer, mentions self-bows, thought to be plain wooden bows, as training weapons and recommends an exaggerated practice range of 300 yards (274 meters). Modern tests have shown the effective range of these bows to be 55–165 yards (50–150 meters), with a maximum range of 180–250 yards (165–230 meters). Naturally, as with all missile weapons, effectiveness was determined as much by the skill of the archers as by the technology of the bow.

Vegetius does not describe the war bow. Many scholars believe these were not self-bows but composite bows, constructed from wood, sinew, and horn. They arrive at this conclusion based on the later use of composite bows, for which there is no known origin, and because of the archaeological finds of ear- and grip-laths that are thought to be from composite bows. Several artistic portrayals also seem to depict composite bows, based on the way they are bent when strung. These demonstrate that the bowstring could be drawn both by the fingers—the so-called Mediterranean release—or the thumb—the Mongolian release. Bracers on the left wrist and stalls or rings for the fingers or thumb are also depicted, as are quivers. Finally, during the period of barbarian invasions, the Romans used horse archers who could fire at full gallop when skirmishing against an opponent, but who could also use a sword or spear when directly attacking an opponent's troops.

Two types of arrowheads have been identified from archaeological excavations. The long, thin bodkin arrowhead is thought to have been used as an armor piercer, with the suggestion that the triple- or quadruple-vaned trilobate arrowhead was more effective against unarmored targets. Both could be tanged or socketed and, as such, either bound or glued to a reed or cane shaft, which was kept from splitting on impact by the addition of a solid wooden piece in the middle. Rare archaeological examples of these arrows found at Dura Europos in Syria have also shown that part of the surface of the Roman arrow was roughened and the fletching was attached by glue.

Slings, long a weapon used in ancient warfare, continued to be used into the late Roman period. In fact, Vegetius deemed them to be more effective than the bow. The excavation of one possible sling pouch shows them to have been made of thick and rough cattle hide decorated with geometric patterns. Both stone and lead slingshots have also been excavated, but none can be conclusively dated. Artistic depictions show that the sling was swung over the head or at the side of the body, and as with the bowstring grip, there seems to have been no standard method for Roman soldiers. Modern experiments have determined that the sling had a range between 165–440 yards (150 and 400 meters).

LATE ROMAN ARMOR

Soldiers who accompanied Julius Caesar's march into Gaul in the first century BC were the most superb fighting men of their time. From narrative descriptions and artistic renderings it can be seen that they were protected by a bowl-shaped helmet, which also protected the neck; a large oblong shield, measuring approximately 51 by 25 1/2 inches (130 by 65 centimeters) (the scutum); and a solid bronze breastplate (the lorica). The workmanship of the various armor pieces was often extremely skilled. The helmet and breastplate were made of bronze beaten to shape, while the shield was constructed from layers of wood, usually three, glued together. Each layer was made of strips 2.4–4 inches (6–10 centimeters) wide; the outer pieces were laid horizontally, the inner piece was laid vertically, and the whole was covered in canvas and calf hide. A long wooden boss ran the entire length of the shield. Although no metal was used in the construction of the Roman shield, it was heavy, weighing an estimated 22 pounds (10 kilograms). However, because of its shape and size, the soldier did not necessarily have to wear greaves, and this gave him greater freedom of movement and, generally, a fairly quick speed.

Helmets

The bronze helmet of earlier Roman soldiers also changed during the second and third centuries; it was replaced by a more carefully designed helmet, made from an iron or bronze skull-plate or cap with either bronze or iron reinforcing bars crisscrossed or ribbed over it. This skull-plate or cap continued down over the back of the neck, ending in a neck-guard that angled out several inches over the soldier's back. The front of the skull cap ended in a peak formed by turning out the metal of the skull cap or adding a separate bronze or iron bar to the front of the helmet. The sides of the face were covered by ear- and cheek-pieces made of single bronze plates and attached to the helmet by a hinge at their upper edge and fastened together at the chin. Gravestone carvings and other illustrations show that this was a particularly favored helmet style throughout the third and fourth centuries, although from the same sources it appears that older models did continue to be worn. Some helmets were also fitted with a mail aventail to further protect the neck, and mail coifs were known, although evidence of both is rare. Roman soldiers would also have worn a padded or quilted "arming cap" made of leather or wool under their helmets.

Shields

Although some late Roman shields were still the same length and width as previous ones, they were now more rectangular and curved to fit the body. A mid-third-century rectangular shield excavated at Dura Europos measures 40 by 33 inches (102 by 83 centimeters). They continued to be made of wood glued together in layers—the Dura Europos shield was made of strips measuring 1.2–3.1 inches (3–8 centimeters) wide and 0.6–0.8 inches (1.5–2 centimeters) thick—and covered in leather. However, they now had applied gilded or silvered decoration, a large metal domed boss, and rims of wrought iron or bronze around the edges. Oval shields also appeared at this time. An example from Dura Europos measures 42–46.5 by 36–38 inches (107–118 by 92–97 centimeters) and is constructed of 12–15 poplar wooden planks 0.3–0.5 inches (0.8–1.2 centimeters) thick glued together. A horizontal bar, riveted only on each side, reinforced the inside of the shield and provided a wooden grip that was anchored on the front by a large domed boss measuring 7.3–8.5

inches (18.5–22 centimeters). The shield was covered in leather or fabric, like earlier examples.

Armor

During the second and third centuries AD, Roman armor changed, and the hard, solid, and immobile breastplate was replaced by a more flexible cuirass (a lorica segmentata). Six or seven thick horizontal bronze strips were attached by hooks and buckles onto a leather undergarment to cover the lower chest and stomach area to below the waist. The shoulders were covered with several curved strips of bronze secured to a pair of front and back metal plates that were attached to two sets of horizontal strips that protected the lower part of the body. This allowed the wearer much more freedom of movement than did the solid lorica worn by Caesar's legionnaires, and it could also be taken apart easily for transportation and repair. The lorica segmentata was still in fashion at the time the Arch of Severus was built in Rome; the arch depicts soldiers wearing it in 203 and it seems to have been used at least through the middle of the third century. There is little evidence, however, that it was worn by soldiers during the barbarian invasions of the fourth and fifth centuries, perhaps because of its technological complexity and the cost of its manufacture.

The Arch of Severus portrays not only soldiers wearing technologically complex, expensive lorica segmentata cuirasses but also the more easily constructed and cheaper lorica squamata and lorica hamata armor; evidence also suggests that these had completely replaced the earlier armor by the end of the third and the beginning of the fourth centuries. The lorica squamata was made of a large number of metallic scales attached to each other by leather laces and affixed to a linen undergarment by linen thread. While not as frequently depicted in artistic renderings as the other Roman armors, several finds of this armor have established that the scales were made either of bronze or, more frequently, iron. These measure about 0.6 inches (1.5 centimeters) long and 0.5 inches (1.3 centimeters) wide and are pierced by six holes, two in the center top and two each on the right and left edges. It is not known how a soldier put on this scale armor, and it is not believed that sleeves were attached to the torso-covering cuirass.

The lorica hamata was constructed of metal rings. Artistic depictions and archaeological excavations of this mail armor indicate that it was made of alternating rows of rings—measuring 0.3 inches (0.7 centimeters) in diameter and 0.04 inches (0.1 centimeter) thick—punched out of sheet metal or made of wire, with a connecting row of metal wire rings in between. The lorica hamata had the ring ends of each row riveted together or a row of riveted rings alternating with a row of welded rings. Each of the rings was interlocked with four others, two in the row above and two in the row below; 35,000 to 40,000 rings were needed to make an entire armor, including elbow-length sleeves that were always attached to the shirt. The lorica hamata was extremely flexible and durable, and it was pulled on over the head.

Both the scale armor (lorica squamata) and mail armor (lorica hamata) covered the torso from the shoulder to at least the middle of the thigh, and some seem to have stretched as far down as the knee. They were worn by the infantry and cavalry. And while they were lighter than the earlier lorica segmentata armor, they were also less protective, sacrificing defense for expense and comfort. Greaves seem to have been regularly worn with both types of armors.

Underneath all late Roman armors a garment known as a *thoracomachus,* in Greek, or *subarmalis,* in Latin, was worn. An anonymous late-fourth- or early-fifth-century military manual, the *De Rebus Bellicis,* identifies the *thoracomachus* as a thick cloth garment that added protection to the armor, but at the same time also helped spread the weight, cut down friction and rubbing, and reduce the heat of wearing it. There are no artistic depictions of this garment, and, not surprisingly, none have survived, but it is thought that they were made of wool, felt, or linen and were padded or quilted. In wet weather a leather garment—made of Libyan hide, says the author of the *De Rebus Bellicis*—or, later, a hooded felt cloak was worn over the armor.

But how protective were the two later Roman armors—the lorica hamata and the lorica squamata—and what did the soldiers think of wearing them? During the fourth century, Ammianus Marcellinus writes that he had seen Roman "infantrymen with shields and crests gleaming with glittering rays, clad in shining mail," but in the early fifth century, Vegetius is less positive about the Roman soldiers' attitude toward their armor:

> But when, because of negligence and laziness, parade ground drills were abandoned, the customary armor began to seem heavy since the soldiers rarely ever wore it. Therefore, they first asked the emperor to set aside the breastplates and mail and then the helmets. So our

soldiers fought the Goths without any protection for chest and head and were often beaten by archers. Although there were many disasters, which led to the loss of great cities, no one tried to restore breastplates and helmets to the infantry. Thus it happens that troops in battle, exposed to wounds because they have no armor, think about running and not about fighting (as quoted in Arther Ferrill, *The Fall of the Roman Empire: The Military Explanation* [London: Thames and Hudson, 1986], 128–129).

But did this matter in facing the barbarians? The Romans seem to have been very careful in admitting the Visigoths to the Empire as *foederati,* forbidding them from bringing their weapons and confiscating any that were found. Of course, some Visigoths no doubt smuggled in their weapons or bribed Roman guards to allow them to keep them. Still, these cannot have been very numerous, and in fact there seem to have been several attempts by the Visigoths to obtain Roman arms during their 376–378 war against the Empire. Certainly, such desperation does not necessarily mean that Roman weapons were seen as superior to those normally carried by the barbarians—although previous attempts to acquire weapons from Roman arsenals by barbarian raiders might suggest as much.

BARBARIAN ARMS AND ARMOR

So at least initially, the Roman troops who were defeated by barbarian armies did so against warriors armed with similar weapons to those they used. The Ostrogoths and Vandals faced the Romans using weapons they had either acquired or copied from them. However, while Visigothic armies were largely infantry, with few cavalry and even fewer archers, both Ostrogothic and Vandal military forces had more cavalry and archers than the Romans. In fact, the Vandals, although they were the most nomadic of any of the early invading tribes, quickly became a cavalry-dominant force, although the reason for this has never been completely understood. Their interest in acquiring or imitating Roman arms and armor was determined by their own military needs. Barbarian heavy infantry dressed like Roman heavy infantry, barbarian heavy cavalry dressed like Roman heavy cavalry, and lighter barbarian troops and skirmishers dressed like the same lighter Roman soldiers. To be certain, the barbarians

Carson City
City
Library

Carson City

Library

Date 5/18/2019

Time 10:15:35 AM

Fines/Fees Owed $0.00

Total Checked Out: 2

Carson City

Library

Date: 5/18/2019

Time: 10:35:35 AM

Fines/Fees Owed: $0.00

Total Checked Out: 2

Checked Out

Title: Manufacturing engineering and technology
Barcode: 31472702193446
Due Date: 06/15/2019 23:59:59 (*)

Title: Medieval weapons : an illustrated history o
their impact
Barcode: 31472701459772
Due Date: 06/15/2019 23:59:59 (*)

Page 1 of 1

CARSON CITY LIBRARY
Check us out at
www.carsoncitylibrary.org
CLOSED: May 27, 2019 reopening
May 28, 2019 at 1:00 PM

seemed to prefer some Roman weapons over others, with *spathae* preferred over *gladii,* and lances and javelins preferred over *pila.* Slings never seem to have caught on, but archery, both on foot and on horse, flourished. This may be an indication of what was also happening in the Roman armies of the time. It should be noted that standardization of weapons and armor was never an issue; indeed, both mail and scale armor seem to have been used equally by soldiers fighting side by side in the same armies.

It was not long, however, before the various barbarian tribes began to develop and make their own weapons, perhaps because of the fall in the number of arms produced by Roman smiths as the economy of the Empire declined. Some historians suggest that this meant a decrease in overall quality of weapons and armor, but this has not been confirmed by archaeological finds from the period. In fact, the opposite may be true: barbarian arms and armor of the fifth century may have been superior to Roman arms and armor in several ways. Infantry soldiers continued to use spears (although not *pila*) as their chief weapon, but these were fitted with stronger iron heads. Archers began to fire iron-tipped arrows. And the cavalry and infantry both began to use longer two-edged swords. In the Eastern Roman Empire similar changes to weapons occurred, but who influenced who in this case cannot be determined. The Romans, especially in the Western Empire, were unable to adapt, and such a tactical failure may have added to their ultimate "fall."

As in many other areas, the Franks were very different from other barbarian societies in their choice of weapons. Being used so often to supplement Roman troops along the Rhine River in the fourth and early fifth centuries meant that the Franks used Roman arms and armor. Yet before long some, especially military and political leaders, appeared to have given up using heavy armor, choosing instead to carry more weapons. This surprised many who came in contact with them and who otherwise expected more traditional defensive attire from such a militarily successful tribe. For example, in 470 Sidonius Apollinaris recalls his first meeting with Frankish soldiers:

> Their swords hung from their shoulders on baldrics, and round their waists they wore a belt of fur adorned with bosses . . . In their right hands they held barbed lances and throwing-axes, and in their left shields, on which the light shone, white on the circuit and red on the boss, displaying both opulence and craftsmanship (as quoted in

R.H.C. Davis, *A History of Medieval Europe from Constantine to Saint Louis* [London: Longman, 1970], 108–109).

And Agathias, writing a century later, records a similar impression of the Franks:

> The military equipment of this people is very simple . . . They do not know the use of the coat of mail or greaves and the head the majority leave uncovered, only a few wear the helmet. They have their chests bare and backs naked to the loins; they cover their thighs with either leather or linen. . . . Fighting on foot is both habitual and a national custom and they are proficient in this. At the hip they wear a sword and on the left side their shield is attached. They have neither bows nor slings, no missile weapons except the double edged axe and the *angon* which they use most often (as quoted in Bernard S. Bachrach, "Procopius, Agathias and the Frankish Military," *Speculum* 45 (1970): 436).

Spears

The use of the barbarian spear precedes the barbarian invasions of the Roman Empire and may be the single weapon least affected by similar Roman weapons. They especially interested Tacitus, writing about the Germans in the first century AD:

> Only a few of them use swords or large lances: they carry spears called *frameae* in their language—with short and narrow blades, but so sharp and easy to handle that they can be used, as required, either at close quarters or in long-range fighting. Their horsemen are content with a shield and spear; but the foot-soldiers also rain javelins on their foes: each of them carries several, and they hurl them to immense distances (Tacitus, *The Agricola and the Germania,* trans. H. Mattingly [Harmondsworth, England: Penguin Books, 1970], 105–106).

Already it seems that these barbarians understood the three uses of the spear even before they invaded the Empire—as a lance, as a thrusting weapon, and as a javelin—an assessment that was confirmed by later witnesses.

However, what has not been confirmed, by archaeological finds, artistic renderings, or other literary sources, is Tacitus' description of the barbarian spears. There is little doubt that the spear was important, as he suggests, but, as with other weapons used by both barbarians and Romans at the time, it seems there was not the standardization in these weapons that Tacitus implies, even among, let alone between, the barbarian tribes. As many as twelve different types of spearheads have been found in Anglo-Saxon archaeological excavations, and these have been further grouped into four main categories: derivative forms of Germanic spear-types before the Anglo-Saxon settlement in England, leaf-shaped blades, angular blades, and corrugated blades. It is likely that chronological and regional differences must account for some of the variations in spearhead types. However, on the whole it must be concluded that the Anglo-Saxons saw no need for standardization or even consistency. Archaeological excavations of spearheads from continental Europe show a similar diversity. These spearheads are larger and thicker compared with Roman examples.

Of special and specific interest is the Frankish spear known as the *angon*. Agathias describes the weapon:

> The *angons* are spears which are neither short nor long; they can be used, if necessary for throwing like a javelin, and also, in hand to hand combat. The greater part of the *angon* is covered with iron and very little wood is exposed. Above, at the top of the spear, on each side from the socket itself where the staff is fixed, some points are turned back, bent like hooks, and turned toward the handle. In battle, the Frank throws the *angon,* and if it hits an enemy the spear is caught in the man and neither the wounded man nor anyone else can draw it out. The barbs hold inside the flesh causing great pain and in this way a man whose wound may not be in a vital spot still dies. If the *angon* strikes a shield, it is fixed there, hanging down with the butt on the ground. The *angon* cannot be pulled out because the barbs have penetrated the shield, nor can it be cut off with a sword because the wood of the shaft is covered with iron. When the Frank sees the situation, he quickly puts his foot on the butt of the spear, pulling down and the man holding it falls, the head and chest are left unprotected. The unprotected warrior is then killed either by a stroke of the axe or a thrust with another spear (as quoted in Bernard S. Bachrach, "Procopius, Agathias and the Frankish Military," *Speculum* 45 (1970): 436).

Although this description is probably fanciful, most historians accept it as accurate. A similar spear is described in a tenth-century poem, *Waltheri,* but the anonymous poet claims that this spear has three cords attached to its end so that, when stuck into an enemy soldier's shield, three Frankish warriors might be able to pull on these and force him to drop it—though why an enemy soldier would allow three Frankish warriors to pull on these cords is not stated. From these descriptions, some believe the *angon* was a descendant of the Roman *pilum;* however, such a link is not supported by written, artistic, or archaeological evidence.

Swords

The spear may have been the most widely used weapon of the early Middle Ages, but the sword was certainly the most celebrated and was the weapon of choice for the elite of barbarian society. From very early, the sword became a part of every cavalryman's arsenal, its ownership generally preceding even that of a warhorse. But they were also used by large numbers of infantry; the Visigothic Code of Ervig (680–687) even made ownership of a sword mandatory for all men joining the army, Visigoth or Roman, infantry or cavalry. Of course, although the sword was usually purchased, it might also be given to a particularly valiant acolyte by his master or acquired by taking it from a fallen or captured opponent, and it is quite early in the Middle Ages that such acquisitions become part of almost all heroic literature.

Although it has been proven that barbarian soldiers used short swords, with archaeological examples averaging 15 3/4 inches (40 centimeters) in length—no doubt Roman *gladii* or a weapon based on them—these warriors preferred the longer *spatha*-type weapon. Heavy, undoubtedly meant to be used with two hands, and two-edged, with a center of gravity near to the point, archaeological evidence has shown these to be quite long, 29 1/2–39 inches (75–100 centimeters). However, the blades of these swords are also narrow, 2.4 inches (6 centimeters) wide on average, which has given rise to the scholarly opinion that they were not very strong or well made. Historians point to Tacitus' derision of the first-century Germanic swords that he had seen, stating that they were not common because barbarian iron "is not plentiful." While this may have been the situation when Tacitus was writing, it may simply have been the quality and abundance of the swords of the tribe he was studying, and by the fourth and fifth centuries this was clearly no longer the case. Swords were both numerous—contemporary chroniclers report that almost all barbarian soldiers bear one—and well made—with blades made of finely forged iron of a quality equal or superior to contemporary Roman swords. Swordsmiths were highly paid artisans whose craftsmanship was beginning to come into its own—although their Carolingian and Viking descendents outshone their achievements.

Another myth that should be dispelled is that swords, especially long swords, were only owned by the tribal elite or chieftains and as such were symbols of their wealth and power. Historians have suggested that burials of this type of sword with their owners, as in the grave excavated at Sutton Hoo, and thus not passed down to others indicate that these were more than mere weapons. This has arisen largely from a misreading of these burial sites; not all were of wealthy or powerful individuals. In fact, the large number of graves found may indicate that such a burial was a tradition for honoring soldiers of any class, and may also indicate an abundance of these weapons rather than a scarcity. However, the fact that there are excavated instances of swords that have been "ritually killed," bent, or otherwise damaged before being placed in a warrior's grave so that they could not be reused, may in fact suggest the rarity of these blades.

A type of sword specific to this time was known as a seax or scramasax—a single-edged weapon that could be up to 33 1/2 inches (85 centimeters) long and between 1.6 and 2.6 inches (4 and 6.5 centimeters) wide. But unlike the long swords of the period, the lower range of whose length they equaled, these were lighter in weight and could be used with only one hand. Small versions, measuring around 7.8 inches (20 centimeters) long, have also been found.

All barbarian swords had large pommels and cross guards of various sizes and shapes and made of the same metal as the blade. Some pommels were also covered in a thin sheet of bronze or silver. Grips were covered in wood and leather and sometimes had metal elements. Scabbards differed little in construction from their Roman predecessors—wood covered with leather and decorative and reinforcing metal elements. Blades, hilts, and scabbards were frequently decorated; especially popular was the inlaying of gold, silver, and bronze, and decorative effects such as gold cloisonné and the attachment of jewels. The most wealthy of barbarian leaders owned extremely decorated swords; that of Childeric, the fifth-century Merovingian chief whose extremely rich tomb was excavated at Tournai in 1653, had both gold inlay and cloisonné decoration on both the hilts and scabbards of two swords found in his grave—a *spatha* and a scramasax—the only parts of the weapons remaining.

Daggers were also used by many barbarian soldiers, with artistic and archaeological remains confirming their stylistic and technological connection to earlier Roman ones.

Axes

No evidence suggests that Roman soldiers used axes as weapons, although they certainly used them as tools. Barbarians used them both as tools and weapons. The latter seemed to have been quite novel in the late Roman period, as they were particularly commented on by contemporary chroniclers. These writers report that barbarian warriors used axes both in close infantry fighting and as missile weapons, and that they were easily able to destroy any armor or helmets and penetrate shields. When used as infantry weapons, axes were swung with one or both hands, and when used as missile weapons they were thrown. One tactic, used especially by Frankish soldiers—whose term for such an axe, *francisca*, has been adopted by historians as a name for all of them—was to throw their axes in unison at approaching troops, thus disrupting their charge. Procopius, writing in Byzantium during the sixth century, describes this use of the weapon:

> Each man carried a sword and shield and an axe. Now the iron head of this weapon was thick and exceedingly sharp on both sides while the wooden handle was very short. And they are accustomed always to throw these axes at one signal in the first charge and shatter the shields of the enemy and kill the men (as quoted in Bernard S. Bachrach, "Procopius, Agathias and the Frankish Military," *Speculum* 45 (1970): 436–437).

Although not mentioned by the term *francisca* until Isidore of Seville in his famous and influential early seventh-century encyclopedia, it has been suggested that it is from this that the Franks derived their tribal name. However, recent historians have suggested the opposite, that the *francisca* was so named because of its use by Frankish soldiers.

The fact that these weapons were thrown suggests that *franciscae* were relatively small, a fact confirmed by artistic renderings and archaeological finds. A large number of axes have been found in warriors' graves, and their average weight was about 2.6 pounds. (1.2 kilograms), with the head weighing between 10 ounces–2.2 pounds

(300–1000 grams). These axe heads measure 7–7.8 inches (18–20 centimeters) high, and it is estimated that their handles measured in the region of 15.7 inches (40 centimeters) long. For example, the *francisca* head found in Childeric's tomb measures 7.8 inches (20 centimeters) and weighs just over two pounds (935 grams). Modern experiments have shown that when an axe like this is thrown it rotates about its own axis; the head will be uppermost, and therefore do the most damage to an enemy, at about four yards with a single rotation, eight yards with a double rotation, and twelve yards with a triple rotation. Soldiers had to be skilled enough to judge the speed and distance of a charging enemy to take complete advantage of the small cutting edge when throwing their axes.

Forged from a single piece of iron, barbarian axes, *franciscae,* had a fairly distinct shape: the upper head had an S-shaped curvature, the lower edge of the blade had a simple elbow, the lower part of the head swung strongly to the handle, and the upper edge of the blade formed into a point or rounded.

The throwing axe remained important to barbarian soldiers until the beginning of the seventh century, when it began to decline in use, possibly because of a drop in the number of skilled throwers, but more probably because of an increase in the use of archers by the Franks. By the end of the seventh century it had effectively disappeared. The handheld axe, however, continued to be favored as an infantry weapon throughout the rest of the Middle Ages, although it tended to have a longer handle and larger head and was usually wielded with two hands.

Bows

At the time of the barbarian invasions of the Roman Empire, it is unclear just which tribes were armed with the bow or the extent to which it was used. However, late Roman authors comment on the proficiency of the Visigothic archers and indicate that they were of great effect in their victory at the battle of Adrianople in 378 as well as in other conquests. Certainly, judging from the large number of arrowheads found in Visigothic grave sites in Spain, the bow was an extremely widely used weapon. It appears that the Visigoths shot a short arrow with an iron head, of varying shapes, from a bow of only around 5 feet (150 centimeters) long. It was of composite construction, meaning that the stave was a combination of wood, horn, and sinew. Strips of sinew were softened in boiling water so that they could be molded into the required shape; the strips were glued onto the outside of a wooden piece cut to the desired length of the bow to which strips of horn were then glued to the inside. The combination of materials, the sinew strong in tension and the horn strong in compression, produced a highly effective springlike stave. Nocks, cut with a groove into which the bowstring fitted, were glued to the tips of the arms. They were built so that the arms, in the relaxed state, bent forward and the bowstring, made of linen (flax) or hemp, pulled them back to the firing position, from which they sometimes get the name "recurved bow."

Recurved bows could be shot from the standing position by an infantry soldier or from horseback. A Visigothic army usually contained both types of troops, as did the Vandals, although foot bowmen were more numerous. In the armies of their fearsome enemies, the Huns, the opposite was true—their prevalence for mounted archers was noted throughout the late Roman world as discussed later.

The Ostrogoths, Franks, Angles, and Saxons, although they used the bow, did not do so as often as the Visigoths or Vandals, let alone the Huns. The Franks were said to have preferred the throwing axe as a missile weapon, although the large number of arrowheads found in Frankish grave sites may cause a reassessment of that view. The Ostrogoths seemed to have held the bow in such low esteem that Totila, the king of the Ostrogoths during the sixth-century Byzantine invasion of Italy, refused to allow his army to use bows against the eventually victorious invaders—however, this cannot be said to have caused their defeat.

Grave sites in England have shown that the Angles and Saxons also used the bow; yet the very small number of arrowheads found in these graves—about 1 percent of Anglo-Saxon warriors' graves contain arrowheads—suggests that the weapon was not valued as much as other weapons. An Old English riddle on the bow indicates that the Anglo-Saxons knew and used these weapons; however, the first word of the riddle, when read backwards, gives an earlier form of the Anglo-Saxon word for bow, *boga*—the only riddle to give such an internal clue—which may indicate that it was not as popular as some other weapons:

> Agob *is my name, one must work it out;*
> *I am a fair creature fashioned for battle.*
> *When I bend, and shoot a deadly shaft*
> *from my stomach, I desire only to send*

that poison as far away as possible.
When my lord, who devised this torment for me,
releases my limbs, I become longer
and, bent upon slaughter, spit out
that deadly poison I swallowed before.
No man's parted easily from the object
I describe; if he is struck by what flies
from my stomach, he pays for its poison
with his strength—speedy atonement for his life.
I will serve no master when unstrung, only when
I am cunningly notched. Now guess my name

> (in Kevin Crossley-Holland, ed. and trans.,
> *The Exeter Book Riddles* [Harmondsworth, England:
> Penguin Books, 1979], No. 23).

Of course, a simpler answer may be that the bow was seen more as a lower-class weapon than those that appear more frequently in what are likely to be graves of wealthier soldiers.

Cavalry Arms

In ancient military strategy and tactics, cavalry played a secondary role to infantry; on the battlefield, its role was to skirmish with enemy cavalry, to chase off their missile troops, or to provide mobile missile fire to harass their infantry. At sieges, cavalry became responsible primarily for reconnaissance and foraging. Therefore, cavalry soldiers needed to be well trained as horsemen, but not particularly as fighters; their horses needed to be fast, but not particularly well trained or even well bred. The Romans used few cavalry, preferring to fight on foot. Before the end of the third century, they were rarely used as a frontline force, serving primarily as a means of transportation and harassment.

Emperor Diocletian, who ruled the Empire from 284 to 305, was a former Roman general determined to reform Rome's military units, among other things making them more mobile so they could respond more quickly to foreign threats. His changes included keeping centralized garrisons of troops as rapid response units in forts a few miles from the border; this necessitated a change in cavalry strategy, although not in tactics, and resulted in an increase in the number and status of mounted troops. This strategic change was realized by the time of the campaigns against the barbarian invaders of the fourth and fifth centuries, although the Romans rarely succeeded against similar cavalry forces of the Visigoths, Vandals, and Huns. Early Franks, Angles, and Saxons seemed to have preferred to use cavalry simply as a royal or chieftain bodyguard, without involving them directly in combat. Yet, as can be seen by the story of the two Merovingian duelers, Dragolen and Guntram, the Franks could fight on horseback if so desired; on the other hand, the Anglo-Saxons seem never to have adopted the wide use of cavalry.

By the end of the fifth century Visigothic and Vandal cavalry had become far better armed and armored, essentially what historians might describe as "heavy cavalry." They used lances—to thrust—and long swords—to slash down at enemy soldiers. Before the invention and proliferation of the stirrup, they were supported only by their saddles. Because modern horsemen have found it difficult and un-stable to carry out such actions without stirrups, modern historians were led to believe early heavy cavalry simply could not have wielded their weapons very effectively. Yet the Visigoths and Vandals man-aged to fight as heavy cavalry and the Huns fought successfully as mounted archers, so it must be concluded that soldiers who fought on horseback before the proliferation of stirrups in Europe *must* have been able to wield their weapons effectively, presumably using their knees and legs to anchor their bodies to the horse.

Their saddles, too, obviously helped the barbarians fight from horseback. By the time of the barbarian invasions, the Romans had adopted a type from the Sassanian Persians known today as the "four-horned saddle." Made from wood, it enabled the Roman cav-alry soldier to stay on his mount for the longer campaigns Diocletian had anticipated in his military reforms. But it was not a particularly good saddle on which to conduct battlefield warfare. By the time of Constantine the Great, within a generation of Diocletian, it had al-ready begun to change—he had after all fought several significant battles, including that at Milvian Bridge in 312 where he had won control of the Empire, and thus he judged that he had a fairly good idea of what a mounted warrior required. In 428, the emperor Theo-dosius II attempted, in a legal code, to standardize the weights of these new saddles. He failed, but by his time the use of the "four-horned saddle" had come to an end. Barbarian warriors do not ap-pear to have favored any one type of saddle; they used many differ-ent forms, including the Roman one, though the Huns seem to have favored a particular type designed especially for mounted archery.

Cavalry weapons during the early Middle Ages differed little from similar ones used by infantry; lances and swords were probably longer and bows shorter, but the technology of these weapons remained the same. What seems to have been different was the horse. Diocletian's military reforms required an improvement in the stock of Roman warhorses, and it has been thought that the Visigoths and Vandals rode into battle on the same type of horses. This was one of the Roman industries that continued with very little disruption into the Middle Ages. Of course, this is only an assumption based on the absence of evidence indicating otherwise. Actually, little is known about the horses ridden by barbarian soldiers who fought in early medieval wars, although because they were required to carry horsemen wearing quite heavy armor, it is believed that the horses were strong and that speed was possibly sacrificed for strength. It is also assumed that these horses were smaller than more modern cavalry mounts as illustrations show the legs of medieval soldiers dangling well below the belly of their horse, but artistic renderings before the advent of perspective are difficult to interpret.

Armor

The complaints of Vegetius as to the poor attitudes of Roman soldiers toward wearing their armor may not have mattered, at least initially, as the enemies they faced then may not have been well protected by armor either. In the first century, Tacitus reported that most Germanic warriors owned neither breastplate nor helmet, and their shields were not strengthened with metal or leather. They regularly went into battle naked to the waist or with only a short cloak, protected by only a light wooden or wicker shield. Therefore, Tacitus perceived Germanic soldiers to be generally inferior to their Roman equivalents whose armor, at the time of his writing, was substantially better. Although controversial, this perception has been generally accepted. However, it has not been determined why the Germans did not wear armor or helmets or, in many cases, carry a shield. Was this because of the Germans' scarcity of metal, as Tacitus contended? Was it because the barbarians used tactics that simply did not necessitate the same armor as the Romans? Or did they simply face enemies who also fought without armor?

The lack of armor seemed to have carried on into the very earliest invasion of the Roman Empire, by the Visigoths, who, as noted already, were forced to surrender their arms and armor to the Romans on entering the Empire. The Visigoths, therefore, initially fought without helmet, shield, or body protection. Eventually they did outfit themselves better by raiding arsenals, acquiring arms from defeated soldiers, and enlisting in mercenary service in Roman armies, but before the end of the fourth century the number of armored Visigothic warriors remained small and was most often confined to the elite or chieftains. According to contemporary sources, the only armor that seems to have been plentiful was shields, and it is apparent that these had improved since Tacitus' time with the addition of a pointed iron boss in the centre. Still, it is reported that these shields were relatively thin and easily smashed by Roman swords and spears.

After the fourth century, all types of armor began to be more available to all barbarian soldiers. During this period the use of armor definitely increased, and the barbarians began to establish and develop arms industries. Some of the armor produced was quite luxurious and elaborate—for example, Totila, a sixth-century Ostrogothic king of Italy, is said to have worn golden armor—but this was obviously made more for status than military use. Basic armor was far more common, especially mail cuirasses, fashioned after the Roman lorica hamata, and scale armor, like the Roman lorica squamata. Unfortunately, none of these have survived, although they are frequently portrayed in various artistic media. Thus, the actual technology of early medieval armors must remain speculative, with most historians relying on a connection that links them to similar Roman armors. It is also assumed that early medieval soldiers wore a garment, like the Roman *thoracomachus,* under their armor.

Frankish and Anglo-Saxon armor did not differ much from that worn by the barbarians in the south of Europe. In fact, the Franks probably initially had more armor than the Visigoths, Ostrogoths, and Vandals, because of the large numbers who served in Roman armies along the Rhine; however, there is also little firm evidence to support such claims. Eventually, the Franks adopted mail armor, although that does not seem to have occurred before the rise of the Carolingians. On the contrary, Anglo-Saxon armor was not plentiful, and it was said to have been almost exclusively worn by elite soldiers and chiefs, although that may only be because they are the ones who are written about or portrayed in art. What these few early English soldiers wore was a short-sleeved mail shirt, reaching to the mid-thigh or to the knee. In the Exeter riddles it is called an "excellent garment"; to Beowulf it was a "tangled war-net"; and Aldhelm, another author of riddles, describes it as not fearing "arrows drawn from a long quiver." Finally, in the Anglo-Saxon poem, "The Battle of Maldon," a mail shirt is so valuable that Byrhtnoth, the military leader defeated in the poem, was stripped of it by a conquering enemy, who then presumably reused it himself or gave it to another soldier. It would appear that mail armor was absolutely essential for the protection of a noble warrior.

In all early medieval societies the use of armor increased markedly by the end of the sixth century. Evidence for this comes not only in the increased portrayal of it in literature and art but also in its greater occurrence in excavated graves of soldiers. It can also be seen in the attempts to regulate armor beginning in the late seventh century. The first to do so was Ervig, a Visigothic king, who some time between 680 and 687 issued a legal code demanding among other things that "some" of his soldiers "shall wear armor." These laws were followed in 750 by a similar edict ordered by Aistulf, a king of the Lombards, which required the richest and most powerful of his warriors to be outfitted with armor, as well as a shield and weapons.

Helmets

After the first barbarian invasions, helmets became much more plentiful. Those brought into the Empire by the barbarians were often only simple iron skull caps or metal frameworks covered with leather or another fabric. Of course, compared with those used by the Romans, these provided negligible protection, so very quickly barbarian soldiers discarded these and used or imitated Roman types of helmets.

However, even Roman helmets were eventually rejected for a new type of helmet, the so-called spangenhelm. Perhaps the most original of all barbarian armaments, excavated examples from England and continental Europe generally consist of four parts: the cap, two hinged cheek-pieces, and a section of mail protecting the back and sides of the neck. The cap was made of a wide metal band encircling the head, with a narrower second metal band attached to the first by rivets and running from back to front. This second band was further linked to the wide circular band by two short bands running down toward the ears. The spaces left open by this framework were filled by plates of metal or horn attached to the bands by rivets. In some, semicircular holes were cut into the front of the helmet for the eyes, and a long, thin piece of iron descended between them to serve as a nose guard. In others, most notably the Vendel-style helmets, the eyes and upper nose were protected by a metal sheet, with a smaller nose guard descending down from it, or, as in the Sutton Hoo helmet, the eyes, nose, and much of the chin are covered by a larger metal sheet. The metal cheek-pieces, hinged onto the wide browband, covered both the ears and cheeks and were attached together under the chin by a leather or cloth strap. A mail neck guard, made in a manner similar to armor, was attached to the back of the browband. They were frequently decorated by inlaying, engraving, or overlaying, the latter including copper-alloy eyebrows added above the eyeholes, or by other means, such as adding the figure of a boar on the crown.

Although it used to be believed that early medieval helmets were rare and only found in the graves of chieftains and other elite soldiers, so many of these helmets have been excavated that such a belief must now be questioned. Further evidence from artistic sources supports this view, and it appears that most soldiers in the early Middle Ages must have owned and used a helmet.

Shields

The only piece of armor used by almost all barbarian soldiers was the shield. Indeed, in artistic and written media the early medieval shield, known typically as a buckler, became a symbol of military occupation. The most common barbarian buckler was round, or elliptical, convex, and made from strips of wood secured together and covered by leather. They measured on average 31–36 inches (80–90 centimeters) in diameter and were 0.3–0.5 inches (0.8 to 1.2 centimeters) thick. An iron boss measuring some 6–6.7 inches (15–17 centimeters) in diameter, with an average height of 2.4–4 inches (6–10 centimeters)—although sometimes it could be quite a bit larger—was placed in the center of the outside of the shield and anchored a grip made of wood, hide, or fabric on the inside. Many shield bosses found in grave sites are also decorated with applied metal decoration. In fact, the iron boss is often the only evidence that a shield was buried with its warrior. The poem "The Battle of Maldon" states that the shield of one of the Anglo-Saxon warriors, Atherich, had a metal rim, which burst under the blow of his enemy's sword. Shields are also noted in Anglo-Saxon riddles, written in both Latin and Old English, where they are frequently described as scarred but not broken by the blows of enemy weapons.

SIEGE WEAPONS

Most medieval military engagements of any period were not fought on the battlefield but against fortified sites. Without capturing these fortifications, the conquest of foreign lands was impossible. In ancient times, forced starvation of the besieged site was a frequently used tactic, often with success, although it depended on the abundance of food supplies in the fortress or town and on the availability of relief troops. But driving a town or castle into starvation could be protracted; it often required more than a year and sometimes longer to gain victory. A second means of ending a siege victoriously was through treachery, gaining the fortification's surrender by convincing someone inside to open a gate or gates. Again, this could take quite a long time. The ten-year siege of Troy was not created by Homer simply as a literary metaphor; it also reflected ancient reality. Even after ten years it required a trick, the Trojan horse, to take the heavily fortified city and end the confrontation. A similar, although less dramatic, siege of Rome ended after ten years when one of the wealthy families responsible for guarding the city decided to open a gate to the Ostrogothic besiegers in a vain hope to protect their riches.

Other ancient methods of conquering fortified sites were also time consuming. Chief among these was mining, in which the attacking force would attempt to tunnel under the walls and then collapse the tunnels to bring down a section of the walls above. Nor did the direct assault of a fortification using scaling ladders and battering rams often bring success, as these attacks could be easily countered by defenders inside the fortification. Some were built on terrain that could not be easily surmounted, such as the Judean fortress at Masada that, in the first century AD, held out for nearly three years before the Romans could construct an earthen ramp to reach its walls.

As early as the fourth century BC, Greek military engineers recognized the need to construct heavy weapons, artillery pieces, with enough power to breach the gates and walls of a fortification. Eventually the torsion catapult was developed. From these a missile, typically a large stone or bolt, could be launched with enough force to cause a breach in the wall or to weaken it so that continual impact would ultimately cause a breach. Of course, it was hoped that this would not be required, and that the mere display of such force would induce those besieged to yield to their attackers. And this often happened.

The Romans adopted Greek torsion catapults—the larger weapons known as ballistae, and the smaller, and more portable weapons, *cheiroballistae*—which had, by then, been significantly improved by the famed Macedonian military leaders, Philip II and Alexander the Great. These catapults had arms fastened to two tightly twisted skeins made of sinew set on a heavy stock fitted with a slider placed in a dovetailed groove and able to slide freely back and forth. On each side of the stock was a straight ratchet with two pawls fitted into them and attached to a clawlike trigger mechanism. A missile would be placed against a thick bowstring strung between the two arms and, after having been drawn back by the ratchets, would be shot by releasing the trigger.

To these catapults the Romans added *onagers*, which used only a single horizontal spring and one arm swinging upwards. At the end of the single arm was a sling in which a missile, usually a stone ball, was placed for launching. The trigger was a piece of rope used to anchor the arm ready for loading, which was mounted on two large and heavy horizontal beams held apart by a number of crossbeams. Technologically simpler than the ballistae or *cheiroballistae, onagers* may have been more powerful; apparently, they also appeared only during the barbarian invasions and are mentioned by only one contemporary author, Ammianus Marcellinus.

At this time, the Romans seem to have had a large amount of artillery. Indeed, they might have had catapults defending nearly every one of their fortifications, and it is reported that several arms factories continued to supply artillery for use during the early invasions. It is similarly recorded that in some military engagements these catapults thwarted barbarian attacks against Roman fortifications. For example, Ammianus explains how one Gothic attack was halted when a single large stone fired from an *onager*, despite hitting no one, caused such mass confusion that it eventually routed the attackers. This artillery, whose adoption was not ultimately successful in defeating the barbarians, caused such heavy death and destruction among them that it postponed the final outcome. Procopius, writing about the defense of Rome in 537–538, provides such a witness:

> [A]at the Salerian Gate a Goth of goodly stature and a capable warrior, wearing armor and having a helmet on his head, a man who was of no mean station in the Gothic nation . . . was hit by a missile from a catapult which was on a tower at his left. Passing through the armor and the body of the man, the missile sank more than half its length into a tree, and pinning him to the spot where it entered the tree, it suspended him there as a corpse (Barton C. Hacker, "Greek Catapults and Catapult Technology: Science, Technology, and War in the Ancient World," *Technology and Culture* 9 (1968): 45–46).

However, once the barbarian tribes had overrun the Empire, they seem not to have adopted this technology from their conquered foes. Some historians have contended that the barbarians were simply unable to use or to continue to build Roman-style catapults. They argue that there is some evidence of early barbarian use of artillery, for example at the siege of Thessaloniki by the Goths in 269 and at Tours by the Alemanni or Franks a century later. However, both of these engagements were early in the invasions of the Roman Empire, and their artillery failed to prove effective as the defenders were able in both cases to burn the catapults by hurling blazing missiles at them. After the fifth century there is no further mention of them in historical sources, and they seem to have passed into obscurity.

Other historians argue that the reason for the barbarians' rejection of Roman catapult technology is that they accepted an alternative artillery, the traction trebuchet. Here a rotating beam was placed on a fulcrum supported by a wooden tower and base. On one end of the beam was attached a sling for the projectile and on the other a number of ropes that, when pulled in unison, turned the beam and fired a stone shot with considerable accuracy and force. As evidence, they point to an eyewitness account of the siege of Thessaloniki by the Avaro-Slavs in 597, written by John, the Archbishop of Thessaloniki. In this account, John describes siege machines of the Avaro-Slavs, known to him as *petroboles* or "rock throwers," possibly indicating that they were traction trebuchets:

These *petroboles* were tetragonal and rested on broader bases, tapering to narrow extremities. Attached to them were thick cylinders well clad in iron at the ends, and there were nailed to them timbers like beams from a large house. These timbers had the slings from the back and from the front strong ropes, by which, pulling down and releasing the sling, they propel the stones up high and with a loud noise. And on being fired they sent up many great stones so that neither earth nor human constructions could bear the impacts. They also covered those tetragonal *petroboles* with boards on three sides only, so that those inside firing them might not be wounded with arrows by those on the walls. And since one of these, with its boards, had been burned to a char by a flaming arrow, they returned, carrying away the machines. On the following day they again brought these *petroboles* covered with freshly skinned hides and with the boards, and placing them closer to the walls, shooting, they hurled mountains and hills against us. For what else might one term these extremely large stones? (As quoted in Speros Vyronis, Jr., "The Evolution of Slavic Society and the Slavic Invasions in Greece: The First Major Attack on Thessa-loniki, AD 597," *Hesperia* 50 (1981): 384).

It is further suggested that the technology for these siege weapons was transferred to the Avaro-Slavs by a captured Byzantine soldier named Bousas a decade before the siege of Thessaloniki. Whether these were actually traction trebuchets or not, they do not seem to have impressed anyone enough to make them anything other than the rarest of early medieval weapons.

THE ENEMY: THE HUNS

The Huns first appeared at the end of the fourth century when they attacked barbarian tribes living to the north and west of the Danube. These barbarians then crossed the river and attacked the Roman Empire. They brought with them a style of warfare not entirely un-known to either the barbarians or the Romans, although neither had seen it on such a large scale. This description of the Huns, also from the pen of Ammianus Marcellinus, somewhat distorts the history of the Huns, but it does show the curiosity of the Roman people toward these soldiers:

> They are ill-fitted to fight on foot, and remain glued to their horses, hardy but ugly beasts, on which they sit like women to perform their everyday business. Buying or selling, eating or drinking, are all done by day and night on horseback and they even bow forward over their beasts' narrow necks to enjoy a deep and dreamy sleep. When they need to debate some important matter they conduct their conference in the same posture . . . They sometimes fight by challenging their foes to single combat, but when they join battle they advance in packs, uttering their various war-cries. Being lightly equipped and very sudden in their movements can deliberately scatter and gallop about at random, inflicting tremendous slaughter (Ammianus Mar-cellinus, *The Later Roman Empire (A.D. 354–378)*, trans. Walter Hamilton [Harmondsworth, England: Penguin Books, 1986], 411–412).

Initially, the Romans hired the Huns to help them fight the other barbarian tribes who had attacked their borders. As the Huns be-came a more permanent presence in the Empire, the Romans, who had been unable to handle the speed of the barbarian invasions before this, still held the balance of power on the frontier, although this balance was shifting away from them. This, in turn, created a previously unseen unity among the Visigoths, Ostrogoths, Vandals, and other barbarians to survive against these two enemies, the Romans and the Huns. Content at first to remain on the frontiers of the old Empire, the barbarians penetrated farther and farther into Roman territory until they occupied southern Gaul, Spain, and North Africa. However, even before those final migrations came about, in about 405 a large group of Huns, perhaps the majority of them, had turned their backs on the Romans and began to fight against both the Eastern and the Western Empire.

So very early on in the history of the Early Middle Ages both the barbarians and the Romans felt the full force of the Huns' method of fighting wars, for they fought very differently than either the barbarians or the Romans. Obviously, some of this difference was in their attitude, as the Huns are reported to have fought with a confidence and a ferocity that had rarely been seen in soldiers before this time— certainly, if Vegetius is correct, Roman soldiers lacked this. Some of the difference was also attributable to the Huns' training and discipline: they were able to perform military maneuvers on the battlefield with a speed and dexterity that could only have come from years of being on horseback, a characteristic that Ammianus gives them in his description above. Yet a major reason for the difference between the Hunnic art of war and that of the barbarians or Romans was their use of the mounted archer as the primary component of their strategy and tactics.

The Huns used light cavalry, all of whom carried composite bows, and some also carried spears and swords. This cavalry almost always operated as mounted archers. They would not ride directly into an opposing force as in a charge, but would ride around them, firing as they passed. The contemporary writer, Claudian, describes the tactic: "Their double nature fitted not better the twi-formed Centaurs to the horses that were parts of them. Disorderly, but of incredible swiftness, they often return to the fight when little expected" ("Against Rufinus," in *Claudian,* trans. Maurice Platnauer [Cambridge, MA: Harvard University Press, 1922], I:51). These soldiers were especially skillful, capable of shooting their bows with great accuracy from either side of their horses at full gallop. They could also fire across the rear of their horses to protect themselves and their companions as they withdrew from an attack or in case of retreat. Their bows were not overly powerful, certainly not compared with the bows carried by Byzantine foot soldiers or by later, mounted archers. They appear to have been unable to shoot an arrow capable of penetrating the armor worn by their opponents, although against unarmored enemies or unprotected parts of armored soldiers their barbed arrows could be devastating. The Huns only used infantry as auxiliaries.

Despite contemporary and modern popular opinion that the mounted archers of the Huns wore no armor, it is currently believed they did indeed wear it during battlefield confrontations. However, the Huns favored scale or lamellar armor and not the mail that was becoming more prevalent throughout the fourth and fifth centuries. This preference is remarked on by several late Roman writers who seem surprised by it, perhaps giving an indication that scale armor was not considered to be as protective as mail at the time, or perhaps they believed the Huns should have been able to afford the more expensive mail coats. A simpler answer could be that mail was more fashionable among Romans than scale, but the opposite was true with the Huns. One late Roman author, writing in the fifth century, also describes a Hun who wore no sleeves on his scale armor, provoking some surprise. This might indicate a general trend, especially among these mounted archers who may have thought the weight and bulkiness of such armor impeded their ability to fire their bows accurately. No doubt both scale armor with or without sleeves was used by Huns; again, there was no standardization.

Judging from his earlier comments, Ammianus Marcellinus had a low opinion of the beauty of Hunnic horses—being "ill-shaped"—although he seems to have held their abilities in higher esteem—calling them "hardy." It is certainly clear from his statement that their owners greatly valued their horses, better known as "steppe ponies." While little is known about the horses that were ridden by other barbarian tribes who fought in these early medieval wars, much more is known about Hunnic horses, especially that they were light, short, and fast. They could also go for long distances without tiring, although Ammianus remarks elsewhere in his narrative that most Hun cavalry soldiers traveled with several horses during times of war, changing mounts frequently to preserve their horses' strength. Moreover, the Huns' horses were most often mares, as their milk could sustain the life of the warrior on campaign if needed. Mares are also easier to control than stallions. These may in fact have been the ancestors of the modern Mongolian horse, the mares standing an average of 50 inches (127 centimeters) high and being able to be milked four to five times a day, providing 0.11 pounds (50 grams) of milk each time.

After his defeat at the battle of Chalons in 451, Attila's star began to fall rapidly. This most feared of all barbarian military leaders had been forced to turn back from an invasion of foreign lands, virtually the first time that such had happened to a Hun army since 405. Attila tried to regroup in Hungary, but even after he had done so, when he turned his army south into Italy, he could not regain his former military status. His army, hampered more by disease than by enemy forces, was forced to turn back once again. Attila did not live much longer. He died in 453, after a night of drinking and carousing, reports a contemporary critic, Jordanes. Attila was a man whose excesses in life, more than any military activity, brought about his premature death. A Hunnic civil war followed Attila's demise, fought between his two sons over leadership of the tribe. Peoples previously subjected to the Huns, both barbarians and Romans, took advantage of this turmoil and the now extremely weakened Hun army could do nothing in response. By the end of the next decade, the Huns had begun retreating from Europe back toward the steppes. Some remained in what was later to be called Hungary, but those who did were forced to appeal to their former enemies for protection against invaders of their lands. It certainly was a comeuppance.

CHAPTER TWO

The Carolingian Era, 750–1050

HISTORY

Charlemagne

Pippin III named the Frankish royal dynasty he founded after his father, Charles Martel, but it would be his son, also named Charles, who would give the dynasty its dominant military character. Charlemagne—Carolus Magnus, Charles the Great, Karl der Grosse, Karel de Grote, Carlomagno, Carlo Magno—ruled the Carolingian Frankish kingdom from 768 to 814. In all but one of those years, 791, he mustered his military forces and took them on campaign—that this absence of military activity was remarkable can be seen by the fact that it was specifically noted in the official narrative record of the kingdom, the *Annales Regni Francorum* for that year. Charlemagne fought against Aquitanians, Avars, Saxons, Andalusian Muslims, and Lombards, and in all these actions he was successful. Indeed, on only one occasion was even a small part of his army defeated, when the booty-laden rearguard, led by Roland, was ambushed leaving Spain at Roncesvalles in 778, an event that within two centuries spawned a great literary myth.

By the time of his death, Charlemagne had more than doubled the size of the kingdom he had inherited forty-two years before, encompassing modern France, Belgium, Holland, Switzerland, Austria, most of Germany, more than half of Italy (down to Rome), and northern Spain. Furthermore, as each of his victorious military campaigns was against a non-Catholic enemy, all of his wars were waged for the benefit and with the blessing of the church. In 800, this service was formally recognized on Christmas Day, when Pope Leo III crowned him as the first Holy Roman Emperor.

No sooner had Charlemagne ascended the Frankish throne than he began his military career. Following barbarian tradition, at his death Pippin III had divided his kingdom between Charles and his younger brother, Carloman, a situation that suited neither of them. Yet before they could settle their differences militarily, a rebellion arose in Aquitaine, in the lands inherited by Charles. The people there, only recently subjugated by Pippin, clearly saw in his death an opportunity for self-rule, especially as Charlemagne's youthful reputation was not one of a warrior. But without the assistance of his brother, who had promised support but clearly regarded the rebellion as Charles's business alone, the new king responded with a military acuity that would characterize his entire reign. Einhard, his biographer, describes Charlemagne's leadership in this action: "Charlemagne pressed on energetically with the expedition which he had put into the field, refusing to withdraw from a campaign already started or to abandon the task once undertaken. In the end, with no small perseverance and continued effort, he brought to complete fruition what he was striving to achieve" (Einhard, "Life of Charlemagne," in *Two Lives of Charlemagne,* ed. and trans. Lewis Thorpe [Harmondsworth, UK: Penguin, 1969], 59). Charlemagne then pursued the rebel leaders until they were caught and executed, displaying the ruthlessness toward defeated enemies that also characterized his reign.

Having put down the Aquitanian rebellion with such ease, Charlemagne immediately turned to other military activity. Carloman's death in 771, following which his wife and sons fled to Italy, left Charlemagne in complete control of his father's entire kingdom and obviated the need for war against his brother. But there were plenty of enemies to be found outside his realm. The first of these, the Saxons, who lived on the northeast borders of the Carolingian kingdom, also proved to be the most troublesome. Charlemagne's armies seemed never to have much difficulty in defeating Saxon forces, first in 776, nor to convert them to Catholicism—his justification for these and other conquests. Yet once he had removed his main army from their lands, the Saxons always rose up against the substantially fewer forces he left behind and returned to their former religious practices. Thus, Charlemagne was forced to return several times to Saxony, in 782–785, 793, 797, and 804. In each of these campaigns, he became increasingly ruthless as he felt the need to answer their continued revolts with an increased strength. In 772 Charlemagne was satisfied to just defeat them in battle, forcing them to accept Christian baptisms, taking a few hostages, and destroying the religiously significant Donar Oak at Geismar. In 782–785, after defeating them yet again, he forced their leader, Widukind, to be baptized with himself standing as godfather, and he massacred 4,500 rebel prisoners of war. In 793 and 797, Charlemagne added deportation to the punishment of forced baptisms and executions of rebel leaders, relocating thousands of Saxons throughout the rest of his realm. Finally, in 804, Charlemagne offered the simple choice to all Saxons: be baptized and peaceful, or be executed.

When not fighting the Saxons, Charlemagne undertook campaigns against others along his borders. In 778, this was against the Muslims in Spain. Although there is some question as to what Charlemagne's aims were in carrying out such an expedition—was his intention to occupy all of Spain or was he merely trying to cut down on the number of raids into southern Francia by Muslim forces—it proved to be successful enough to ensure a continued military interest in the region. Over the next few years Charlemagne frequently sent armies into northern Spain. Sometimes these campaigns resulted in impressive victories—for example in 778 when he captured Barcelona and razed Pamplona, and in 801 when he recaptured Barcelona—while others led to relatively few gains, usually only in booty. In Spain in 778, Charlemagne also suffered his single significant loss when his baggage train, following the main army through Roncesvalles Pass out of the Pyrenees, was attacked and looted by Basques as revenge for the destruction of Pamplona. Such an event might have fallen into the historical abyss had not a later, anonymous poet used it as the central feature of his crusader propaganda epic, *The Song of Roland,* a literary masterpiece named after the leader of the baggage guard. Making the victors of Roncesvalles Muslims instead of Basques, increasing their numbers to more than 100,000, introducing an evil Carolingian traitor, Ganelon, and inventing a decisive vengeful counterattack by a 200-year-old Charlemagne may have destroyed the facts of the battle, but it ensured its legacy.

In 790–792, Charlemagne campaigned against the Avars, whose lands stretched from Hungary to the Bavarian borders of the Carolingian kingdom, and whose alliance with the rebellious Duke of Bavaria, Tassilo, added a military justification to that of Catholic conversion always used by Charlemagne. Perhaps having learned

the lessons of conquest and pacification from his dealings with the
Saxons, Charlemagne dealt fiercely and decisively with the Avars.
Noting that this campaign was carried out "with more vigour than
any of the others and with much greater preparation," Einhard
writes:

> Just how many battles were fought and how much blood was shed is
> shown by the fact that Pannonia is now completely uninhabited and
> that the site of the Khan's palace is now so deserted that no evidence
> remains that anyone ever lived there. All the Hun nobility died in this
> war, all their glory departed (Einhard, p. 67).

So great was the booty taken by Charlemagne from the wealthy
Avars that it funded the building of his own palace complex at
Aachen, including the construction of the Notre Dame Cathedral
there.

But it was probably the conquest of the Lombards that Charlemagne himself was most proud of, for he adopted the title King of
the Lombards after its successful completion. Charlemagne's campaign, which ultimately added Italy, from the Alps to Rome, to the
Carolingian kingdom, was initiated in 773 by Pope Hadrian I, who
beseeched the relatively newly crowned king for assistance against
the Lombards. It was not that the Lombards, who had held Rome
since the time of the Byzantines, had begun to mistreat their Italian
subjects more or to even treat the pope with less respect than previously. Hadrian's plea was prompted instead by the fact that the Lombards were Arian Christian and not Catholic. As such the pontiff
deemed them to be heretics. Surely, he felt, they should not have political suzerainty over the headquarters of the Catholics.

Of course, Charlemagne, who truly believed his responsibility as
the leader of a powerful military extended to the conversion of non-
Catholics, by force if need be, could not refuse a summons from his
ecclesiastic overlord. He responded quickly, mustered his army and
marched them through the Alps. His siege of the Lombard capital,
Pavia, began in late spring 773 and lasted for nine months, during
which time the Carolingian soldiers suffered more from disease than
from their opponents, especially as the weather of northern Italy
worsened with the approach of winter. Ultimately, the siege was successful, and Charlemagne accepted the surrender of the Lombards
from their king, Didier. Charlemagne went on to Rome, where he
was acclaimed its liberator, champion, and—although he left much
of the local political control to the pope—governor.

This was not to be the last time Charlemagne would march into Italy at the head of an army, however. In 800, Hadrian's successor, Pope Leo III, requested military assistance against local Roman forces, ecclesiastical as well as political, opposed to him and his pro-Carolingian policies. In traveling to Rome this time he met no armed opposition as Leo's enemies chose to submit to the Carolingian king rather than face him. In recognition of this deed and his leadership of virtually the whole of Western and Central Europe, Leo III crowned Charlemagne as the first Holy Roman Emperor. Although there is some dispute over whether Charlemagne wished for or initially welcomed this crowning, as it essentially meant that the Pope held some power over the secular and the ecclesiastical world, there is no doubt that he liked the honor and bore the title for the rest of his reign. In 803 he even made his nobles and military leaders take oaths of fidelity to him as Holy Roman Emperor, many of whom had previously taken similar oaths to him as king.

CAROLINGIAN MILITARY ORGANIZATION AND OBLIGATION

Charlemagne accomplished these military feats because he, like his father and grandfather, understood the power of diverse, well-trained, well-equipped, and well-led professional forces. He also continually sought to improve his army despite his many victories, which might have suggested that he could have adopted a more economically conservative policy and maintained the status quo. As numerous laws (capitularies) from Charlemagne's reign attest, he was constantly seeking to improve and standardize his army, especially in their personnel, command structure, training, provisioning, and arms and armor. The numbers of soldiers Charlemagne employed at any time during his reign certainly called for this. Exactly how large this Carolingian force was, however, is debated by modern historians. Some believe Charlemagne's standing force of professional, regular soldiers numbered in the tens of thousands and that when the militias, mercenaries, and other irregular troops were added for any of his numerous campaigns, the total force operating throughout the entire realm, in offensive and defensive strategies, garrisoning, policing, training, engineering, and quartermastering duties, as well as in actual fighting, numbered more than 100,000. Others contend that the economy of the Carolingian kingdom and later empire could not support such a force, although this contention, even they admit, is based on socioeconomic sources and data that are far from definite and require a certain amount of sociological paradigmatic manipulation to "prove" Charlemagne's inability to draw on such a large military force. Without the kind of demographic records and muster rolls that we have for other periods, the size of the Carolingian army will have to remain in dispute, though all do agree that it was large, the greatest organized military force in Western Europe since the fall of the Roman Empire.

How Charlemagne raised such a force is also an issue not completely determinable by the extant sources. Although in the past he has often been portrayed as the father of "feudalism," that term has found much modern criticism—at its best it is more of an idealistic theory to describe the social and economic structure of Carolingian society—such a title bestowed on this very important ruler has little value today. However, it can be seen from a number of Charlemagne's capitularies that he relied on some form of military obligation to fill his ranks as well as to relieve the royal treasury from the responsibility of paying for the arms, armor, and provisions of those in the kingdom wealthy enough—and thereby concerned enough with the preservation of their economic well-being to feel not only militarily but economically obligated to defend their lands—to supply these themselves. Charlemagne also required all property-holders of the realm to participate in military service—either they themselves had to serve in the army or they had to arm and pay for a suitable replacement. An example of one of these capitularies is dated 808:

> Every free man who has four *mansi* (a measurement of land) of his own property, or as a benefice from anyone, shall equip himself and go to the army, either with his lord, if the lord goes, or with his count. He who has three *mansi* shall be joined to a man who has one *mansus,* and shall aid him so that he may serve for both. He who has only two *mansi* of his own property shall be joined to another who likewise has two *mansi,* and one of them, with the aid of the other, shall go to the army. He who has only one *mansus* of his own shall be joined to one of three who have the same and shall aid him, the latter shall go alone; the three who have aided him shall stay home (Stewart Easton and Helene Wieruszowski, *The Era of Charlemagne* [Princeton, NJ: D. Van Nostrand and Company, 1961], 141).

Landowners—landlords or, more simply, lords—with more than five *mansi* of land were also required to provide additional men, retinues, to serve as cavalry or infantry soldiers. Even subject peoples were required to fill the ranks of Charlemagne's army, though they were always commanded by Frankish leaders. Allies and mercenaries were, of course, always welcome to fill out the numbers of Carolingian soldiers.

As suggested, Charles Martel must be credited with increasing the role and importance of cavalry in Western European armies. But it was his grandson, Charlemagne, who must be recognized as the leader who made the cavalry a dominant arm of his military organization. In fact, historians have generally agreed that Charlemagne's was the first Western medieval army that used cavalry as its dominant force in battle. However, it is worth noting that the Carolingian cavalry never outnumbered the infantry and, in fact, may never have exceeded 10 to 20 percent of the total number of soldiers in any army, even on the battlefield, let alone at sieges or in garrisons. Still, very early in his reign, Charlemagne recognized that the defensive requirements of his large empire and his desire to conquer lands beyond its borders required a large and dominant professional cavalry.

It is clear that the Carolingian cavalry were especially favored soldiers, an elite professional force. They had to function in a disciplined way, especially tactically, where battlefield maneuvers could be so easily disrupted by a soldier who was unable to follow the movements of his unit. They also had to be uniformly well armed and armored. The first extant law to state this policy was the *Capitulare Missorum* of 792/3, which demanded that all benefice and office holders, titled "nobles" in the Carolingian realm, possess a full coat of armor and shield as well as a horse and offensive weapons. This was followed in 802/3 by a capitulary again charging these horsemen to have their own helmets, shields, and armor coats, known to the Carolingians as byrnies. Finally, in 805, the law was made even more specific. In this capitulary, Charlemagne required anyone of his empire who held twelve *mansi* of land to have his own armor and to serve as a horseman in his army; if he failed in this duty, both his land and his armor would be taken from him. Infantry soldiers were not so well protected, although the Capitulary of Aachen, proclaimed in 802–803, did require them all to carry a shield.

The weapons carried by Carolingian soldiers, especially the cavalry, were also regulated and standardized. Like their Frankish ancestors, their principal weapon was the spear. The *Capitulare Missorum,* for example, stipulated that all horsemen must carry one, and similar commands were repeated in capitularies of 804 and 811. In addition, the cavalry were to have their own swords. So prominent were these swords that in many Carolingian narrative and literary sources they are portrayed before the lance as the cavalry soldier's primary weapon. Cavalry were also required to carry a dagger. Finally, there is also evidence that some Carolingian cavalry were armed with bows and arrows.

Carolingian Tactics and Strategy

Charlemagne's cavalry was the dominant part of his army because it played the most prominent role on the battlefield. At least, that is how most historians have portrayed Carolingian military tactics. In battle, although the Carolingian cavalry could and did dismount to fight as infantry, their primary tactic seems to have been the charge, although one not yet delivered using couched lances. What little evidence there is suggests that the spear may have been used as a throwing weapon when used by cavalry—although it could also have been used for thrusting down at an enemy. A likely scenario may have been that, when fighting infantry, the Carolingian cavalry charged and after first throwing their spears, at suitably close range, continued the attack using their swords. Alternatively it is possible that they could have thrown their spears and then turned back for another to repeat the charge. When fighting against cavalry opponents, similar tactics were probably used, though at an equal level. However, the point of the charge, here and later in the Middle Ages, may have been less to come into contact with the enemy than to cause them to flee in disorder from the battlefield. Intimidation of poorer, less well-armored infantry and cavalry by wealthy, expensively clad cavalry was the key here. Should even part of the enemy line flee at the prospect of facing these heavy horsemen, the whole of the force would be severely weakened. The cavalry would then be able to ride through the gaps left in their opponent's line, meeting little effective opposition. Subsequent charges would eventually cause the whole of the enemy army to flee, and victory would be won with very few casualties suffered. At the time, no cavalry was more intimidating in Western Europe than Charlemagne's.

When not fighting battles, the cavalry could be used for search-and-destroy missions, skirmishing, scouting, scavenging, and other duties that required speed and mobility. During sieges, cavalry was reduced to a supporting role, scouting and skirmishing where and when necessary.

Even if it was not the most dominant part of the Carolingian army, the infantry were enormously important in all military activities. They were present in all battles, in far greater numbers than the cavalry, and served as support troops to those delivering the primary attacks on the enemy. Throughout the Middle Ages, when the cavalry faltered—admittedly not often during Charlemagne's reign—the infantry provided a defensive formation behind which the cavalry could regroup if needed. Thus, there was an obvious need for discipline and training among Carolingian infantry soldiers. Should they flee from the battlefield, whether the cavalry had or not, the battle was likely lost. Should they stand solidly in their formation, again whether the cavalry had fled or not, the battle was as likely won. Carolingian infantry also served in patrols and as garrison troops, besiegers, and construction crews for fortifications and other defenses or public buildings.

Following his father, Pippin III, Charlemagne traditionally mustered his army yearly at the Marchfield, so designated not because of the time of year it was summoned but because of its bellicose purpose. This assembly was called every year, even when Charlemagne undertook no campaigns. At that meeting, Charlemagne would instruct his lords and other generals of his military purposes. Sometimes he kept the army together in a single force, while at other times it was broken down into two or three separate forces. On those occasions, one army might campaign in Saxony while another campaigned in Spain; a third army might have defensive or construction responsibilities. Until later in his life, as his health weakened, Charlemagne placed himself at the lead of one of these armies. His sons often commanded the others. Campaigns usually ended within the year, most often before the fall harvest, although if needed, such as during the siege of Pavia, soldiers remained in the field until their goals were achieved.

Communication between and among all of Charlemagne's military units seems to have been remarkably efficient during these military seasons. Charlemagne used signal fires and towers to send short messages while riders delivered longer dispatches. Responses to emergencies were quickly made, and it was not unusual to see these separate armies join together to face an imminent threat, even if it meant a long march through a large part of the kingdom. Service in the Carolingian army was difficult, long, and sometimes dangerous, but soldiers were well treated, honored, well fed, and, seemingly, more economically well-off over other, nonmilitary Carolingians.

Even though it is the battles that are more renowned at this or any other time in the Middle Ages, the most frequent military activity of Carolingian soldiers was the siege. Even a small, unfortified town needed to be besieged if the inhabitants desired to hold out against their attackers. Of course, a larger, fortified site stood a better chance of withstanding besiegers, but that, too, was determined almost solely by the willingness of the population within not to surrender. It seems that Carolingian kings, including Charlemagne, did not possess artillery of any sort and thus were forced to rely on starvation or treachery to bring them success. This meant sieges could take a very long time, as when Charlemagne besieged Pavia for more than nine months, even if there was no potential relieving force, as was also the case at Pavia. Chances were always good that a besieging army might become more quickly fatigued, hungry, or diseased than those inside the town and raise their siege.

Therefore, it was generally whoever had the strongest determination, the besiegers or the besieged, who claimed victory at the end of a siege. Again at Pavia, this proved to be Charlemagne who, despite losing much of his army to disease, refused to be driven away from the city. It should be noted, however, that most places besieged by the Carolingians surrendered quite quickly, no doubt either apathetic over whoever their governor might be or fearful of reprisals by kings known for their ruthlessness should they try to hold out and ultimately fail.

Successors to Charlemagne and the Eventual Fall of the Carolingian Empire

In 806, recognizing his age and fearing that his health was deteriorating, Charlemagne met with his three surviving sons, Charles, Pippin, and Louis, and proposed a division of the kingdom between them, following the tradition of partible inheritance. His sons, who had taken only a little part in governing before, although they had been leaders of the army since their teenage years, were anxious about this division and the lands that might be theirs. At the same time, as seemingly with all partible inheritances, a sibling rivalry began to brew, as each brother worried that the other's lands might surpass theirs in quantity or quality. Charlemagne did not die in 806, however, and by 814, when he did die, only one of his three sons survived, Louis, known during his lifetime as Louis the Pious.

"The Pious" as a cognomen undoubtedly indicates a special relationship that Louis had with the church. However, it could also be taken in a more insulting way, as someone who placed his religious devotion over his political and military responsibilities. Louis was not the man his father was, "the greatest and most distinguished of all men" (Einhard, 52), as described by Einhard, who used his biography of Charlemagne, dedicated to the new king, to remind him exactly what large shoes he had not been filling.

As a military leader, Louis was far from being his father, both in ability and strategy. Brittany and Aquitaine never seemed to have accepted him as their king, despite his inheritance of those lands and even despite his carrying the Imperial title. On several occasions, Louis was forced to undertake campaigns into those provinces to put down rebellions, and the number of these obviously indicates their overall futility. On each campaign, his armies were met by compliance and submission, but as soon as they had left, the rebellions would return.

Nor could Louis effectively garrison these provinces because of the almost constant amount of military activity on the Carolingian Empire's borders. The most persistent of those attacking these borders, the Vikings, will be discussed at length later. As early as 820 the Vikings attempted to move from their previously preferred targets, the British Isles and Ireland, to the European continental mainland. The 820 invasion into the mouth of the River Seine was repulsed by Carolingian troops, but it was one of the few successful defenses made by Louis' soldiers against them, and within a decade Viking raiders could be found sailing almost unhindered along almost all of the rivers of the Carolingian realm.

Other persistent military threats to the security of Louis' reign were the Bulgarians, who attacked the southeastern Carolingian provinces in 828, and the Muslims, who crossed over the Mediterranean and attacked Italy in 837 and 840 and southern France in 838. These enemies, like their Viking counterparts in the north, seem to have had little notion of conquest, but rather sought to enrich themselves with plunder acquired by hit-and-run raids. So it was in 838 that Marseilles was sacked and burned but not conquered.

It was obviously difficult to defend the Carolingian lands against such random and ruthless military activity, and most historians find little fault in the failure of Louis the Pious, or his successors—for raids by the Vikings, Bulgarians, and Muslims, later joined by the Hungarians, continued for the next two centuries—to defend his people against such activities. Should he have been actively waging other wars successfully, Louis would probably not be judged so harshly for initiating the decline of the Carolingian Empire. But it is during his reign that the civil wars that plagued the realm until its eventual fall began.

To avoid repeating the negligence of his father in instructing him and his brothers on the art of governance by sharing his offices and landholdings, early in his reign Louis included his own sons in ruling his kingdom. At his very ascension to the throne, he placed Lothar, Pippin, and Louis "the German" in governing positions and later he did the same with Charles the Bald, whose youth and circumstances of birth—being born to Judith of Bavaria, Louis' second wife, rather than his first, Irmengard, the mother of the other three—had kept him from joining his brothers in the early acquisition of power. However, what might be thought of as a nice way to ease an heir into his role as ruler, when split between several sons, simply became a platform for inciting jealousy and rivalry. It had happened this way with the Merovingian kings and was to do so also with the Carolingian ones. Of course, the problem was partible inheritance, a barbarian tradition that almost always ensured fraternal warfare, as it did with the sons of Louis the Pious.

In 830 the Carolingian Empire suffered its first fraternal civil war when Pippin and Louis the German revolted against their brother, Lothar, and father, Louis the Pious, because of the latter's perceived favoritism of the former. It was more than a year before peace was restored, when Louis the Pious agreed to direct more of his favor toward the two rebellious sons. Of course, this had little chance of correcting the problem, as Louis discovered in 833 when Lothar rose up against him, Pippin, and Louis the German, leading to his deposition and imprisonment for a year.

Nor did the deaths of Pippin or Louis in 838 and 840, respectively, put an end to these fraternal bellicosities. Instead, Pippin's death brought Charles the Bald into the fray when he received a part of the redivided Carolingian lands, which was perceived as a direct insult to Louis' sons by his first wife. Louis' death prompted so much rivalry between Lothar, Louis the German, and Charles the Bald that it was not until 843 with the Treaty of Verdun that a division of the Carolingian Empire could be agreed on, and this occurred only after an alliance had been made between Louis and Charles against Lothar.

Of course, the Treaty of Verdun did not stop the Carolingian civil wars either. Indeed, it was less than a year after the treaty had been signed that Charles the Bald mounted a campaign into Aquitaine against his nephew, Pippin (known as Pippin II), the son of Pippin I.

Pippin II, who had supported Lothar against Louis and Charles, had been excluded from the Treaty of Verdun's land settlements but had nevertheless occupied and declared himself king of Aquitaine, a province given to Charles the Bald in the Verdun agreement. Hence Charles invaded Aquitaine, but he was unsuccessful and was forced to accept Pippin's kingship there, although Pippin agreed to do homage to his uncle.

By 850, fatigued by the constant military bickering between himself and his brothers, Lothar decided to retire as Holy Roman Emperor and King of Italy, both of which titles he gave to his son, Louis II, who had won some military legitimacy for his defense of Italy against Muslim raiders his father had been busy fighting with his brothers. This unprecedented move rewarded the former emperor a peaceful final five years of life, but, unfortunately, his example was not followed by Louis the German, Charles the Bald, or Pippin of Aquitaine who continued to fight for the next two and a half decades. Defeats of one another became frequent and were always followed by peace treaties, but these were never decisive. Soon, Louis II and his brothers, Lothar II and Charles of Provence, joined in the fraternal conflicts. The Carolingian Empire that Charlemagne had nearly doubled in size through his military conquests was shattered.

With each outbreak of civil war the Carolingian Empire became weaker and weaker. The Vikings continued to raid, seemingly without resistance, throughout the lands. They attacked Paris almost at will, being paid off on two occasions and sacking this largest city in Western Europe on another. Smaller towns, villages, and monasteries had no chance against them, especially as no effective defense of any part of the kingdom could be mounted by the warring grandsons and great-grandsons of Charlemagne. Even when some strategic gains were made, such as when Charles the Bald decided to fortify some bridges along the Seine and to appoint some more militarily astute leaders as marcher lords to better protect the inland population in response to the sacking of Paris in 860, these plans were rarely completed and often short-lived. Only two (or possibly three) fortified bridges were actually constructed in 861and only Baldwin I, "the Iron Arm," was actually planted in a marcher province, in Flanders, in 863, before Charles was back paying off the Vikings not to attack Melun in 865. At the same time, Charles the Bald was so concerned about the possibility of rebellions against him that, during the time of the greatest number of Viking raids, he was disarming the people and tearing down their fortifications.

Rebellions by the Bretons also continued during this period, and they were joined by those living in Catalonia, on the Spanish March, so that neither province could actually be said to have been Carolingian by the beginning of the tenth century.

By 877 the grandsons and many of the great-grandsons of Charlemagne had died. Louis II died in 875, Louis the German in 876, and Charles the Bald in 877. In most instances they were succeeded by several of their own sons, partible inheritance still holding sway. These successors continued the civil wars that had by this time become so characteristic of the Carolingian kingdom that few historians write about the period with anything other than derision and ridicule. This only reflects contemporary attitudes, however, as the cognomens given the late Carolingian kings by their own chroniclers seem proof enough of their incompetence and impotence: Charles the Fat, Louis the Stammerer, Charles the Simple, Louis the Fat. And while Charles the Fat did restore Charlemagne's kingdom nearly to its former size for four years (from 884 to 888), more by the fluke of having all his cousins die at the same time rather than by any military activity, the Empire was no longer a threat to outsiders while, at the same time, being extremely vulnerable to any military or raiding force that wished to enter its borders.

By the beginning of the tenth century most of the nobles of the various Carolingian kingdoms had become frustrated by those ruling them and their incessant fraternal military squabbles. Year after year they and their retinues would be mustered to fight against other Carolingian Europeans at the same time their own lands and peoples were being ravaged by very fearsome raiders. Several tried to refuse to participate in these civil wars, but the threat always existed that they might be seen to be rebels and therefore enemies to all Carolingians. The loss of lands and titles as a potential punishment meant that few of the lesser nobles could ignore their lords' summons for long. Greater nobles had a better chance to avoid civil war participation because of their size and wealth, but even they could not refuse military service without good reason.

Only by unifying their efforts were the nobles able to contend against the selfish goals of their Carolingian overlords, and uniting together generally meant that some nobles would have to acknowledge the comparative power of rival nobles. Thus, it was not until the second decade of the tenth century before a group of nobles was able to decisively remove from power one of the Carolingian kings. This occurred in 911 when the successor to Arnulf, king of the East Franks (Germany), appropriately named Louis (or Ludwig) the

Child, followed his father to the grave without children. While some of the East Frankish nobles wanted to transfer their allegiance to one of the other Carolingian kings, most did not. They decided instead to choose their own non-Carolingian king and, after much debate, resolved to do so by election among themselves. This action set a precedent for choosing the king of Germany, who would often be named Holy Roman Emperor as well, that would last until Napoleon Bonaparte dissolved the Empire in 1806.

Of course, this meant that when a king died his successor would not necessarily be his son. Instead, the greater nobles of the realm, serving as electors, would meet and decide who among them would succeed the deceased king. From a modern viewpoint this system might seem more democratic and therefore present more of a consensus and fewer disagreements than a direct patrilineal succession, and the first election seemed to verify this. Conrad I, the Duke of Franconia, was easily elected and reigned as king of Germany from 911 to 918. Franconia was Germany's second most powerful duchy, but as Henry, the Duke of Saxony, the most powerful duchy, was quite old and expected to die soon, the electors passed him by. A similarly easy succession was had in 918 when the electors chose the new Duke of Saxony as King Henry I, over the successor to Conrad's Franconian duchy, a choice with which even Conrad agreed. But incontestable elections were unusual. Most often, if there were two (or more) strong candidates who vied for the German kingship, which obviously only one of them could hold, the loser and his supporters generally became bitter and dissatisfied with the selection, sometimes even waging civil war against the new king. While this did not occur in the early elections, it did at least twice later in the twelfth century.

Another problem that came with the election system of naming a new German king was that he, by tradition, was an inheritor of Charlemagne's title, Holy Roman Emperor. However, this happened only if he was deemed worthy of being named Holy Roman Emperor by the pope at the time of his election. Therefore, the pope often made his preference for a new emperor known, although to be historically accurate only very rarely did the wishes of the papacy matter to the German electors. What resulted, simply, was that a number of German kings were not also made Holy Roman Emperor.

Nobles from West Francia (what had become France by this time) did not name their first non-Carolingian king until later than their German cousins, in 987, nor did they opt for an elected king. Perhaps this was because they could see the problems that elections caused or might cause. But more than likely it was because at the death of their last Carolingian king, Louis V, there was one clearly dominant leader among them, Hugh Capet, the Duke of the Franks whose power base lay in the lands around Paris. At the death of the childless Louis, Hugh Capet immediately and without opposition named himself king. More importantly, he did this with the assistance and blessing of the chief ecclesiastical prelate of the kingdom, the archbishop of Reims, who agreed to this exchange of power when crowning Hugh king by declaring that he received the throne of France "by divine right." In other words, despite not inheriting the title at birth, God had determined that Hugh Capet was to be king of France. This declaration, seemingly no more than an addition to the ritual of naming a new king, thus set a precedent in France that was tied to the kingships of no other European kings: God desired that Hugh Capet and his successors be the rulers of West Francia; therefore, anyone in opposition to them was also opposing God. One would think that such a belief should not have affected subsequent baronial opposition to a French king, especially a weak one, and yet, despite some of the lords being more powerful than the kings they served under—such as the Dukes of Normandy, Counts of Aquitaine, and Counts of Flanders—very few rebellions against the Capetian dynasty are recorded during their uninterrupted rule from 987 to 1328.

From the end of the tenth to the end of the fifteenth centuries European warfare was most often fought between Christian states— perhaps simply an extension of the fraternal struggles of those Carolingian kings who eventually divided Charlemagne's realm into the lands that became modern Europe. The other major cause of medieval warfare was the defense against outside forces. Most often, these were small in number, whose whole military purpose was to raid, and in doing so also to destroy almost all they came in contact with. There were no chronological limits to this type of warfare, nor did these raiders come from only one geographical group or sociological type of people. The Vikings, discussed below, are the most famous of these, but even during their own period they were not the only raiders attacking Europe.

In parts of Europe during the tenth century raids from the Hungarians (or Magyars) were feared as much if not more than those of the Vikings. Beginning in the late ninth and lasting until the middle of the tenth centuries, raiding Hungarian horsemen made their presence felt, especially in the areas of central Europe near to their Hungarian homelands. Ironically, these raiders may first have glimpsed what became their targets when they were employed as mercenaries by Arnulf, king of the East Franks, in his 892 campaign against the Slavs in Moravia. Seven years later, in 899, they returned to the west on an expedition of their own. The Hungarians first advanced south to Pavia, which they sacked, and then wintered in Lombardy. The following year, 900, they raided Bavaria, and the year after Carinthia. After a five-year period of peace, in 906 the Hungarians returned to the west when they raided Saxony; in 907 they again raided Bavaria; in 908 Saxony and Thuringia, and in 909 Swabia. Civil wars in their homelands prohibited further raiding for eight years, but when they resumed, the Hungarians returned to the west with ruthless violence. From 917 until 926 these renewed raids were increasingly destructive, and they stretched farther, into Basle, Alsace, Burgundy, Lombardy, and Provence. But after 926, and for reasons that cannot be fully explained by the historical sources, Hungarian attacks became less frequent, although the raiders remained a threat to those living on German lands within close proximity. Again, in 950, Hungarians began to mount raids into the west. However, then they faced a more determined defender in Otto the Great, king of Germany since 936. After numerous small victories, in 955, Otto decisively defeated the Hungarians at the battle of Lechfeld, driving them back into Hungary.

Anglo-Saxon England

England was the only major European land that had not been directly affected by Charlemagne's military policies at the time of his death in 814. There had certainly been contact between the Carolingian kingdom and the people of England. In fact, in 781, Alcuin, a religious scholar, was lured away from his school in York to become the head of Charlemagne's school in Aachen. But Charlemagne never expressed an interest in campaigning against the different kings there, perhaps because the Anglo-Saxon people were already Christian or, possibly, and more simply, because the English Channel and North Sea stood in the way of any plans for conquest, at least until William the Conqueror would launch his invasion in 1066.

Anglo-Saxon England might have been quite easy for the Carolingian armies to conquer. Until the end of the tenth century there was little unity among the various kingdoms there, and this was undoubtedly the primary problem faced by the people there. Instead of working together to promote, for example, the herding of sheep, and the trading of wool, aspects of later medieval English economy that would bring the population wealth and prestige far exceeding their demographic numbers and geographical limitations, the political and military disunity of the island's peoples meant a large amount of intra-kingdom disputes and warfare. In a hypothetical year it was possible that the king of Northumbria might fight the king of Strathclyde, the king of Mercia might fight the king of Wessex, and the king of Essex might fight the king of East Anglia. And a following hypothetical year, things might be reversed, for example, with Wessex fighting Essex, East Anglia fighting Northumbria, and Mercia fighting Strathclyde. Added to this disunity were the equally disunited Scots and Welsh who could be counted on to mount frequent raids into kingdoms that further disrupted any peace or prosperity for those living along the Welsh and Scottish marches. At times, the Northumbrian and Strathclydian kings tried to maintain the old Roman Hadrian's Wall, while, in the eighth century, King Offa of Mercia tried to build a lengthy earth-and-wood ditch-and-rampart fortification, now known as Offa's Dyke, across the southern Welsh marches to better protect his people living there from Welsh raiders.

This disunity exacerbated a second major problem the Anglo-Saxons faced when, at the end of the eighth century, Vikings began to land on English shores almost exclusively to rob and plunder whatever they could before returning with this booty to Scandinavia. Initially, these unexpected attacks from abroad came as quite a shock to the Anglo-Saxon people, as expressed in the first record of a Viking raid reported in *The Anglo-Saxon Chronicle* for the year 787:

> And in [King Breohtric's] days there came for the first time three ships of Northmen from Hörthaland. And then the reeve rode there, and he wanted to take them to the king's town, for he did not know what they were. And these men killed him. That was the first time that ships of the Danes had sought the land of the English (*Anglo-Saxon Chronicle*, vol. I, *Two of the Saxon Chronicles Parallel*, eds. Charles Plummer and John Earle [Oxford: Clarendon Press, 1899], 55 [authors' translation]).

Such ignorance of Viking purpose did not hold for long, however, as after a second raid of 793 took away the undefended riches of the Anglo-Saxon monastery at Lindesfarne, Viking ships began appearing more and more frequently, along all coasts and up all navigable rivers. Of course, England was not the only target of Scandinavian Vikings. Nor did England offer any less resistance against the Vikings than did any other target, at least among the British Isles. But England's proximity to Norway and Denmark, as well as its large number of unfortified, and virtually undefended, monasteries, villages, and towns, meant that it had more than its fair share of early raids. No doubt the disunity of the military response further added to the Vikings' early ease of invasion and raiding.

For a while, Viking raiders were content to feast on the fairly rich pickings of monastic and small urban areas located near the sea or along the many rivers spread throughout the English countryside. The fact that they were filled with unarmed ecclesiastics or poorly armed farmers added to the ease of the raiders' actions, and they took untold amounts of plunder and booty back to Scandinavia. Eventually, the Vikings began wintering in England, establishing base camps from which they could raid longer and farther inland than ever before, leaving those who were previously safe because of their locations away from rivers and sea more vulnerable to attacks.

Obviously, the English did try to defend themselves. Many kings and local leaders attempted to oppose the early to mid-eighth-century Viking invasions. But they had little success, although most historians blame this lack of success on the disunity and disorganization of the Anglo-Saxon governmental and military leadership than on the Vikings' military capabilities. Most often any defense mounted was that of local militias seeking to protect their own homes, lands, and families. Just as often these brave defenders met their own ends at the hands of the invaders, and these raids continued without much of a deleterious effect.

Finally, one of the English kings, Aethelred, king of the West Saxons (Wessex), put together an army that began having success in opposing the Scandinavian invaders. After his death in April 871, his brother Alfred, who succeeded him as king, defeated the Vikings in battles fought at Englefield, Ashdown, and, fighting the so-called "Danish Great Army," at the battle of Edington. During the next few years, with a well-organized army and confident leadership, Alfred began to push Viking colonists out of the English areas that had been conquered. By 886, he had completely removed them from London and surrounding areas of Essex, prompting a reinforcing invasion of Danes under their king Haesten. But in 895, this, too, was turned back when Alfred's strategy of blocking the River Lea drove them into a flight from their camp near London. The following year, the Vikings in England chose to retreat to the north and northeast of

England, behind an artificial border that became known as the "Danelaw." Alfred also restored education, laws, and courts as main components of his English kingship. By the time of his death in 899, Alfred had earned the cognomen "the Great."

None of the victories Alfred won forced the Viking colonists entirely from England. There is, in fact, some question as to whether they were meant to do this, especially as none of the peace treaties signed between Alfred and his opponents even required it. By this time, a large number of the Scandinavians had settled in England and had ceased being foreign raiders. When the first of these settlements had been founded, or even why some Scandinavians, especially from Norway and Denmark, had decided to leave their rural existences in their homelands to take up equally rural existences in the British Isles cannot be known. For it was not only England that gained a large number of settlers, but also Scotland, the Orkney, Shetland and Faroe Islands, Wales, and Ireland. Certainly by 866 when they had established their chief colony within the Roman walls of Eboracum, which they renamed Jorvik—and from which its later name, York, was derived—colonies were numerous throughout northeastern and eastern England.

Yet these Scandinavian settlers had done more than simply move into the area. They had integrated themselves into the institutions, the culture, and the society of the people already living there. In doing so, they had become Christian, and they had begun to write using a Latin script. But they, in turn, had their own influences on the indigenous population. They began to affect the language, changing it from a Germano-Celtic to an Anglo-Scandinavia mixture. Place names became Scandinavian. And governing nobles took on Scandinavian titles. Most importantly, for later history, these settlements adopted a Scandinavian legal system, an adoption that to great extent gave a rationale to the name of this Scandinavian-settled area, the Danelaw. By the end of the ninth century, when Alfred began to gain military victories against Vikings in the south of England, it would have been impossible for him to remove all Scandinavians from Anglo-Saxon England. In reality, by this time Anglo-Saxon England had become Anglo-Scandinavian England.

For more than a century, from 878 to 980, the non-Scandinavian parts of England were largely at peace with their Scandinavian neighbors, both those living across the seas and those living in the Danelaw. There were some Viking raids, but almost all were made into the Anglo-Scandinavian north of England by Viking leaders mostly wishing to extend their political control over more than their own regions of the British Isles. Almost all failed in these endeavors. In the south of England, away from most Anglo-Scandinavian influence, the royal descendants of Alfred had prospered. Edward "the Elder" (899–924) followed by Aethelstan (924–939), and Edgar (959–975) were strong and powerful rulers who also managed to receive recognition of the supremacy of their kingship over the Viking leaders of the Danelaw, Scotland, and Strathclyde. Aethelstan even raised Hakon, the son of the Norwegian king, Harald Finehair, as his own "foster-son" in his English court. Even poorer kings, Edmund (939–946), Eadred (946–955), and Eadwig (955–959), despite having shorter reigns and struggles within their own courts, did not encourage a breakdown in peaceful relations with either the Anglo- or foreign Scandinavians.

But after the death of Edgar in 975, and the murder of his son, Edward "the Martyr," in 978 by supporters of Edward's stepbrother, Aethelred II, England fell into a period of political unrest and instability. Perhaps this was what prompted renewed Viking attacks from 980 on, although historians generally believe the problems of English rule, while certainly injurious to English defensive capabilities, were only coincidental to a renewed drive by recently united Scandinavian principalities, especially the kingdoms of Norway and Denmark, to increase their non-Scandinavian lands. Raids were mounted in 980 against Southampton, the Isle of Thanet, Cheshire, and parts of southwest England. These were followed by attacks on London and other key southern English locations, many of which ended only after a ransom, the "Danegeld," was paid. In 991, the Battle of Maldon was fought and lost, becoming the subject of a famous Old English vernacular poem. In 994, the Norwegian king, Olaf Tryggvason, who had won at Maldon and profited from Danegeld, returned to England in the company of the Danish king, Svein Haraldsson, known to history as "Forkbeard" because of his uniquely shaped beard. Despite being driven back from London, the two gained much booty and Danegeld from their military campaign. In the ensuing years, Olaf converted to Christianity and did not return, but Svein's appetite for the conquest of England had only been whetted. He returned annually. Peace in Anglo-Saxon England disappeared, as two passages from the *Anglo-Saxon Chronicle* exemplify:

> **997.** Here in this year the [Danish] army traveled throughout Devonshire into the mouth of the Severn, and there they raided, both in Cornwall and in North Wales and in Devon; then they went up at

Watchet, and there wrought much evil by burning and by the slaughtering of men, and after that traveled back throughout Penwith Tail to the south side, and traveled then into the mouth of the Tamar, and then went up until they came to Lydford, and burned and killed everything that they met, and burned down Ordwulf's monastery in Tavistock, and brought incredible war-booty with them to the ships.

1001. Here the [Danish] army came to the mouth of the Exe and then went up to the stronghold and were determinedly fighting there, and the men determinedly and ardently withstood them, then they traveled through the countryside, and did what they were accustomed: killing and burning. Then there was gathered an immense army of Devon people and Somerseters, and then they came together at Pinhoe; and as soon as they joined battle the English army gave way and many were slaughtered there, and then rode over the countryside; and each following occasion was always worse than the one before; and they brought much war-booty with them to the ships, and traveled from there into the Isle of Wight, and there traveled wherever they wished, and nothing withstood them. No navy on sea or army on land dared approach them, however far inland they went. In every way it was a heavy time, because they never left off their evil (*Anglo-Saxon Chronicle*, vol. I, 131, 141 [author's translation]).

Many similar passages can be found. All suggest that England had become a kingdom completely overrun by ruthless Scandinavian soldiers. Aethelred II was completely powerless to defend his people. Even when he did raise an army, it fled or was quickly and violently defeated. Nor did the paying of Danegeld prove to keep the attackers away for long, and when the Vikings returned to the same area the following year, as they nearly always did, and found that the people had no further funds to pay them, they seemed to have raided with even greater ferocity.

Ultimately, the English people decided that they no longer wished to endure the continual violence. Exiling the useless Aethelred in 1013, they submitted to Svein, hoping that, as king of England, the raids of his countrymen might cease. But Svein died in February 1014, and for two years the violence continued. Finally, in 1016, Cnut, Svein's son, took over the kingdom. He would rule until 1042, bringing renewed prosperity to England, mostly because, with his ascension to the English throne, the Viking raids had finally ended.

ARMS AND ARMOR

It is rare that the study of warfare, and by implication of arms and armor, intrudes on the wider study of the development of Europe since the fall of Rome. Although wars and warfare were a vitally important part of that history, they are often viewed with disdain and are either ignored or pushed to the side. Only in two cases has this not been the case. The paradigm of early modern warfare that goes by the name the "Military Revolution," although it may be discredited and dismissed by many military historians, was found to be a means for them to bring their arguments, skills, and subject closer to the more mainstream historical debate. The argument introduced by Lynn White, Jr., that the introduction of the stirrup in the early eighth century led to the rise of the feudal system in Western Europe had much the same effect. White linked the invention of the stirrup to the rise of a military elite and by extension to the rise of a system, feudalism, that affected Western Europe for the next thousand years.

His arguments did not stand for long without criticism and, once they had been thoroughly chewed over and spat out, most medieval historians were unconvinced of the connection between the stirrup and feudalism. However, White's thesis brought the stirrup to center stage and forced researchers to take a good look at its introduction and use. Without stirrups, the control of a horse was difficult and limited a rider's ability to wield some weapons. It could be learned, but training generally had to begin at a young age and practice continued throughout adulthood. The stirrup allowed soldiers easily and with less training to use the horse's speed and dexterity as a fighting tool.

So where did the stirrup come from? With the exception of an isolated but undisputed illustration of stirrups from the ninth century BC Assyrian Empire, there is no ancient evidence of stirrups. And even although they were well known in China, India, Korea, and Japan during the early Middle Ages, they seem not to have diffused to Europe or the Middle East until at least the late seventh or early eighth century. They first appear in Persia from where they spread quickly to Byzantium and then to the Franks. Over time they, and other armies they encountered, began to recognize the value of stirrups in cavalry warfare. Although their effects may never have been quite as White suggested, eventually stirrups became a very important feature of mounted warfare.

No army may have used the stirrup better than the Carolingians. Charlemagne's force, where heavy cavalry appeared in greater numbers and began to play a more prominent role than in previous medieval armies, was extremely well armed and armored. The armor and equipment of the Carolingian armies is nowhere better summarized than in the life of Charlemagne written by Notker the Stammerer, a monk of St. Gall in modern Switzerland. Although his description is somewhat poetic and overblown, it provides us with a good idea of just what a well-equipped soldier would have worn and used:

> Then came in sight that man of iron, Charlemagne, topped with his iron helm, his fists in iron gloves, his iron chest and his Platonic shoulders clad in an iron cuirass. An iron spear raised high against the sky he gripped in his left hand, while in his right he held his still unconquered sword. For greater ease of riding other men keep their thighs bare of armor; Charlemagne's were bound in plates of iron. As for his greaves, like those of all his army, they, too, were made of iron. His shield was all of iron ("Notker the Stammerer," in *Two Lives of Charlemagne,* ed. and trans. Lewis Thorpe [Harmondsworth, UK: Penguin, 1969], p. 146).

Armor

Notker the Stammerer's description of Charlemagne goes on to say that his army all wore "the same armor, and their gear was as close a copy of his own as it is possible to imagine." This, confirmed by other more contemporary sources, suggests that the armor worn by soldiers of Charlemagne's armies was homogeneous. It is clear that most soldiers wore a mail shirt, carried a shield, and had a helmet of fairly uniform appearance, but they were far from identical. This can be seen in a Carolingian pyx, now found in the Treasury at Aachen, which depicts eight soldiers on its base. All of these vary just a little: some wear armor that descends to the elbows and knees, others barely off the shoulders or down the thighs; some carry oval shields, others more round ones; some have helmets with more prominent brims and crests, others with less pronounced features. Perhaps this variation came from fashion or choice. Perhaps it was an economic decision. Certainly not everyone could afford all this armor and equipment. A mid-eighth-century source lists a helmet, body armor, sword, scabbard, leg defenses, lance, shield, and horse as the full equipment of a horseman, for a total cost of 44 solidi, at a time when a cow was valued at 3 solidi!

The main defense worn by both mounted and foot soldiers was the mail shirt, the byrnie, which extended from the neck to the thighs or knees. It was worn fairly loose with short sleeves reaching to the mid-arm or elbow, and, unlike later examples, does not appear to have had a slit between the legs at front and back. The opening at the neck was round and quite wide, rather like a modern T-shirt, with no defense for the neck itself, and it was worn over an undershirt of some sort. Soldiers do not seem to have worn any form of additional protection on their lower legs and feet or on the lower arms or hands. Occasionally, soldiers are shown wearing a short cloak fastened at the shoulder and the waist.

Mail armor was made and worn for a very long time. As seen in the previous section, mail was known to the Romans and went on to be used into the early modern period. Throughout the whole period of its use, mail was always made in the same way, although there are some small variations in actual manufacturing detail. It was basically formed from rings of iron, each of which was linked through four others—two above and two below it—making a pattern of rows of rings, which faced alternately one way and then the other. The rings that make up almost all mail made in the West were manufactured in one of two ways. The first, today called riveted, is where the ends of the rings were overlapped slightly and flattened. A hole was then punched through the overlapping ends and a small rivet was used to close it up. The second type of ring was made "solid"—that is, it was made as a continuous ring. Just how solid rings were made is still open to some debate, but certainly later on they were made by wrapping a thin wire around a mandrel twice and then hammer-welding the whole together to form a solid ring. It has also been suggested that solid rings could have been made by punching and cutting them out of solid sheet iron although there is little, if any, evidence for this type of manufacture.

Where solid rings were used to make mail, they were alternated with riveted rings in a very characteristic fashion, one row of riveted rings, the next of solid, then one of riveted and so on—basically the riveted rings were used to fasten rows of solid rings together. Butted rings, where the ends of the rings were not connected one to another but were simply butted up close and not joined was only used in the East, in India, the Middle East, and North Africa, for example, and probably also on some early Roman examples.

The wire used to make rings varied considerably in its cross-sectional shape from round to flat. Rings could also vary in size, although a garment was normally made from rings of all the same size, from just a quarter of an inch (6 millimeters) to around half an inch (12 millimeters) or slightly more, but most were in the region of a third to half an inch (8–10 millimeters). In nineteenth-century analysis of medieval mail, references are found to a number of supposed different forms of mail construction, for example banded mail, chain mail, and double mail, but it is now clear that there is only one form—mail, pure and simple.

To create a completed mail garment, the armorer added or subtracted rings and/or rows in a manner very close to knitting and was able to build up complex shapes and forms to fit the torso, head, and arms. Mail armor was usually worn over some form of underclothes, either normal everyday garments or special, padded clothes that would have helped to cushion heavy blows and provide additional protection. As a defense against attack, it was always flexible and easy to wear, yet it was, surprisingly, quite heavy—much of the weight of a mail shirt was borne by the shoulders. Although mail offered good protection against slashing and cutting blows, it was somewhat less effective against attacks from sharp-pointed weapons such as arrowheads. However, before the advent of plate armor, mail offered the best and most effective protection from the dangers of warfare.

Although it is clear that most armor in this period was mail, some was likely scale, although evidence for this is limited and somewhat contradictory, and there is no agreement among modern historians. While a number of pictorial representations of armor appear to portray scale armor, none has ever been found in archaeological excavations.

Helmets

Together with the mail shirt, Carolingian soldiers, again both mounted and on foot, wore very open helmets. These consisted of a fairly shallow skull that fitted closely to the head and flared out just above the level of ears to form a brim, narrow at the sides but more pronounced over the back of the head to protect the neck, and which turned slightly upward at the front in a very characteristic fashion. They were not fitted with cheek-pieces and most appear to have had a rib or crest running from front to back, although whether this was a construction feature or just decorative is not clear.

This type of helmet was worn in the ninth and tenth centuries in Carolingian Europe, but in Scandinavia and England the helmet was very different and largely a continuation of those before this time. A superb example of the type of helmet in use there is that found in York and dating from around 750–775 AD, the so-called "Coppergate helmet." It consists of a broad iron band that encircles the head at eye level and is cut out for the eyes. Another broad iron band is secured to this and goes over the head from front to back, also extending down the front of the face to form a nose guard, a nasal. A further two bands on either side complete a cross-shaped framework, the triangular spaces of which are then filled with iron plates. To the lower edge of the helmet are attached two iron cheek-pieces by means of simple iron hinges that have a copper alloy strip around their edges. A fringe of mail protects the neck at the rear and is attached through holes around the back of the helmet and to the rear edge of the cheek-pieces. The mail is composed of both solid and riveted rings. A decorative copper alloy strip around the tops of the eyes, rather resembling eyebrows, continues down over the nose guard. Two decorative copper-alloy strips run over the skull, one from front to back, the other from side to side. The lower edge of the skull is also bound with a copper alloy strip. Inscriptions on this very obviously high-status helmet say that it was made for an otherwise unknown warrior named Oshere. It is also noteworthy that the Coppergate helmet incorporates Christian inscriptions and decoration in place of the more pagan boar's head of earlier helmets.

It is not clear just how long this type of helmet with its close-fitting skull, nose-piece, and cheek-pieces, continued in use, although many of its features can be found on helmets for the next three centuries. The method of manufacture, often also called spangenhelm, with its iron framework and triangular panels and nasal can be found in helmets from the eleventh century.

Horses, Horse Armor, and Stirrups

Cavalry tactics and numbers in Carolingian armies are still somewhat unclear. It is clear that there was always an elite group of cavalry that fought on horseback. However, modern estimates of the size and composition of Carolingian armies vary considerably, although historians agree that infantry always outnumbered the cavalry.

Still, there is little doubt that cavalry numbers had increased since earlier times and that these needed to be provided with horses. To fill these needs, contemporary sources claim that stud farms were highly organized and well funded. It is clear also that this period saw considerable improvements in horse stock. Stronger and sturdier horses were bred, more able to carry armored cavalry, and in ever-increasing quantity.

Carolingian warhorses did not wear any form of armor and were not protected in any way. Saddles were quite small and had low cantles at the front. Nailed horseshoes were introduced in the late ninth century, although they did not have any great effect on the cavalry tactics—they were probably most useful in the wetter climate of northern Europe where they could better protect horses' hooves.

As already mentioned, this period saw the introduction of the use of stirrups. However, it is clear that they were not adopted widely nor quickly—it took time for them to be accepted—there are quite late references to the young leaping into the saddle while older soldiers used a mounting block. As is the case right through to the late medieval period, stirrups were worn very long, with riders' legs either straight or very slightly bent at the knee, unlike the modern fashion of wearing short stirrups with a bent knee.

Shields

Most Carolingian soldiers, even in the lowest rank, carried a concave, circular shield for protection. These were, in the main, quite large, up to about 32 inches (80 centimeters) in diameter, and made from wood probably covered in leather. An iron boss reinforcing the center of the shield protected the hand holding the shield while an additional strap allowed it to be slung over the shoulder when not in use. Few other details about Carolingian shields can be determined from the scarce, solely pictorial evidence.

Spears and Lances

The most common weapon used by almost all Carolingian soldiers was the spear. These ranged from perhaps eight or nine to perhaps as many as thirteen feet (2 1/2 or 3 to 4 meters) long with a long head. They also had a slender tapered form with two cross-wing projections at the base. These projections are generally suggested to have prevented the blade from penetrating too deeply, but this may not be the case. An alternative possible explanation is that they enabled the use of the spear as both a thrusting and a parrying weapon, akin to the later pollaxe (see Chapter 4), a view supported also by the appearance on some of langets, iron extensions from the head running some way down the haft. These provided reinforcement to the shaft and protected it from sideways blows from an attacker.

Just how these weapons, the lance and spear, were used is a difficult question to answer for much of the medieval period as the evidence is very limited—mostly to pictorial representations. While in some of these it is clear what is going on—for example where the illustration shows the actual moment of attack—in many it is impossible to be sure just how they are being used—are these weapons just being carried, are they about to be thrown, or are they being used as a thrusting weapon? The answer is probably that this type of weapon was used in many different ways, depending on the occasion, the threat, and the enemy encountered—and there is evidence for all the ways that they could be used. What is impossible to know is whether there were specific strategies that were used and practiced—for example, was there an initial charge by mounted troops using lances?

The lance and spear were used extensively throughout Western Europe during this period with minor regional variations in shape and form, although all consisted of a long double-edged blade mounted on a wooden shaft.

Swords

Almost all Carolingian soldiers would also have carried a sword. The weapon is especially prominent in Charlemagne's many capitularies that refer to weaponry, especially for the cavalry. When a warhorse was owned so too should a sword. Thus it is not surprising that in illustrations and excavations the numbers of these weapons have increased rather dramatically. Nor should it be surprising that the sword began to gain a reputation as the weapon of honor for the noble and wealthy soldier.

In the early Carolingian period it appears that swords themselves were not substantially different than previous Frankish examples. Both the longsword and the sax were carried, as attested to by both literary and archaeological sources, and both measured and were made the same as the earlier weapons. However, by the end of the eighth century the seax began to disappear and the longsword began to change both in shape and manufacture.

The longsword blade was usually of simple broad shape and could be single- or double-edged with a rounded point made for slashing and cutting rather than thrusting. The hilt was usually out-fitted with only a simple straight cross guard and pommel. Of particular interest in this period was the manufacture of what are known today as *pattern-welded swords*. They were made by building up the blade of a weapon from many smaller pieces of iron, either from the same source or else very slightly different in composition, the latter containing slightly more phosphorous than the former, for example. These pieces of iron were then welded together, twisted and worked in such a way that the resultant surface of the blade exhibited a discernible and visible pattern akin to waves or ripples or somewhat like woven patterns, especially herringbone work. To the central core of this pattern-welded material a steel edge could be welded on, producing a very high-quality sword. The reason blades were made this way, requiring as it did a great deal of time and enormous skill, is not known for certain. It has generally been thought that the use of separate pieces of iron twisted and welded together improved the blade by combining their hardness and toughness. Yet it is also possible that they were made in this manner because it was difficult to obtain large enough blooms of material to make entire blades for the increased number of swords the larger armies of that period required.

What is known for certain is that swords were extremely expensive to make, whether pattern-welded or not. This is undoubtedly why the weapon became a powerful and vital symbol—of manhood, of valor, of authority, of honor—that found its way into the contemporary literature and culture. An example of this can be found in the Anglo-Saxon poet, Cynewulf's, description of the fiery sword which guarded Eden: "The hard-edged blade with its woven patterns quivers and trembles; grasped with terrible sureness, it flashes into changing hues" (Hilda Ellis Davidson, *The Sword in Anglo-Saxon England: Its Archaeology and Literature* [Woodbridge, UK: The Boydell Press, 1994], 123).

It was common for swords of this period to bear an inscription of some sort, often on the blade itself, although the cross guard was also sometimes marked. Inscriptions on the blade were commonly made by cutting a groove into the blade and inlaying it with silver. Although a very many remain indecipherable to us today, inscriptions could be either Christian symbols or the name of the owner or maker. For example, the inscriptions INGELRII and ULFBERHT are both known from several swords and probably refer to the smith or workshop where they were made.

Daggers

Some historians have suggested that the seax (scramasax) did not entirely disappear at the end of the eighth century, but rather became a supplementary weapon to be carried in addition to the spear and sword: the dagger. During the Carolingian period, it seems that many warriors began to carry daggers. However, again the evidence for their use is scarce and it is not always clear whether they were subsidiary weapons to the spear and sword or not.

Axes

Axes continued to be widely used throughout Europe at this time. Indeed, in Scandinavia and England they were almost as popular and "honorable" as the sword. In the Carolingian Empire axes did not have the same appeal or carry the same symbolism, but they were still used. As earlier, they could be either small and used with only one hand or relatively large and wielded with two hands. Occasionally in contemporary illustrations a double-headed axe is also depicted, with a similar-sized head on either side of a central socket, although these are rare. Axes were used primarily by foot soldiers, although one-hand axes could also be effective weapons from horseback. Very high-status axes were often decorated with inlays of silver.

Slings

The sling was seemingly used throughout this period—an illustration from the ninth century shows one being used in hunting, and it would appear that they were used in warfare as well. Unfortunately, their use by lower-status soldiers only—and their string or cord construction—means they are rarely, if ever, mentioned in the sources and do not survive, or are rarely identified, in archaeological contexts.

Bows

The evidence for the use of bows in the eighth to eleventh centuries is somewhat scarce and not always easy to interpret. By the time of Charlemagne and the establishment of the Carolingian Empire with its professional army, the bow returned to favor, and with an importance not previously seen among the Franks. This may have been the result of Charlemagne's wars against the Avars and Slavs, tribes that had continued to use the bow since ancient times. Their proficiency in the weapon, although not decisive, may have inspired the Carolingians to adopt it. In the 802–803 Capitulary of Aachen, Charlemagne ordered that the bow should become the army's chief infantry weapon. Infantry soldiers were ordered to carry it, a spare string, and twelve arrows, presumably the contents of one quiver. He followed this in 806 with a decree demanding that each horseman should also be equipped with a bow as well as several quivers of arrows. Both decrees were further confirmed in 811.

Although the earlier Franks had used the longbow, perhaps as long as 6 1/2 feet (2 meters), the bows adopted from the Avars and Slavs were likely the recurved bow. Whether the two were used side by side or whether the recurved bow supplanted the earlier type is unclear. An illustration from the late ninth century seems to show a horseman shooting a recurved bow, for example, but other sources confirming this are very limited. The arrow was probably about 3 feet (90 centimeters) long and there is some evidence that earlier Carolingian arrowheads were simple but changed to a barbed type in the tenth century.

Bows were clearly used outside the Carolingian areas of Europe, but the available evidence is too slight for us to be sure just what type these were. However, it seems certain that they were the ordinary longbow and not the recurved type.

Siege Weapons

Evidence for the use of siege equipment is, like much in this period, difficult to interpret. Certainly battering rams and scaling ladders were used. But whether Carolingian armies possessed other forms of siege engines is not entirely clear. Yet, it would appear that some form of large throwing machine was used in the defense of Paris against the Vikings in 885–886. According to the poem *De bello Parisiaco* (The Attack on Paris), by Abbo of Saint-Germain-des-Prés, the defending Franks deployed a type of defensive apparatus known as a manganum or mangonel, the mechanics of which seem to have been similar to the traction trebuchet—

a rotating beam engine throwing huge stones against the opposing Vikings:

> The Franks prepared some heavy pieces of wood each with an iron tooth at the end, so as to damage the Danish machines more quickly. With coupled beams of the same length they built what are commonly called *mangonels,* machines for throwing vast stones, which could blast the lowly race of barbarians often blowing out their brains, crushing crowds of them and their shields. Not one shield that was hit did not break; not one unfortunate who was hit did not die (David Hill, "Siege-craft from the Sixth to the Tenth Century," in *Aspects of the "De rebus bellicis": Papers Presented to Professor E.A. Thompson,* ed. M. W. C. Hassal, 113–115 [Oxford: British Archaeological Reports, 1979]).

Unfortunately this is the only source that mentions any form of throwing machine until the twelfth century.

Greek Fire

Fire has always been a major component in warfare since the very earliest times. When most things were made from natural flammable materials, fire was a very potent weapon—torches made from sticks or twigs or burning bundles of wood, for example. However, the use of fire took a leap forward in the early eighth century with the invention of Greek fire—an enigmatic material, the discovery of which has always been attributed to a Greek named Kalinikos. Greek fire is now suggested to have been a low-boiling-point distillate of a natural deposit similar to modern gasoline, although its exact composition is obscure. The Byzantines, who were the early users of the weapon, forced the fluid under pressure out of a simple pump device over an open flame igniting it—rather like a modern flamethrower. Thought to have been used on board ships as a means to fight other ships, there is actually little known about Greek fire. Some historians have suggested that it was kept as a military secret and that this would explain its relative rarity and obscurity, but such an argument is hard to sustain. Other reasons for its obscurity may have been the difficulty of production and scarcity of supply or the problems of its use—one was as likely to cause damage to oneself as to the enemy. However, Greek fire does seem to have been a real substance and to have been used in the warfare of the period, although to a very limited extent.

THE ENEMY: THE VIKINGS

No doubt the single greatest threat to Europe from 750 to 1050, if not for the entire Middle Ages, was the Vikings. Yet, it is one of the real mysteries of history as to why Viking raiders suddenly burst out of Scandinavia in the late eighth century, although the destruction of the Frisian fleet by Charlemagne at about the same time certainly left no effective deterrent to their sea travel and may have been a factor in launching their invasions. Still, it is hard to believe this alone can explain the large number of voyages that were launched from Sweden, Norway, and Denmark between 789 and 1066 and extended along almost all of the coasts of continental Europe, England, Ireland, the Baltic lands, east to Russia, south to Italy, North Africa, and Byzantium, and west to the Faroe and Shetland islands, Iceland, Greenland, and North America.

The first reference to any attack of the Vikings was that made in 789 on the southeastern coast of England, although little seems to have been gained from this raid. Four years later, however, Viking ships again appeared off the coast of northeastern England, and this time there was no question as to the profit of their violence. The *Anglo-Saxon Chronicle* records their attack on the prestigious and wealthy Lindisfarne monastery:

> 793. Here, terrible portents were come over the Northumbrian land, which miserably frightened the people; there were huge flashes of lightning, and fiery dragons were seen flying in the air. Much hunger soon followed these signs, and a little after that in the same year, on January 8, the raiding of heathen men miserably destroyed God's church on Lindisfarne Island by looting and the killing of men (*Anglo-Saxon Chronicle*, vol. I:55–57 [authors' translation]).

Immediately, it seems, news spread throughout Scandinavia of the enormous amounts of rich booty that could be acquired with relatively little effort by raiding lands easily reached by ship. Soon Vikings were along the shores of England, Ireland, and northern Europe, carried there in dragon-prowed ships, content to feast on undefended monastic and small urban targets. These fairly rich locations waited, it must have seemed to these Vikings, for someone to raid them. And the fact that they were filled with unarmed ecclesiastics and farmers added to the allure for these raiders who then returned to their homes with large amounts of plunder and booty. No doubt this gave reason to their journeys away from families and fields, while at the same time inspiring new Viking raiding voyages. Eventually, the Scandinavians even wintered in England, Ireland, France, and the Low Countries, establishing base camps from which they pushed their raids further and further inland than ever before.

For the first fifty years, Ireland, Scotland, and northern England provided the richest objectives. Attacking lands filled with monasteries and without many fortifications or militias meant that there was little opposition to these violent raids. However, by around 834 the ancient Irish civilization had been virtually destroyed and the countrysides of Scotland, northern England, and Ireland were almost completely devoid of monasteries that had not been attacked by Vikings. They were forced to turn to continental Europe for their booty. Of course, those lands were almost constantly embroiled in fraternal civil wars, which left few troops to stop these attacks. There the Vikings also found larger and richer targets. By 840, the Vikings had raided the Low Countries towns of Noirmoutier, Rhé, Duurstede—which was eventually sacked no fewer than four times—Utrecht, and Antwerp. In 843, they wintered for the first time in Francia, capturing Nantes, ravaging the valleys of the rivers Loire and Garonne, sailing south to the Mediterranean, and even, on their way home to Scandinavia, threatening the Muslim cities of Lisbon and Cadiz. And, in 845, a Viking force of more than 120 ships sailed up the River Seine and sacked Paris.

The number of rivers on the European continent provided the Vikings with the means to reach a large number of inland sites, and during the last half of the ninth century, they raided up the rivers Rhine, Meuse, Scheldt, Somme, Seine, Marne, Loire, Charente, Dordogne, Lot, and Garonne. No town, village, or monastery of any size anywhere close to a waterway was immune from attack. Nor did it seem that there was any coastal European site too distant from Scandinavia to keep the Vikings away, for as the century progressed they became increasingly bolder and more adventurous. One expedition, from 859 to 862, sailed so far that the Vikings passed through the Strait of Gibraltar where they raided Nekur in Morocco, the Murcian coast of Spain, the Balearic Islands, and Rousillon on the coast of France. After wintering on the Rhone delta, these hearty warriors raided upriver to Valence, and then turned to Italy, sacking Pisa and then Luna (which the Vikings apparently were led to believe was Rome), before sailing back past Gibraltar and north to their base in Brittany. Viking runic graffiti, extolling their virtues, attributes, and presence, can also be found on the sculpted lions at

St. Mark's Basilica in Venice and carved into the floor of the Hagia Sophia in Istanbul.

In 866, a large force made up largely of Danish Vikings, what contemporaries called the "Great Army," attacked England. They met little resistance until 877 when the king of the Wessex, Alfred the Great, effectively halted a conquest of England by driving them out of Exeter. Over the next few years there followed three battles between Alfred's troops and the Great Army, at Englefield, Ashdown, and, finally, Edington, all of which were won by the Anglo-Saxons. Alfred the Great also devised a system of fortifications, earth-and-wood ramparts, known as burhs, which surrounded many larger and previously unfortified towns in his kingdom. All of this led to peace treaties being signed, a withdrawal of the Vikings to the north and east—into an area called the Danelaw—and Alfred's assumption of the kingship over the whole of England.

Whether it was because of this setback in England or the increased weakness of the Carolingian rulers after the deaths of kings Louis the German and Charles the Bald, Viking activity increased on the continent at the end of the 870s. In 879 Viking raiders attacked Ghent; in 880 Courtrai and several sites in Saxony; in 881 Elsloo and Aachen, where they even sacked Charlemagne's palace; in 882 Condé; in 883 Amiens; and in 884 Louvain. In 885–886 a large Viking army again attacked Paris with a force said by contemporary chroniclers to have numbered 700 ships and 40,000 men—undoubtedly an exaggeration. However, the Vikings did not sack the city, but were bought off by King Charles the Fat who paid them 700 pounds of silver and gave them permission to spend the summer raiding Burgundy, a land over which he had no power. In 891 the Vikings returned to the Low Countries, where they were defeated by Arnulf, the king of the East Franks, at the battle of the Dyle. Another group, led by Rollo, was still powerful enough to establish a district in the lower River Seine basin, which in 911 was officially given to them by the king of France as the duchy of the Northmen (Normandy).

After 911, Viking activity appears to have slowed. Colonization in the conquered territories, such as that which had occurred in Jorvik after 866, had been taking place for some time during the raids. And by the beginning of the tenth century, Scandinavians had founded communities in Ireland, Scotland, England, Russia, Normandy, the Faroe Islands, the Shetland Islands, Iceland, and, later, in Greenland and in North America. Trading with these communities and other, non-Viking settlements, was practiced more often than raiding, especially with the discovery of cheap Islamic silver which was especially prized in Scandinavia and brought enormous profits.

However, at the end of the tenth century, perhaps because of a decline in the Islamic silver market, Vikings once again started their raiding, especially in England. From 991 on a succession of Scandinavian leaders, mostly Danes, attacked England, and in 1014 one of them, Svein Forkbeard, conquered it and ruled for a short time as king, being succeeded at his death in 1016 by his son, Cnut. But after two of Cnut's sons, Harold I and Harthacnut, died quickly without having produced their own heirs, an Anglo-Saxon king, Edward the Confessor, regained the throne in 1042. It was not until later invasions, led by Norwegian kings Harald Hardrada in 1066, and Olaf III in 1085, were turned back in England that the Viking threat to Europe finally stopped.

By the time their raids had ended, Vikings had been attacking Europe for almost three centuries. So, why did these raids come to an end? First, there was undoubtedly an attrition factor. The Vikings simply could not continue to participate in raids on Europe for much longer than they did as the number of viable targets seems to have dwindled considerably by the later raids. Second, colonization certainly played a role in diminishing and finally ending the invasions. As Vikings began to settle in lands they had previously attacked, these lands no longer became suitable for further raids. That is not to say that the Scandinavian presence in the lands necessarily forbade future raids. Indeed, Vikings who participated in these military activities never were a unified political or military entity, and they seem to have cared little whether they were raiding lands held by Scandinavian colonists or by natives. However, the Vikings who had settled on these lands proved to be more formidable opponents than other inhabitants. This is clearly why Charles the Simple settled Vikings in Normandy, to provide a buffer against further raids. Sometimes other strong military leaders were found to fulfill the same purpose. This appears to have been the situation behind the naming of Baldwin the Iron Arm as Count of Flanders and Reiner with the Long Neck as Duke of Brabant in the ninth century. After their ascension, neither area was threatened much more by raiders.

A third reason for the ending of the Viking raids was that several former raiders seemed to have found it safer and more profitable to become traders and merchants, or to find other occupations. Sailors of skill were always needed, as were soldiers, and Scandinavians were soon welcome throughout Europe and the Middle East for their expertise on the sea and in war. The Byzantine emperors, for example, employed a large number of Vikings in their special body-guard unit, the Varangian Guard.

Fourth, by the end of the ninth and beginning of the tenth centuries most Scandinavians had begun to convert to Christianity. With these conversions the desire to raid monasteries and other Christian sites obviously lessened.

Finally, by the eleventh century, the loose confederations of Viking soldiers who had gone on previous raids began to establish states in their homelands. Norway, Sweden, and Denmark all had kings by this time, and these political leaders frequently needed whatever soldiers they could find—including all who went on raids during the previous two centuries—to fight in their wars and against their rebellions. All of the eleventh-century invasions of England by the Vikings were actually attempted conquests by Danish and Norwegian kings: those of Svein Forkbeard and Cnut were successful; those of Harald Hardrada and Olaf III were not.

> This is how Thorolf was equipped: he had a broad, thick shield, a tough helmet on his head, and a sword called *Long* about his waist, a big, fine weapon. The thrusting-spear he carried had a blade two ells long with four edges tapering to a point at one end, broad at the other. The socket was long and wide, the shaft no taller than might be grasped at the socket by the hand, but wonderfully thick. An iron spike was in the socket and the whole of the shaft was bound with iron. It was the kind of spear that is called a halberd.
>
> Egil had the same kind of outfit. At his waist was a sword called *Adder,* taken in Courland, the very finest of weapons. Neither of the brothers wore a coat of mail (*Egil's Saga,* trans. Hermann Pálsson and Paul Edwards [Harmondsworth, UK: Penguin Books, 1976], 123).

This description of two Viking warrior-brothers is taken from *Egil's Saga,* and although written after the Viking age, is still a nice summary of the arms and armor carried and worn.

The "broad, thick shield" carried by Thorolf and Egil, as throughout the rest of Europe, was made of wood, probably covered in leather. It would also have had an iron boss and probably an iron rim, with possible decorations on the boss and shield that depicted animals and fauna. As its primary position in the *Egil's Saga*'s list of arms and armor implies, the shield was the most common defense used by Vikings, both because of its relatively low cost and, when wielded well, its ability to protect a large amount of the user's body.

The material and style of Thorolf's helmet is not mentioned, only that it was "tough." This makes an interesting point about the perception of Viking arms and armor. More important to the observer (and obviously to the user as well), was the piece's utility. Thorolf's helmet is "tough," meaning no doubt that it would protect his head should any blows be directed toward it. Although archaeological evidence suggests that Viking helmets were made of iron, there is no reason to believe that they could not also have been made of thick leather—both of which would have produced a "tough" helmet. The construction of these helmets were likely similar to the "Coppergate helmet" described above.

Thorolf's sword is named *Long* and Egil's is *Adder*. The fact that they are named indicates their importance to a Viking warrior—in a way that Roland's *Durendal* and Arthur's *Excalibur* indicate their value. Later in the Middle Ages, the naming of swords fell out of practice, but during this period it was common. Such might also indicate a sword's scarcity. These weapons were very expensive, prized possessions to those who carried them, with the best made by swordsmiths of great and far-reaching renown. The origin of Thorolf's sword is not mentioned, but Egil's was "taken in Courland," leaving the impression that swords could be "won" and not just purchased. No doubt improving the quality of one's sword in battle or martial games was also a means of proving status and authority, especially in a society like the Viking society, where the strength and valor of an individual was more important for military leadership than inheritance. Surviving examples show no difference between Viking swords and others used across Europe at the time.

Thorolf's "thrusting spear," called a "halberd" here and elsewhere in Viking sagas was quite a sophisticated weapon. Strangely the author of *Egil's Saga* describes it with more detail than any of the arms and armor, although whether this is because of the weapon's distinctiveness or its relative rarity cannot be determined. The blade is quite long, between 4 and 5 feet (120–152 centimeters), with four "edges," probably indicating a hollow diamond cross-section that ended, as is also indicated in the description, at a sharp tip. The blade is also indicated to be socketed, "long and wide," into which a shaft was fitted. At the socket was a spike, although how long it was is not mentioned. Also not mentioned is its purpose, although its location on the socket would suggest that the halberd could also be used to strike down on an opponent. What is most curious about this weapon is its quite small shaft, "no taller than might be grasped at the socket by the hand." Does this mean the visible portion of the shaft was just a few inches long, and if so that the halberd's shaft was similar to the sword's hilt?

"Neither brother wore a coat of mail," writes the author, a remark that is obviously needed no doubt because Viking warriors of Egil's and Thorolf's status would have normally worn such in battle. The brothers had the mail, but on this occasion were simply not wearing theirs, for whatever reason. As mentioned above, mail at the time was a prevalent defense, very expensive and highly prized, but of enormous importance if a soldier wished to preserve his life.

CHAPTER THREE

The Crusades, 1050–1300

HISTORY

The Normans

In 911 Charles the Simple gave the Viking chieftain, Rollo, the territory surrounding the lower Seine—roughly the area that would become Normandy. Perhaps somewhat surprisingly, within a relatively short period he and his people adopted the same religion, the same language, and the same socioeconomic system as the French inhabitants of their principality, intermarrying with the local peasantry and nobility. Soon the new Dukes of Normandy, as Rollo and his descendants became known, were doing homage to the French king and fighting for him in his battles, obligated by the same code as the king's other barons. But one thing that seems not to have changed was their prowess for fighting and their desire for military gain. In the century following the creation of their duchy, Normans were prized as mercenaries and feared as pirates. However, at this early period they were never united enough to threaten their neighbors. By the middle of the eleventh century this had changed, as shown by two successful Norman invasions. The first was led by Norman adventurers of lesser nobility, the Hauteville brothers, against Sicily and southern Italy. The second was into England, led by the Duke of Normandy, William, known at the time as "the Bastard" because of his illegitimate birth, but by the end of his life as "the Conqueror."

Sicily might seem an odd place for an attack by soldiers from the other side of the continent. Normans first glimpsed Sicily and southern Italy—the two places almost always linked during the Middle Ages—in 1016 when some Norman pilgrims returning from the Holy Land were hired as mercenaries by the Byzantines to fight for them, first against the Italians and later against the Arabs. In doing so, they became wealthy, and these easily acquired riches soon attracted other Normans. Among those new recruits were twelve brothers of the Hauteville family. All were experienced and skilled soldiers, but one of the youngest, Robert Guiscard, gets most of the credit for the conquest.

In 1034 the Hauteville brothers landed with their forces on Byzantine-controlled Sicily, which they then took seventeen years to conquer (1051). They then turned toward southern Italy, also Byzantine controlled, which they captured between 1051 and 1071. They feared little, including the papacy. After the southern Italians had turned to Pope Leo IX to declare a "Holy War" against the Hautevilles, the Normans captured him at the Battle of Civitate in 1053 and imprisoned him in an attempt to force him to renounce the Holy War. Yet a later pope, Nicholas II, perhaps thinking he could not fight these inevitable conquerors, employed Robert Guiscard and his troops at different times against the Germans and Byzantines. And in 1059 he named the Norman leader as his vassal, investing him with the title of Duke of Apulia and Calabria and Count of Sicily in recognition of his service to the church. From then until his death in 1085, Robert reigned as ruler of Sicily—a principality that he continued to enlarge—and defender of the papacy. In 1084, he even defeated the Holy Roman Emperor, Henry IV, at Rome, after Henry opposed Pope Gregory VII—although he could not prevent the sacking of the city by his Norman, Sicilian, and southern Italian soldiers.

From a very young age William the Conqueror showed similar military skill and generalship to that of the Hauteville brothers in the Mediterranean. Coming to the ducal throne in 1035 as the illegitimate heir of Duke Robert the Magnificent, the eight-year-old William soon had to defend his right to that throne. In the next three decades he may have fought in and lived through more battles than any other medieval military leader. Despite Henry I of France's funding of William's enemies, the Norman count won victories at the battles of Val-ès-Dunes in 1047, Mortemer in 1054, and Varaville in 1057. Later, in 1063, he also attacked and conquered the county of Maine in support of his son's claims there, this time fighting against Henry I directly.

Of course, it is William's conquest of England for which he is justifiably called "the Conqueror." Although England held little significance for the European Middle Ages as a whole before 1066, its area of influence before then being almost solely Scandinavian, after his invasion, William and his royal descendants made an enormous impact, both political and military, on the rest of Europe throughout the Middle Ages.

There is some dispute as to why William believed that he had a right to be king of England. Based on the slimmest of historical evidence, one story has the childless King Edward the Confessor name William as his heir to the English throne. Edward had spent some time at the ducal court of Normandy when he was an exiled youth and knew the young duke there, although the historical records show that the contact between the two was never very frequent or influential. Edward did not accompany William on any of his military adventures, nor was there much association between Normandy and England during his reign. The duke was supposed to have visited the king in 1052 during the one-year exile of Edward's chief advisers and in-laws, Earl Godwin and his sons, when Edward is said to have reaffirmed the right of William to the English throne. But when Edward died, on 5 January 1066, he named his brother-in-law, Harold Godwinson, the eldest surviving son of the Godwin family, as his successor. William considered this not only an insult to what he had previously been promised by the dead king but also treason, as, again based on limited evidence, Harold supposedly promised to support William's claim to the throne against all other claims, presumably including his own. There were at least two more claimants to the English crown, King Harald Hardrada of Norway and King Svein Estridson of Denmark. Harald Hardrada, whose claim was the weakest of the four, even went so far as to launch his own invasion of England, which forced Harold Godwinson, only some forty weeks into his kingship, to force-march his army from the southern coast of England, where it awaited the invasion of William, all the way to York in the north. At the Battle of Stamford Bridge, fought on 25 September 1066, Harold Godwinson defeated the Norwegians and King Harald Hardarda was killed in the fighting.

Harold Godwinson was not able to spend much time celebrating this victory, however, as word quickly reached him that, while he was fighting the Norwegians in the north, William and the Normans had landed in the south. Evidence suggests that William anticipated a lengthy defense of his newly gained foothold in southern England. Harold Godwinson, flushed with his recent victory, chose to face the

Norman invaders in battle, on Senlac Hill, north of Hastings, on 14 October 1066. It was a lengthy battle, indeed an "unusual battle," as one historian has described its uncommon length. By its end, William's forces had prevailed and Harold, his brothers, and many of their soldiers were dead. Although there was to be some limited English resistance, by this single victory William had essentially taken England.

Norman Organization and Tactics

Perhaps because of the size of Charlemagne's territories and because of his victories in warfare, Carolingian military organization, strategy, and tactics dominated for the next few centuries. Armies in which the cavalry were the principal attacking force became standard across Europe although, as was the case with the Carolingian forces, cavalry numbers on the battlefield never exceeded those of the infantry. Providing mounts for all of the cavalry meant that a large number of horses had to be bred and supplied. Although the Carolingians had always demanded stallions as tribute from defeated peoples, especially the Avars, these never provided enough horses for their military needs. However, because of an equine epidemic that devastated the Carolingian military herds in 791, and the need to restock the numbers of horses lost, noted in many contemporary sources, the business of horse breeding and supply is better known than almost any other economic institution. It is recognized, for example, that by the end of the eighth century, managed stud farms had been established, owned and operated by well-to-do local magnates and landowners. They controlled not only the management of the stables, pasture lands, and fields that supplied the horses' feed but also the breeding stock (the general practice was to rotate stallions and mares to prevent inbreeding). The high costs of warhorses made these extremely profitable businesses. They operated without much royal oversight, probably because they provided sufficient mounts for the military needs of Charlemagne's army. The owners of these farms were prohibited from raising the prices of their horses during the 791 crisis, however.

Breeders and stablemen also seem to have experimented with breeding warhorses, ultimately improving their strength and endurance, while at the same time removing lesser steeds. Over a long period, but certainly by the twelfth century, the medieval destrier, a strong, heavy warhorse, had been bred from Bactrian or Arabian stock. From illustrations and the remains of bones it can be surmised that an average destrier stood 17 hands tall (68 inches or 173 centimeters). With its strong bones and strong, short back, a destrier was capable of carrying a heavily armored soldier into a battle or a tournament—rarely would a knight use the same horse for both. (In comparison, nonmilitary horses measured 12–13 hands tall [48–52 inches or 122–132 centimeters] during the Middle Ages).

When and from where the Normans acquired their cavalry skills cannot be ascertained from medieval sources, although it seems clear that they were not acquired until after Normandy was founded in 911, which may indicate a French rather than a Scandinavian influence. What is certain is that by the time of the ducal ascension of William the Conqueror in 1035, Norman horsemen had become well known and militarily respected throughout Europe.

William the Conqueror is justifiably considered to be one of the most famous generals of the Middle Ages—the Battle of Hastings was only one of his several military adventures. Because William's ascension took place when he was only a child, and no doubt also because of his illegitimacy (although he had been legitimized at birth by his father, Robert), several Norman nobles apparently thought they might strengthen their position and landholdings without fear of military reprisal from the duke. But William did respond, and he did so with great military strength and tactical proficiency. He was still reacting to the rebellions of Norman nobles as late as the 1060s when he successfully put down a rebellion by Conan of Brittany—an event shown in the *Bayeux Tapestry*—in which William and his military entourage appear only on horseback without any infantry.

Of course, William the Conqueror's army did include infantry. Spearmen, swordsmen, and archers are all depicted in the *Bayeux Tapestry,* although it is quite clear in the narratives reporting the Battle of Hastings that the cavalry was the most important. But his was not the only eleventh-century Norman army so organized. The Norman invasion force of Sicily and southern Italy was also cavalry dominant, and the cavalry was used effectively in all campaigns and against all enemies: Byzantines, Muslims, Germans, southern Italians, and Sicilians. For example, at the Battle of Civitate in 1053, although Pope Leo IX's army outnumbered the Normans almost two to one, the initial charge of Norman cavalry caused most of Leo's infantry to flee from the battlefield and they quickly defeated those remaining. The southern Italians and their German mercenaries preferred to fight on foot, wrote William of Apulia, because they could not maneuver their horses as expertly as the Normans.

As at Civitate and Hastings, the cavalry charge was the tactic of choice for Norman generals. To successfully deliver it against other charging horses or a solidly formed infantry line, however, required training and strict discipline. Should horsemen not be able to ride together or turn in unison, disorder would result, which might, at the very least, disrupt the impetus of the charge, or at worst, cause fatalities. This was especially important when one considers that the primary purpose of the medieval cavalry charge was not necessarily a clash between two units of cavalry. On the contrary, the most successful cavalry charge was often against infantry in an effort to make them flee in panic, disorder, and confusion, as happened at Civitate.

If the initial charge did not succeed further charges were needed which meant that cavalry had to be able to turn and regroup—maneuvers that required skill and training. At the Battle of Hastings, Harold Godwinson's infantry, tightly formed in a shield wall, proved to be much more disciplined than the infantry at Civitate. They did not flee at the initial charge of William's cavalry, forcing them to charge again and again—hence it was a very long battle. Clearly, the Norman cavalry were well trained and highly disciplined—but so were the Anglo-Saxon infantry, whose lines did not break. However, in the end Harold's infantry were defeated, lulled out of their position by yet another intricate battlefield maneuver that could only have been performed by well-trained cavalry, horsemen who ignored both their fatigue and frustration to execute one of the most difficult cavalry tactics: the feigned retreat. This demanded both skill and discipline, for the cavalry had to *look* as if they were running away from the battle, only to turn and charge again, in complete order at exactly the right moment. Such a maneuver must not be performed too early and rarely more than once in a battle. In fact, it is likely that, should it not achieve its purpose (the breaking of the opposing line in celebratory pursuit), the battle would be over, and the cavalry would retreat, this time in earnest, from the field.

At Hastings, the feigned retreat worked. While some Anglo-Saxon soldiers remained in their lines, a sufficient number broke away and pursued the retreating Normans, destroying the integrity of the infantry shield wall. Only too late did they realize that the cavalry had turned around and begun to charge again. Few of the troops who ran down the hill after the Normans could muster the speed or strength to return to their lines and were ridden down and slain. Those infantry who had remained on the hill now found their shield wall weakened, and although Harold Godwinson tried to reform the remaining Anglo-Saxon soldiers into a much smaller line, they proved to be too fatigued and disorganized to resist the Normans for long. Shortly thereafter their king was killed and the battle lost.

The Crusades

In response to the Viking and Hungarian invasions of the eighth to tenth centuries, many men took up the profession of soldier, their employment secured by the continuing invasions. However, when these raids began to decline their skills became less necessary, and soon, it seems, large numbers of soldiers were unemployed. Unwilling to return to agricultural work, some of these men tried to make a living by doing exactly what they had been paid to defend against, terrorizing the general population.

As the clergy, monks, women, and poor were often the targets of these lawless men, their defense became an issue for leaders of both church and state. The initial response was the "Peace of God," proclaimed throughout Europe in the second half of the tenth century. Although varying somewhat, depending on who was proclaiming it (the church) and who was enforcing it (the state), the basic purpose was to protect those who could not protect themselves, as well as to protect certain material things, such as church buildings, church property, and alms for the poor. This is exemplified in the Peace of God proclaimed in 989 at the Synod of Charroux in southern France:

> We, assembled there in the name of God, made the following decrees:
>
> 1. Anathema against those who break into churches. If anyone breaks into or robs a church, he shall be anathema unless he makes satisfaction.
>
> 2. Anathema against those who rob the poor. If anyone robs a peasant or any poor person of a sheep, ox, ass, cow, goat, or pig, he shall be anathema unless he makes satisfaction.
>
> 3. Anathema against those who injure clergymen. If anyone attacks, seizes, or beats a priest, deacon, or any other clergyman, who is not bearing arms (shield, sword, coat of mail, or helmet), but is going along peacefully or staying in the house, the sacrilegious person shall be excommunicated and cut off from the church, unless he makes satisfaction, or unless the bishop discovers that the clergyman brought it upon himself by his own fault (Brian Tierney, ed. and trans., *The Middle Ages*, vol. 1, *Sources of Medieval History*, 4th ed. [New York: Alfred A. Knopf, 1983], 135).

Yet, the Peace of God seems not to have been very effective, as witnessed by the fact that Catholic ecclesiastical leaders, again in concert with noble lawmakers, were required to introduce a similar proclamation, known as the Truce of God, less than a century later. The Truce of God focused more on banning military activity at certain times of the year and of the week and less on protecting certain people. It prohibited fighting during Lent and from Wednesday sunset to Monday sunrise. The Truce of God was also more specifically detailed and legalistic than the Peace of God, trying to protect everyone at least some of the time, as seen in this example proclaimed in 1063 in the Bishopric of Terouanne in the southern Low Countries:

> Drogo, the Bishop of Terouanne, and Count Baldwin [of Hainault] have established this peace with the cooperation of the clergy and the people of the land.
>
> Dearest brothers in the Lord, these are the conditions which you must observe during the time of the peace which is commonly called the Truce of God, and which begins with sunset on Wednesday and lasts until sunrise on Monday.
>
> 1. During those four days and five nights no man shall assault, wound, or slay another, or attack, seize, or destroy a castle, burg, or villa, by craft or by violence.
>
> 2. If anyone violates this peace and disobeys these commands of ours, he shall be exiled for thirty years as a penance, and before he leaves the bishopric he shall make compensation for the injury which he committed. Otherwise he shall be excommunicated by the Lord God and excluded from all Christian fellowship. . . .
>
> 5. In addition, brethren you should observe the peace in regard to lands and animals and all things that can be possessed. If anyone takes from another an animal, a coin, or a garment, during the days of the truce, he shall be excommunicated unless he makes satisfaction. If he desires to make satisfaction for his crime he shall first restore the thing which he stole or its value in money, and shall do penance for seven years within the bishopric . . .
>
> 6. During the days of peace, no one shall make a hostile expedition on horseback, except when summoned by the count; and all who go with the count shall take for their support only as much as is necessary for themselves and their horses.
>
> 7. All merchants and other men who pass through your territory from other lands shall have peace from you.
>
> 8. You shall also keep this peace every day of the week from the beginning of Advent to the octave of Epiphany and from the beginning

of Lent to the octave of Easter, and from the feast of Rogations [the Monday before Ascension Day] to the octave of Pentecost.

9. We command all priests on feast days and Sundays to pray for all who keep the peace, and to curse all who violate it or support its violators (Tierney, 135–136).

Of course, the Peace and Truce of God were highly idealistic. Had they ever been fully effective, warfare in the rest of the Middle Ages would have been nearly completely eliminated. It was not, and there is even some debate as to whether these attempts at peace actually had much effect on the warriors against whom they were directed. The fact that the Normans did most of their fighting in the period of the Truce of God certainly seems to indicate its limited effectiveness.

From the eighth to the eleventh centuries there was little military activity between the Christians and the Muslims, and what there was took place in southern Italy, Sicily, and the Greek Islands. In most of these encounters Europeans were successful, primarily the Byzantines in Greece and the Normans in Italy and Sicily. Perceiving that these enemies may be vulnerable gave some European leaders hope to regain lands that had been lost by Christians centuries before. In the early eleventh century the Christian kings of northwest Spain, lands that had never fallen to Muslim conquest, began a *reconquista*, a reconquest of the Iberian peninsula, a fight which was to be long, lasting until 1492, but which ultimately freed all of Spain and Portugal from Muslim control.

There is no doubt that many dreamed of a *reconquista* of the Holy Land—the Middle Eastern area so called because it held the holiest sites of Christendom.

However, the reality was that only a major campaign undertaken by a very large army could have any chance of ousting those holding the Holy Land. There was also no real need or desire to do so before the middle of the eleventh century, as the Muslims controlling those sites were usually very friendly to visiting Christian pilgrims. After all, the pilgrims were good for the local economy. Trade and educational ideas flowed between the Christians and Muslims with very little difficulty between the eighth and eleventh century.

However, control of the Holy Land became a concern once again in the middle of the eleventh century with the rise of a powerful and pugnacious Muslim group that came into the Middle East from the mid-Asian steppes, the Seljuk Turks. They did not have the same tolerance of Christians as the Fatamid Egyptians, who controlled much of the Middle East at this time. For example the Seljuks massacred a large group of German pilgrims in Syria in 1064–1065. Even more startling than that atrocity, however, was the defeat of a large Byzantine army by the Seljuk Turks at the battle of Manzikert in 1071, a defeat which forced the Byzantine Empire to surrender almost all of Asia Minor to Muslim control. In response to this defeat and the loss of further land, the Byzantine emperor, Alexius I Comnenus, petitioned Pope Urban II to aid the Byzantines in regaining their lost territories by summoning an army of Catholic soldiers to campaign against the Turks in the Middle East.

Such a request appealed to the pope in two ways. The first was obviously the conquest of the Holy Land. Second, by recruiting soldiers to fight elsewhere, he hoped that the violence and warfare that had plagued Europe for the past 150 years would diminish. On 27 November 1095, at the Council of Clermont, which was attended by a large number of ecclesiastic and political leaders, Urban II called for a crusade. It was an emotional call to arms, as seen in Robert of Rheims' description:

> From the confines of Jerusalem and the city of Constantinople a horrible tale has gone forth and very frequently has been brought to our ears, namely, that a race from the kingdom of the Persians [the Muslims], an accursed race, a race utterly alienated from God, a generation forsooth which has not directed its heart and has not entrusted its spirit to God, has invaded the lands of those Christians and has depopulated them by the sword, pillage and fire; it has led away a part of the captives into its own country, and a part it has destroyed by cruel tortures; it has either entirely destroyed the churches of God or appropriated them for the rites of its own religion . . . The kingdom of the Greeks [the Byzantine Empire] is now dismembered by them and deprived of territory so vast that it cannot be traversed in a march of two months. On whom therefore is the labor of avenging these wrongs and of recovering this territory incumbent, if not upon you? You, upon whom above other nations God has conferred remarkable glory in arms, great courage, bodily activity, and strength to humble the hairy scalp of those who resist you.
>
> Let the deeds of your ancestors move you and incite your minds to manly achievements; the glory and greatness of King Charlemagne and of his son Louis, and of your other kings, who have destroyed the kingdoms of the pagans, and have extended in these lands the territory of the holy church. Let the holy sepulchre of the Lord our Saviour, which is now possessed by unclean nations, especially incite

you, and the holy places which are now treated with ignomy and ir-reverently polluted with their filthiness. Oh, most valiant soldiers and descendants of invincible ancestors, be not degenerate, but re-call the valor of your progenitors . . .

Jerusalem is the navel of the world; the land is fruitful above oth-ers, like another paradise of delights. This the Redeemer of the hu-man race has made illustrious by His advent, has beautified by resi-dence, has consecrated by suffering, has redeemed by death, has glorified by burial. This royal city, therefore, situated at the center of the world, is now held captive by His enemies, and is in subjection to those who do not know God, to the worship of the heathens. She seeks therefore and desires to be liberated, and does not cease to im-plore you to come to her aid. From you especially she asks succor, because, as we have already said, God has conferred upon you above all nations great glory in arms. Accordingly undertake this journey for the remission of your sins, with the assurance of the imperishable glory of the kingdom of heaven (Dana C. Munro, *Urban and the Cru-sades* [Philadelphia: University of Pennsylvania Press, 1895], 5–8).

Whether the pope expected that a large number of soldiers would answer his call to fight in the Holy Land is not known. Certainly the Byzantine emperor did not anticipate the numbers of Western Euro-peans which formed the First Crusade, as he seemed to have been completely unprepared for those willing to "take up the cross" (the crusaders affixed a crucifix to their tunics and shields). Urban's ap-peal was extremely successful—immediately after Clermont, bishops and priests began preaching the crusade throughout Europe, appeal-ing to all military professionals to fight against the Turks. Unfortu-nately, itinerant preachers, such as Peter the Hermit and Walter the Penniless, who served the poor also took the message of the crusade to their congregations. Soon two armies of European Christians were marching toward Byzantium. One included many renowned lords and knights: Raymond of Saint-Gilles, Count of Toulouse; Hugh of Ver-mandois, brother to King Philip I of France; Robert, Count of Flanders: Stephen, Count of Blois and son-in-law of William the Conqueror; Robert, Duke of Normandy and son of William the Con-queror; Godfrey of Bouillon, Duke of Lower Lorraine, and his brother, Baldwin; and Bohemond Guiscard, the son of Robert Guis-card, and his nephew, Tancred. Traveling with the soldiers was Adhe-mar, the bishop of Le Puy, titular leader of the crusade. However, the second army contained no well-known military leaders or soldiers. In-stead, it was filled with a large number of unarmed peasants, including women and children, who had also answered the call, expecting that their faith alone could defeat the enemies of God. Together the two groups may have numbered more than 100,000.

By the beginning of 1097 these armies had reached Constantinople. The numbers in the peasants' army, which arrived first, surprised Emperor Alexius Comnenus. Indeed, they were potentially more of an economic problem than a military aid. He fed the peasants and quickly ferried them to the other side of the Bosporus where shortly thereafter they were massacred by a Muslim army. The Byzantine emperor then greeted the surprisingly large numbers of soldiers arriving with the second army a couple of weeks later. He was probably hoping at best for one or two thousand soldiers to serve as a part of his forces, not an entire army itself. At the same time, if this Western European army was successful, he wanted his due. Therefore, he refused to allow the crusaders to proceed on their journey until they had taken an oath of fealty to him, promising that any lands which they captured from the Muslims would be returned to him. The crusaders reluctantly agreed, although to most of them such an oath and promise to a man for whom they had little regard meant nothing.

The march across Asia Minor was not easy. Although it began with a victory over an army of Seljuk Turks outside the walls of Nicaea, it soon became apparent that the crusaders had grossly misjudged the distance they would have to travel and the climate of Asia Minor. They had difficulty living off the land, and there was little water. Some gave up and returned home, but most kept on marching toward the Holy Land. Finally, early in 1098, they reached the first large enemy city, Antioch—a strongly defended, walled city with a large citadel towering over it. Though the crusaders were weakened by starvation, theirs was a determined army on a religious quest. Besides, their only means of escape was to return across Asia Minor. After several months of siege, they were able to gain access to the city—but not the citadel—when they bribed one of the captains of a gate tower. Immediately they began to gorge themselves on the fresh fruits and victuals, which led to an outbreak of dysentery.

As the crusader army suffered, they were besieged themselves by a large Turkish relief army. Ironically, as starvation began to affect the now-besieged crusaders, the dysentery actually began to clear up. Then, on 28 June 1098, one of their accompanying priests, Peter Bartholomew, claimed to have found the lance of Longinus (the lance that had pierced Christ's side on the cross), the location of which he said he saw in a dream. Taking this as a sign of the divine favor of their quest and by further sightings of Saint George and other military saints, the crusaders sallied out of the city and defeated a much larger Muslim force.

That the Seljuk Turks and Fatamid Egyptians had been fighting their own war for several years before the crusaders appeared in the Holy Land undoubtedly helped the latter at Antioch. Both Antioch and Jerusalem were places they had fought over—the Turks had captured Jerusalem in 1070, but the Fatamids had regained it early in 1099, when the crusaders were marching from Antioch toward the city. Thus, when the crusaders, now possibly numbering no more than 20,000, reached Jerusalem, they faced a weakened city and a fatigued population. But the walls of Jerusalem remained strong, and the inhabitants were determined. It was not until 15 July 1099, after a major assault of the walls using siege towers, that the crusaders finally captured it. In response to the ardent defense, and fueled by rumors of great treasures hidden in the city, the crusaders massacred everyone in the city. Raymond d'Aguiliers, chaplain to Raymond of Saint-Gilles and an eyewitness to the massacre, writes:

> . . . wonderful sights were to be seen. Some of our men (and this was more merciful) cut off the heads of their enemies; others shot them with arrows, so that they fell from the towers; others tortured them longer by casting them into the flames. Piles of heads, hands, and feet were to be seen in the streets of the city. It was necessary to pick one's way over the bodies of men and horses. But these were small matters compared to what happened at the Temple of Solomon, a place where religious services are ordinarily chanted. What happened there? If I tell the truth, it will exceed your powers of belief. So let it suffice to say this much, at least, that in the Temple and porch of Solomon, men rode in blood up to their knees and bridle reins. Indeed, it was a just and splendid judgment of God that this place should be filled with the blood of the unbelievers, since it had suffered so long from their blasphemies. The city was filled with corpses and blood (August C. Krey, *The First Crusade: The Accounts of Eyewitnesses and Participants* [Princeton, NJ: Princeton University Press, 1921], 259–260).

In the years immediately after the fall of Jerusalem, the crusaders extended their control to lands and towns neighboring those they had captured. Refusing to give these to the Byzantine emperor or to make them papal fiefs as Pope Urban II desired, crusader leaders set up their own kingdoms: Bohemond Guiscard became king of Antioch and the area around it; Baldwin of Bouillon, who had taken an army northeast of Antioch to Edessa and captured it, established a kingdom there; Raymond of Saint-Gilles became king of Tripoli after the city was captured in 1109; and Godfrey of Bouillon, who by the fall of Jerusalem had become the leader of the crusaders, became the king of Jerusalem. But most of the crusaders wanted to return home. They had been traveling for more than three years, often under extremely harsh conditions, and only a few wanted to remain in the Holy Land. By the turn of the twelfth century, the kingdom of Jerusalem had only 300 soldiers to defend it, and other crusader kingdoms had even smaller numbers. Still, initially there were few problems for the resident crusaders, especially as they periodically received reinforcements from Europe: younger warriors who wanted to make their names and fortunes in the Holy Land. For a while the crusaders also continued to be successful. Caesarea fell to them in 1101, Tartous in 1102, Acre and Jubail in 1104, Tripoli in 1109, Beirut and Sidon in 1110, and Tyre in 1124. They also began building large stone castles, the size of which had never been seen in Europe. Some of these castles were large enough to sustain their garrisons for five years, or, it was hoped, as long as it was needed to receive relief from Europe should they be attacked. Finally, to increase crusader numbers, three military monastic orders were established in the Holy Land: the Knights Hospitaller, the Knights Templar, and the Teutonic Knights.

Then in 1144 the city and kingdom of Edessa, located some distance from the other kingdoms, poorly manned, and with no natural defenses, fell to a new Seljuk Turkish army. Immediately, a Second Crusade to the Holy Land was called throughout Europe. Again crusade preachers went forth, the Cistercian monk, Bernard of Clairvaux being perhaps the most famous of these. It was said that when he preached for soldiers to fight the crusade, wives hid their husbands and mothers hid their sons, so effective were his sermons:

> The earth trembles and is shaken because the King of Heaven has lost his land, the land where he once walked . . . The great eye of Providence observes these acts in silence; it wishes to see if anyone who seeks God, who suffers with him in sorrow, will render him his heritage . . . I tell you, the Lord is testing you (R. H. C. Davis, *A History of Medieval Europe: From Constantine to Saint Louis* [London: Longman, 1970], 288–289).

A large number of men again "took up the cross," including two kings, Conrad III of Germany and Louis VII of France.

However, despite this royal participation and the large numbers involved, this Second Crusade could not duplicate the success of the first. In fact, the crusaders had no success whatsoever. As soon as they arrived in the Holy Land, they began to quarrel with the Christians already there whom they blamed for the defeat of Edessa because they had dealt too lightly with the Muslims. In turn, the resident Christians resented these new arrivals, no matter what their rank or status, for trying to take over the strategic leadership of the crusade. The plan of the resident crusaders was to take an army north to Aleppo, a city held by the caliph of the Seljuk Turks, Nur-ad-Din. But Conrad, Louis, and the other new crusaders saw a closer target in Damascus, a city led by a Muslim ally of the crusaders who was an enemy of Nur-ad-Din. They prevailed, and on 24 June 1148 the second crusaders marched on Damascus. However, even before reaching the city, the two kings began to argue over who was to take credit for the victory, which, in fact, never came. For not only did the attack of Damascus fail, but the citizens of the town were so enraged at the disloyalty of the crusaders that they not only removed their own leader, but they also submitted to Nur-ad-Din. After this defeat, Conrad III immediately set out for home. Louis VII stayed on in Jerusalem, but by summer 1149 he also returned to Europe.

Following his defeat of the Christians, Nur-ad-Din began to extend his control of the region. Surprisingly, he first chose to bypass the crusader kingdoms and attack Fatimid Egypt, which fell to him in 1168. The Christians were therefore surrounded, but in 1174, before Nur-ad-Din could make his move against them, he died. He was succeeded by one of his military leaders, the man who had been chiefly responsible for the conquest of Egypt, Saladin.

Saladin's army will be discussed more completely later in the chapter. Here it is simply necessary to follow his history as it pertains to the defeat of the crusaders at the Battle of Hattin, his recapture of Jerusalem—both of which prompted the Third Crusade—and his victory against that crusade. Saladin was a remarkable man and a remarkable general—perhaps one of the greatest—and a remarkable political leader. Born in Tikrit, of Kurdish background, and nephew to one of Nur-ad-Din's military leaders, Shirkuh, he seems an odd choice to have led the largely Seljuk Turkish army after the death of Nur-ad-Din. And it was certainly true that there was some disagreement as to his ability to lead Muslims of different ethnic groups, though not after he rejoined the main army in Damascus, bringing with him a large number of recruits from Egypt—and therefore reminding all those in Nur-ad-Din's court who doubted his leadership that he was the conqueror of Egypt and held complete control over the Fatamids. What might have been a transfer of leadership decided by war became instead a peaceful acceptance of the military legitimacy of an obvious leader. Those who followed Saladin never regretted their support of him. He married Nur-ad-Din's widow, and founded the Ayyubid dynasty.

It was well known by the time of his ascension to the caliphate that Saladin wanted to attack the crusader kingdoms. Two small, exploratory campaigns before Nur-ad-Din's death, in 1171 and 1173, had revealed the military vulnerabilities of the crusaders, in particular the weakness of the rule of the young king of Jerusalem, Baldwin IV the Leper, whose terrible affliction provided his cognomen as well as an early death and the lack of an heir. Disagreements over political and military policy occurred frequently among the crusade leaders, especially between the cautious regent, Raymond III, king of Tripoli, and the bellicose Guy of Lusignan, Baldwin's brother-in-law, whose belligerence was fueled by the Grand Master of the Templars, Gerard of Ridfort, and one of the truly nasty characters of the entire crusades, Raynald of Châtillon, then Lord of Oultrejourdain and Castellan of Kerak and Montréale castles. Raynald had shown for some time that he had no respect for the tenuous peace that existed between the crusaders and Saladin. By this time, he had already offended the Byzantine emperor, Manuel I Comnenus, by attempting the conquest of Cyprus. He had spent more than fifteen years in a jail in Aleppo after being captured during one of his many raids into Syria and Armenia from his then residence of Antioch. He had planned an attack on Mecca and Medina as one of his many pirating activities on the Red Sea—a number of the soldiers he had sent on this expedition were captured and beheaded in Cairo. He had also made it a practice to attack and plunder the caravans that passed anywhere near Kerak, one of which also contained Saladin's sister. Of course, all of these activities defied the numerous treaties between the crusaders and the Muslims.

Saladin wisely waited for the death of Baldwin the Leper, anticipating that there would be a fight over his inheritance. His patience was rewarded in 1185 when the king died and almost immediately Raymond of Tripoli—who had been Baldwin's regent since 1174—and Guy of Lusignan—his closest male relative, although by marriage only—fought over who was to reign in Jerusalem. Raymond spoke for peace and Guy for war, the latter a position also supported by Raynald of Châtillon and the Templars, whose favor placed Guy on the throne. Immediately afterward, Guy began to muster the crusaders for a campaign against Saladin. Raymond in turn removed his troops and sued Saladin for peace. Thus, the crusader army was split, and Saladin realized that the time was right to pursue his campaign to regain Jerusalem. Luring Guy's army to Tiberias, near the Lake of Galilee (then known as Lake Tiberias), Saladin trapped the crusaders in the valley between the Horns of Hattin, cut off their water supply, filled the air with smoke and arrows, and defeated their charges. Few crusaders escaped. Guy of Lusignan, Raynald of Châtillon, and more than 130 Templars were among those taken prisoner. Saladin had Guy and Raynald brought to his tent and the following was witnessed by the chronicler Baha al-Din:

> Saladin invited the king [Guy] to sit beside him, and when Arnat [Raynald] entered in his turn, he seated him next to his king and reminded him of his misdeeds. "How many times have you sworn an oath and violated it? How many times have you signed agreements you have never respected?" Raynald answered through a translator: "Kings have always acted thus. I did nothing more." During this time King Guy was gasping with thirst, his head dangling as though drunk, his face betraying great fright. Saladin spoke reassuring words to him, had cold water brought, and offered it to him. The king drank, then handed what remained to Raynald, who slaked his thirst in turn. The sultan then said to Guy: "You did not ask permission before giving him water. I am therefore not obliged to grant him mercy." After pronouncing these words, the sultan smiled, mounted his horse, and rode off, leaving the captives in terror. He supervised the return of the troops, and then came back to his tent. He ordered Raynald brought there, then advanced before him, sword in hand, and struck him between the neck and the shoulder-blade. When Raynald fell, he cut off his head and dragged the body by its feet to the king, who began to tremble. Seeing him thus upset, Saladin said to him in a reassuring tone: "This man was killed only because of his maleficence and perfidy" (S. J. Allen and Emilie Amt, eds., *The Crusades: A Reader* [Peterborough, UK: Broadview, 2003], 152–153).

All prisoners who would renounce the crusade and promise not to fight further against Saladin were freed; the 130 Templars, whom Saladin regarded as fanatics, were executed. After this victory,

Saladin moved against the now largely undefended city of Jerusalem, which he conquered on 2 October 1187. Remembering the shocking massacre of all the town's inhabitants by the first crusaders nearly a century before, Saladin allowed all Christians there to be ransomed or, if they could not afford a ransom, freed.

The fall of Jerusalem to Saladin shocked Christian Europe, and a Third Crusade was quickly called. This crusade attracted soldiers from throughout Europe, but especially those in the armies of three kings: Frederick I Barbarossa of Germany, Philip II Augustus of France, and Richard I, the Lionheart, of England. Frederick Barbarossa left in 1189, traveling over land, but few of his force, decimated by disease, fatigue, and apathy, ever reached the Holy Land. Many returned home after the 67-year-old Frederick died when he fell off his horse into the river Salaph in Asia Minor and drowned. The other two kings traveled by ship and arrived safely, but began to quarrel over their respective roles in the fighting. Although the participants in the Third Crusade succeeded in retaking Acre and Jaffa and even defeated Saladin at the Battle of Arsuf on 11 September 1191, they could never achieve the unified attack necessary to recapture Jerusalem. Finally, in October 1191, Philip returned to France and began attacking Richard's territory there. A year later, in October 1192, Richard also returned to Europe, but on his route home he was captured, imprisoned, and held for ransom by Leopold, the Duke of Austria, whose banner he had insulted at the siege of Acre. The Third Crusade failed to accomplish nearly all that its leaders initially set out to do, although it included the best warriors in all Europe.

The Third Crusade was the last Western European campaign in the Middle East to include the participation of more than a single prince. Its defeat, for few considered the capture of Acre and Jaffa to make up for the failure to retake Jerusalem, also seemed to herald a general apathy concerning the Middle East that spread over the next century. The crusaders still held onto three kingdoms—Antioch, Tripoli, and Acre—but there were fewer and fewer European reinforcements. Had the military monastic orders, the Knights Templar and Knights Hospitaller, not been able to supply soldiers to garrison the crusader fortifications and to protect crusader travelers and pilgrims, the remaining kingdoms would have failed much earlier than they did. Europeans started to become cynical of further crusading. Earlier prohibitions against trade with the Muslims began to be ignored, and those who were able to take advantage of that trade, most notably the Genoese and Pisans, profited greatly from it.

The papacy had also lost face. Unable to deliver a victory in more than a hundred years, in 1197 papal control over the call to crusades even became threatened by the Holy Roman Emperor, Henry VI, who made plans to lead an army to the Holy Land without the permission of Pope Celestine III, and to add all that he gained there to his kingdom. But he died suddenly and unexpectedly before he could mount the campaign. A stronger pope, Innocent III, was elected to replace Celestine at his death in 1198, and, determined to reinvigorate the crusades, he immediately called for a fourth one.

However, the Fourth Crusade was doomed from the start. Although not as many as were anticipated, a large force gathered in Venice in 1201 with the goal of traveling to the Holy Land. Yet they never came close to achieving that goal. They tried to arrange passage by sea but, not having enough money, they struck a deal with the Venetians to transport them there. However, first the Venetians compelled the crusaders to attack a Hungarian city, Zara, which—despite being Catholic—threatened the Adriatic trading monopolies of Venice. Following this the crusaders were taken to Byzantium where in 1203 they began to besiege Constantinople, because the emperor had recently signed a trading pact with the Genoese, rivals to the Venetians. Under the guise of asking for money and supplies to proceed to the Holy Land, the crusaders became impatient with the inhabitants' unwillingness to comply with their requests and took the city by storm. The Latin Kingdom of Constantinople, which they established there, lasted until 1261 when an attack from the exiled Byzantine emperor, Michael VIII Palaeologus, acting in concert with the Genoese, restored Constantinople to the Byzantine Empire. The rifts between Byzantium and the West, and between Greek and Roman Christianities, would never be healed.

The result of the Fourth Crusade excited few in Europe, except for the Venetians. Pope Innocent III was especially displeased. Foreseeing the problems this misguided campaign might cause, he wrote the following in a letter to the papal legate who went with the crusaders:

> How, indeed, is the Greek church to be brought back into ecclesiastical union and to a devotion for the Apostolic See when she has been beset with so many afflictions and persecutions that she sees in the Latins only an example of perdition and the works of darkness, so that she now, and with reason, detests the Latins more than dogs? As for those who were supposed to be seeking the ends of Jesus Christ, not their own ends, whose swords, which they were supposed to use

against the pagans, are now dripping with Christian blood they have spared neither age nor sex (James Brundage, *The Crusades: A Documentary History* [Milwaukee, WI: Marquette University Press, 1962], 208–209).

He certainly had cause for anger and was aware that the crusading ideal, to win back the Holy Land, had lost its credibility. It became increasingly difficult, too, to get soldiers to fight against non-Christians in the Holy Land, and the problems of their being diverted on their way to wage war against other Christians only added to the difficulties.

There were few crusades in the thirteenth century—they were almost always unsuccessful and often embarrassed the church that, in growing desperation, continued to call for them. Some, such as the Children's Crusade of 1212, where a large number of adolescent and adult peasants thought that they could simply defeat the Muslims with their "childlike" faith, were stopped by the pope and other ecclesiastical leaders before they got too far—Italy in the case of the Children's Crusade. Others were just poorly planned and executed, including those of Andrew II, the king of Hungary, and Leopold VI, the Duke of Austria, in 1217–1219; those of Emperor Frederick II in 1227 and 1228; or those of Louis IX in 1248–1250 and 1254. Of course, there were some victories, such as Leopold VI's capture of the Egyptian city of Damietta in 1219 and its recapture by Louis IX in 1248—in between those two conquests, it had been retaken by the Egyptians in 1221—or the recapture of an unpopulated and derelict Jerusalem by Frederick II in 1228—it was lost again in 1244. But these did not outweigh the large number of defeats that were suffered, the greatest of which was probably in 1250 when King Louis IX and his entire army were taken prisoner by the Egyptians, necessitating the payment of a huge ransom for their freedom.

The Christians were not even able to take advantage of the Mongol invasion of the Muslim Middle East in the middle of the thirteenth century. The Mongols conquered all of Turkey, Persia, and Syria, destroying Aleppo, Damascus, and Baghdad, but withdrew from the Middle East before attacking any of the crusader holdings when conflicts of inheritance and leadership arose among them. Once the Muslims had recovered from the Mongol defeats, they once again turned their attention to the remaining crusader holdings. The resident crusaders could do little. By the end of the thirteenth century, with no sign of reinforcements from Europe, the remaining crusader kingdoms began to fall: in 1265 Caesarea, Haifa, and Arsuf were taken; in 1268 Antioch fell; in 1289 Tripoli was captured; and finally, in 1291 the last of the crusader kingdoms disappeared when Acre fell to the Egyptians.

The thirteenth century saw a shift in priorities and crusades were called not to the Holy Land but to places in Europe. Two of these are well known: the first a successful crusade against the Albigensians, a heretical Christian sect living in southern France, which took place between 1209 and 1229; and the second against the people of Prussia and Livonia, Baltic coastal lands whose inhabitants had never accepted Christianity. To fight the Baltic Crusades, the Teutonic Knights shifted their emphasis away from the Holy Land to northeastern Europe. This crusade, which began in 1226, did not end until the early sixteenth century when the Reformation and German nationalism reduced the political role of the Teutonic Order to nothing.

However, the call for crusade continued well into the early modern era. By the end of the Middle Ages every king agreed, in principle, to participate in a crusade, only subsequently to break his promise. In addition, by the middle of the fourteenth century a new Islamic foe appeared in the Middle East, the Ottoman Turks. Their presence in the eastern Mediterranean altered the balance of power there and throughout southeastern Europe and the Middle East. Even before the end of the fourteenth century they had occupied not only the Holy Land and Asia Minor but had also soundly defeated a large Anglo-Franco-Burgundian-Hungarian force at the Battle of Nicopolis in 1396. Nor did their conquests end there—they captured Egypt, the Saudi peninsula, and most of North Africa, and they took Constantinople in 1453 and Hungary in 1526. Even when they were defeated, for example at the siege of Vienna in 1529, at Malta in 1565, and at the naval battle of Lepanto in 1571, they remained a potent and dangerous foe.

European Warfare in the Twelfth and Thirteenth Centuries

Following William the Conqueror's victory at the Battle of Hastings he marched directly to the capital, London, and in a very short period established his rule over the entire kingdom. The death of Harold at Hastings was important as it meant that there was nobody to rally support for rebellion, but even more significant was the political and military administration that William quickly put into place.

He also rewarded all those who were faithful to him and those who had distinguished themselves in the conquest with lands, titles, and lordships—his "companions," faithful to him as their leader, and obligated to him for their titles and land. But when William died in 1087, there was some confusion over which of his three sons should rule over England and Normandy. Strangely, at least to modern historians, William had named his eldest son, Robert, as Duke of Normandy and his second son, William Rufus, as King of England. Why had he split his holdings? And why had he given his eldest son the Duchy of Normandy and his second son the Kingdom of England, which, if not a more important political entity, was certainly one more independent from the French crown? Is it possible, as some historians assert, that he saw in William Rufus a stronger leader than Robert? It is an interesting question, but one that is largely unimportant as, within a few years, it turned out that the strongest of all three of William's sons was actually his youngest son, Henry. First, Henry took over the English throne when William was killed in a hunting accident. He then defeated his brother Robert at the Battle of Tinchebrai in 1109 and took over the Duchy of Normandy. Later, he proved his military prowess and his claim to his father's territories by defeating his nephew, William of Clito (Robert's son), at the Battle of Bremûle, despite the presence of the French king, Louis VI, in support of William. He also put down an uprising among his English nobles at the Battle of Northallerton in 1138 (also known as the Battle of the Standard).

The concept of the "divine right" to rule might have prevented the latter conflict, as it had so often kept the French king from noble uprisings, but it had never been declared in England. Nor was it ever acknowledged. As a result, almost every English king during the Middle Ages was forced to contend with baronial revolts and civil war. The earliest, and perhaps most militarily significant of these, came at the death of Henry I when a dispute arose over who would succeed him. Henry's named heir, his nephew Stephen, was immediately opposed by Henry's daughter, Mathilda, who had a number of English noble supporters. What resulted was a devastating civil war that lasted from 1139 to 1153. A second example of this type of baronial chaos occurred in 1215 during the reign of King John when the lords of England forced their monarch to sign the Magna Carta, which awarded them certain powers over the king, a move provoked by John's abuse of taxation and the loss of most of the English lands in France. A third example was during the reign of John's son, Henry III, who, despite surviving an earnest effort to unseat him by one of his lords, Simon de Montfort, was forced to sign away more of his powers to the nobles in the various amended versions of the Magna Carta that appeared frequently throughout his long reign. Eventually this included the establishment of the first English parliament. Put simply, without the "divine right" to rule provision of the French kings, English kings were forced to prove their military leadership. The strong military leaders, such as Henry I, Henry II, and Edward I, were able to ensure peace at home and were successful abroad; while the weak military leaders, like Stephen, John, Henry III, or Edward II, suffered internal uprisings at home and, generally, losses overseas.

Because of the protection afforded by the English Channel, when the English were defeated by foreign powers—most often by the French—the losses were usually at the expense of their holdings on the continent. A curious situation arose when William the Conquerer became king of England. As he was also Duke of Normandy he was obligated to do homage to the king of France for those lands. Perhaps this is why William separated the two holdings between his eldest sons at his death. But the two were reunited by his third son, Henry I, at the turn of the twelfth century. Furthermore, with the succession of Henry II to the English throne after the death of Stephen—the irony of this being that Henry II was the son of Mathilda, Stephen's foe throughout almost his entire reign—the County of Anjou in France was also added to the English royal holdings, and with Henry's marriage to Eleanor of Aquitaine, so too was her inheritance, the duchies of Aquitaine and Gascony and the counties of Ponthieu and Poitou. This meant that when their son, Richard the Lionheart, became king of England in 1089, he held more land in France than all of the other French nobles combined, and certainly more than the king Philip Augustus of France. Of course, this led to the difficulties between those two kings on the Third Crusade, as already discussed, and to Philip attacking these lands after he had returned from the Holy Land. Richard, on his return from the crusades and from his imprisonment by the duke of Austria, spent the rest of his life defending his French holdings. He died in 1099 after being shot by a crossbow during one of these wars. It was John, Richard's brother and successor, who lost them in 1214 when his army was soundly defeated at the Battle of Bouvines by Philip Augustus at the head of a force that included the emperor Otto IV of Germany as well as many of the nobles of France, the Low Countries, and Germany. Philip's impressive victory led to the confiscation of all of the other English lands in France, except for

Gascony, and for the next century there was relative peace between the two kingdoms. Yet this was not to be the last Anglo-French war, as the Hundred Years War would prove.

During the High Middle Ages, despite being legally part of the Holy Roman Empire, Italians frequently sought self-rule, especially after the tenth century when the towns of northern and central Italy became more populous and wealthier. Moreover, only when a Holy Roman Emperor could guarantee the security of his throne would he venture south to Italy to put down any rebellion—a rare occurrence as they usually lacked any political security because of the fact that they were elected, sometimes by only the slimmest of majorities. To travel to Italy was also expensive, long, and difficult and, once on the other side of the Alps, the return was equally expensive, long, and difficult.

On the other hand, Italian cities generally brought huge amounts of taxes into the Imperial coffers, so if an emperor could march into Italy and impose, or reimpose, his authority, it might turn out to be a profitable military endeavor. Nor was it usually too difficult to put down an Italian rebellion once the Germans were through the Alps as any soldiers the Italians could muster or pay for generally lost to the more professional, more experienced, more skilled, better led, and better armed and armored German soldiers.

Thus, much of the medieval history of the Holy Roman Empire and Italy is intertwined, especially during the High Middle Ages. During this period some of the strongest emperors ruled, and, almost always when they did, a German army could be found south of the Alps. The best example of this may be Emperor Frederick I Barbarossa (1122–1190, Emperor 1142–1190). By the time Frederick had been designated as the successor of Emperor Conrad III in 1142, he was an experienced military commander. It may in fact have been the military leadership he showed in 1146 in putting down the insurrection of Duke Conrad of Zähringen on behalf of Conrad III that led to his being recognized as his successor, despite having no direct familial ties to him. This same military leadership may also have been the reason for his unanimous election, a rare event in medieval German politics.

Because of the strength and the cohesion of his political control in Germany, in 1154 Frederick Barbarossa led his first campaign south of the Alps into Italy. It had been a while since the Italians had faced a military threat from the north. Neither of Frederick's two predecessors, Lothair II and Conrad III, had proven strong enough to pursue any more than the most tenuous diplomatic connections with the inhabitants of Italy, leaving them, especially those in the northern and central towns, to virtually rule themselves. However, it was not only allegiance to the Holy Roman Empire that had waned during this period; the collection of taxes and other duties had almost completely ceased, while the passes through the Alps had become so infested with bands of outlaws, that few traders, pilgrims, churchmen, or other travelers could pass through them without being harassed to pay for protection.

By 1154 Frederick certainly wanted to solve these problems, bring Italy back into union with the rest of the Holy Roman Empire, clear up the lawlessness of the Alpine passes, and collect the outstanding taxes. If he thought he could do all of this, however, then his first expedition into Italy must be judged a failure, for although he was able to march his armies all the way to Rome, reaching there in the middle of 1155, he did not bring the rebellious forces in the north to heel, especially not the Milanese or their allies. Nor could he even bring peace among the factions in Rome; although he did succeed in being crowned Holy Roman Emperor by Pope Adrian IV, on 18 June, before returning to Germany.

That the town of Milan led this rebellion is not surprising when one realizes that its wealth was derived largely from its control of most of the Alpine passes—anyone who wished to travel along those treacherous routes had to pass through Milan. This meant that the town was almost always teeming with pilgrims and traders, who spent large amounts on housing, transportation, guides, guards, and victuals from the Milanese merchants. This wealth translated, as it often did elsewhere in the Middle Ages, into a desire for sovereignty. Frequently, this put the Milanese at odds with their German lords. Before Frederick Barbarossa, perhaps the most famous case was the town leadership's opposition to Emperor Henry IV during the so-called Investiture Controversy. In addition, the Milanese always seem to have been able to force other towns in northern and central Italy to join their rebellions, even those that would have been better off had they sided with Milan's opponents or, at least, remained neutral.

When Barbarossa returned north in 1155, having failed to secure Milan's subjugation, his German barons took this as a sign of weakness, and the recently crowned Holy Roman Emperor was suddenly faced with having to quell dissent among them, especially by Henry the Lion, Duke of Saxony and, from 1156, Bavaria. Eventually, through diplomatic as well as military means, Frederick was able to placate or defeat all his adversaries, and by 1158 this had resulted in an even stronger military presence in Germany and a renewed desire to return to Italy.

Frederick's second Italian campaign was far more successful than his first had been. Among his numerous early victories, the greatest undoubtedly was the capture of Milan, which fell to Imperial forces on 7 September 1158 after a short siege. Other rebellious towns fell quickly into line. However, they would not stay that way for long. The premature death of Pope Adrian IV, whose papacy had supported Barbarossa, forced Frederick to involve himself in a prolonged fight over papal succession. This distraction brought further insurrection, and the emperor had to fight numerous engagements against almost all of the towns in northern Italy and Lombardy, including, again, Milan. This time it was not until March 1162 that Milan once more fell to German troops.

Once Frederick returned to Germany, Milan and most of the rest of Italy again declared their freedom, forcing the emperor's third expedition south of the Alps in 1163. On this occasion, his army faced a new alliance of earlier enemies, the Lombard League. The Lombard League had been formed initially by the smaller towns of Verona, Vicenza, and Padua, but soon more substantial allies joined: Venice, Constantinople, and Sicily. In the beginning, Milan stayed out of the League, although probably more out of fatigue than any disagreement with its anti-Imperialist purpose. Facing the unity and military strength of the Lombard League, Frederick's 1163 campaign failed, as did his fourth campaign in 1166. In this latter expedition, it was not only the Italians who defeated the invading Germans, but also disease, in particular fever, which almost annihilated them. Seeing their success, the Milanese joined the League.

Perhaps because of the setbacks of his last two Italian campaigns, Frederick Barbarossa did not campaign an army in Italy again until 1174, when he went there to prevent an alliance between the Lombard League and Pope Alexander III from forming. Although never a friend or supporter of Frederick, since he was named pope in 1159, Alexander had remained neutral in the affairs of northern Italy. In 1174 he began to entertain the Lombard League's petitions for alliance, and with it, obviously, papal approval for their rebellion. Such an arrangement was not in Frederick's interest, and he was determined to stop it. When he was unable to do so diplomatically, he began a new campaign. From 1174 to 1176 Frederick journeyed around Italy, trying his best, though in vain, to defeat the Lombard League. By 1176 he had become frustrated at the lack of progress he had made: the Italians had not been pacified, nor had the pope backed down in his support of them. He pressed on with his campaign, but in doing so he suffered perhaps his greatest defeat on 29 May when a combined force of Milanese, Brescians, and Veronese soldiers crushed a smaller German army at the Battle of Legnano, nearly killing the emperor in the fighting.

By October 1176 Frederick was forced to sign the Treaty of Anagni with Alexander III, recognizing him as pope and giving him a large number of concessions. And the following May, Frederick signed the Treaty of Venice, making a truce with the Lombard League and the Kingdom of Sicily. Over the next few years, he was forced to become more involved in affairs in Germany. Another campaign through the Alps was, at least for the moment, unthinkable, and in June 1183 the emperor once more made peace with the Lombard League, in the Treaty of Constance, which granted nearly complete sovereignty to its members. Although Frederick and some of his successors would return to Italy, most notably Frederick II (Emperor 1212–1250), they were never able to break the desire for independence among those towns that had experienced this self-governance.

Peace was not to be had in Italy, however. Once the common enemy in the Holy Roman Emperor had been pacified, the Italians settled into an almost constant state of civil war. Two parties had formed in the wars with Frederick Barbarossa, the Ghibellines—who supported the emperor—and the Guelfs—who supported the pope. After the turn of the thirteenth century, divisions along these party lines became fierce, splitting regions, cities, and people. Soon Guelf cities opposed Ghibelline cities and vice versa, and this opposition often led to warfare. One of the most violent of these conflicts was the decade-long war fought between Florence (Guelf) and Siena (Ghibelline) from 1250 to 1260. Finally, after several smaller expeditions against each other had failed to bring any conclusion to their hostility, the Battle of Montaperti was fought, and the Sienese defeated the larger Florentine forces. A very precarious peace followed, but later in the century war broke out once more, but this time the Florentines defeated their Sienese opponents in 1289 at the battles of Campaldino and Caprona. But this victory over the Imperial supporters did not satisfy the Florentines, and in 1300 they divided into the Black Guelfs—those who continued to support the pope—and the White Guelfs—those who sought self-rule. Fighting even broke out in the streets. War had become endemic to Italy with perhaps the only unified resolve was the idea that future wars were to be fought not by Italian citizens but by paid soldiers from outside Italy, the condottieri.

Tactics, Strategy, Knighthood, and Chivalry

The waging of warfare on the European continent at the time of the crusades did not differ from that waged in the Holy Land. All European powers, of any size—including the more central lands of France, England, Italy, and the Holy Roman Empire and the frontier lands of Byzantium, Scandinavia, Scotland, Iberia, Hungary, and the various Baltic and Balkan lands—had adopted cavalry as their primary force by this time. Although the number of horsemen in any army never exceeded the number of infantry, it was the military dominance of the cavalry that formed the tactical, strategic, and chivalric policies of the period.

In battles, cavalry soldiers showed the confidence of their skill, wealth, and, often, nobility. It was a confidence borne also by their numbers, the strength of their armor, the intensity of their training, their discipline, the closeness of their formation, and an accumulation of their victories. Ambroise, the late twelfth-century poetic Norman chronicler, describes their military presence on the battlefield:

> *The most beautiful Christian warriors*
> *That ever saw the people of earth.*
> *They were serried in their ranks*
> *As if they were people forged in iron.*
> *The battle line was wide and strong*
> *And could well sustain fierce attacks;*
> *And the rearguard was so full*
> *Of good knights that it was difficult*
> *To see their heads,*
> *If not higher up;*
> *It was not possible to throw a prune*
> *Except on mailed and armored men*

> (Ambroise, *The Crusade of Richard Lion-Heart,*
> trans. M. J. Hubert and J. L. Lamonte
> [New York: Columbia University Press, 1941]).

When formed into a tightly packed, well-disciplined, and trained unit, called by different names throughout the Middle Ages—

échelle, constabularium, bataille, and *conrois*—cavalry could charge with great force and organization. To stand against them took great courage and only a few infantry soldiers of the High Middle Ages seemed to have possessed it. Consequently, battles of the period were often fought by cavalry against other cavalry. Dominant on the battlefield for so long, infantry, for this moment in history, took a secondary role.

The discipline of cavalry forces, and sometimes their training, was largely dependent on their leadership. A good leader most often led his horsed troops to victory, a bad leader often to defeat. During the period of cavalry battlefield domination, leadership was often deter-mined by military obligation, and military obligation was based on what has best been termed "the feudo-vassalic system." Under this system, all men were "obligated" to perform military service to the lords who owned or controlled the fiefs on which they lived and from which they derived their economic livelihoods. There was no unifor-mity in these obligations. Terms of feudo-vassalic responsibilities dif-fered with nearly every contract made between lord and vassal. For example, in medieval Romania, service was given until the age of sixty, unless replaced by a suitable heir before then, and consisted of four months of the year spent in castle duty, four months spent in the field, and four months at home. And in the Latin Kingdom of Jerusalem, military service was for the entire year until death. Out-side of these more war-torn regions, however, feudo-vassalic military service was much shorter, usually being required only in defensive situations—when soldiers were required for militia duty—or when the lord who was owed the obligation desired to go on campaign. Under a particularly bellicose leader, this might mean a military ser-vice that could last much of the year for many years in a row, while under a weaker, more peaceful leader there was a likelihood of never being required to perform military duties.

When summoned for duty, a medieval soldier was required to bring himself and, if he had them, his retinue and to pay for almost all of the arms, armor, horses, and provisions needed to sustain them on their campaign or in their fortification. Theoretically this meant that no paid medieval army was needed during the High Middle Ages. In reality, however, to fill out their numbers, most medieval military leaders had to make promises of financial support or reim-bursement for lost revenues or animals to those called into service. Even this did not always work. For example, in 1300, when Edward I called his already fatigued feudal levy to military service, only forty knights and 366 sergeants responded, and Edward had to give up any thoughts of war that year. At times, medieval forces were also supplemented with mercenaries.

Still, despite the importance placed on them by many military historians, battles were infrequent during the High Middle Ages. Large medieval land battles were usually only fought when one power was invading or trying to stem an invasion—for example Stamford Bridge (1066), Hastings (1066), Manzikert (1071), Northallerton (1138), Arsuf (1191), and Falkirk (1298)—or when leading or encountering rebellions, for example Cassel (1071), the Elster (1080), Brémule (1119), Bourgthérolde (1124), Lincoln (1141), Legnano (1176), Parma (1248), Bouvines (1214), Lewes (1264), Evesham (1265), Benevento (1266), and Tagliacozzo (1268). Leaders only very rarely fought more than one large battle—for example, kings William the Conqueror and Henry I, and emperors Henry IV and Frederick II— and then, it seems, only when ego took the place of caution. Often a leader flushed with victory in one battle met defeat in a following battle, such as Harold Godwinson, Simon de Montfort, and William Wallace. Even that renowned medieval soldier, Richard the Lionheart, was only involved in three pitched battles during his career, including those fought during the Third Crusade.

In reality, the siege was almost always far more important and profitable for medieval leaders for making conquests and capturing land. A leader as militarily astute as King Philip II (Augustus) fought only one major battle during his lengthy reign over France, the battle of Bouvines in 1214, which in fact could be said to have profited him very little as far as actual land gains. Yet his sieges of notable fortifications and towns throughout Anjou, Normandy, and Aquitaine brought him nearly all of the "English" lands in France, except for Gascony.

Interestingly, a medieval battle, while economically very expensive to fight, did not often result in many deaths. As cavalry began to determine what occurred in medieval conflicts some time after the rise of the Carolingians, battlefield deaths became less frequent, as the ransoming of "knights" and other cavalry soldiers began to bring a large profit to anyone who could capture one. At the Battle of Bouvines, for example, fewer than 200 Allied and only two French knights were killed, although perhaps as many as 40,000 fought in the conflict, while at the battle of Brémule, Orderic Vitalis reports that although "nine hundred knights were engaged, only three were killed," something he attributes to the fact that "Christian soldiers did not thirst for the blood of their brothers" (Orderic Vitalis, *The Ecclesiastical History of Orderic Vitalis*, ed. and trans. Marjorie Chibnall

[Oxford: Clarendon Press, 1978], VI:60). Other high medieval battles had similar low numbers of deaths. This could be ascribed to the primary use of short-range weapons in these battles—the spear/lance, sword, and mace—as control of one's weaponry was necessary for the ability to preserve opponents for ransom. However, the nonkilling attitude of soldiers toward their enemies seems far more important, as later high death rates using short-range weapons at the battles of Courtrai (1302) and Nicopolis (1396) would show.

Throughout the eleventh and twelfth centuries, knighthood was being instituted throughout Europe. Called a *miles* in Latin, *chevalier* in France, *ritter* in the Holy Roman Empire, *caballero* in Spanish, and *knight* in English, initially those so elevated were nobles whose land, wealth, title, and status distinguished them from ordinary soldiers. It is difficult to know exactly when the practice of making knights began or where it originated. No document exists that indicates how or why the first knights were made, although it seems more than likely that medieval knights were the result of evolution rather than revolution, meaning that they came to exist as they were in the high and later Middle Ages, not all at once, but over a long period of time.

Knights were, as the terms describing them often confirmed, cavalry, and they had few other duties than to perform as horsemen in battle. However, before too long, more requirements were placed on them with the result that knights began to be more distinct than other cavalry soldiers. Although all knights remained cavalry soldiers, not all cavalry soldiers were knights. To be a knight meant that one had to earn the title through skill and action displayed in warfare or tournaments. Of course, wars were not waged often, and battles fought even less often. So cavalry practice had to be done elsewhere, and training accommodated by other means. This began early in a prospective knight's life, if he was a noble. His teacher in this endeavor would be a knight himself, often the boy's father, if not a relative or close friend. He was trained in riding a horse, couching a lance, using his sword from horseback, and sometimes even throwing a javelin or spear from horseback. This was supplemented by training in the use of weapons when fighting on foot. Roger of Hoveden describes this knightly education, in this case to the sons of King Henry II of England:

> They strove to outdo the others in handling weapons. They realized that without practice the art of war did not come naturally when it was needed. No athlete can fight tenaciously who has never received

any blows: he must see his blood flow and hear his teeth crack under the fist of his adversary, and when he is thrown to the ground he must fight on with all his might and not lose courage. The oftener he falls, the more determinedly he must spring to his feet again. Anyone who can do that can engage in battle confidently. Strength gained by practice is invaluable: a soul subject to terror has fleeting glory. He who is too weak to bear this burden, through no fault of his own, will be overcome by its weight, no matter how eagerly he may rush to the task. The price of sweat is well paid where the Temples of Victory stand (Roger of Hoveden, *Chronica,* ed. W. Stubbs [London, 1869], II:166–167).

Perhaps the best places for a young knight or squire (a knight in training) to practice the art of cavalry warfare was the tournament. When and where the first tournament was held is unknown. Recent evidence has suggested that it might have been as early as the beginning of the eleventh century. Certainly by the early twelfth century, they were being held everywhere in Europe. By that time they had also caught the imagination of many writers and artists, and this would persist throughout the rest of the Middle Ages.

Early tournaments were mostly melees, where teams of cavalry fought a mock battle over a large field. Much of the fighting in these seems to have been with swords and maces. The earliest tournaments might even have been held before lances were couched— indeed, tournaments may well have popularized the use of this method of cavalry combat. Eventually, the joust became more prominent than the melee. During the last two centuries of the Middle Ages melees virtually disappeared. In jousts, two riders divided by a barrier would approach each other with couched lances. Points were awarded for contact with an opponent's armor, shield, and helmet. Rarely was a knight unhorsed, as that was thought to be too life-threatening, but should a lance shatter with audience-pleasing special effects, extra points might be gained.

Some knights made their names on the tournament circuit. Individuals, such as William Marshal and Ulrich von Liechtenstein, were renowned throughout Europe for their jousting skills, even having histories written about them—actually Ulrich von Liechtenstein wrote his own. Some skilled jousters could also make a living on the tournament circuit. Victors would profit from "winning" their opponents' armor and horse, as these were always offered back to their owners for a ransom. There were also times when the church and various governments tried to control tournaments, even prohibiting them. Rarely, though, did these bans last for long, as the urge to joust, and to celebrate jousts, was simply too strong.

Knighthood also acquired its own code of conduct, called "chivalry" by contemporaries as it applied to the horseman, the *chevalier* or knight. The reasons for the existence of such a code of martial honor are not known. Was it instituted by the church at the time of the crusades as a means of regulating the actions of the warrior class? Or was it something which came from within, from a class of knights who decided they needed a set of virtuous qualities or a rule of conduct to offset their bellicose activities and reputation?

While neither the origin nor the reasons for chivalry's existence may be clearly understood, the qualities that defined a chivalric knight are well known. John of Salisbury enumerated them in the twelfth century:

> [a knight's role is] to defend the Church, to assail infidelity, to venerate the priesthood, to protect the poor from injuries, to pacify the province, to pour out their blood for their brothers . . . and, if need be, to lay down their lives (John of Salisbury, *Policraticus*, ed. C. C. Webb [Oxford: Clarendon, 1909], II:16).

Knights were also to honor women, whose participation in the code was to allow their knights to give this honor and to support them with love and, on many occasions, with symbols of their support—a garter or sash.

Medieval chivalry was championed not only by the brotherhood of knights but also by numerous works of art and literature. A very large number of the *Tales of Arthur and his Knights of the Round Table* were written from the twelfth to the fifteenth century, reaching lands and languages that no comparable nonreligious text or genre of text had before. In an era before printing, such a feat must be considered remarkable. It was also undoubtedly sustained by frequent professional sporting events, tournaments, in which the knights often took part.

ARMS AND ARMOR

The *Bayeux Tapestry*

At some time before 1082 in the south of England one of the most remarkable examples of Western art was produced. Now known as the *Bayeux Tapestry*, though in fact it is not strictly a tapestry but an embroidered linen strip, it depicts the events leading up to Duke William of Normandy's invasion and the conquest of England in 1066. What is remarkable about this monumental work, it measures some 224 feet (68.38 meters) in length, is its depiction of the whole panoply of the armies of both Normandy and England. It shows not only the arms and armor worn and used at the time, but the battle scenes give us some of the best information we have as to how armies fought in the eleventh century. It is this feature that is, perhaps, most important. Using it we can begin to see not only how the wars of the decades before 1066 were fought but also how the first crusaders went into battle against the Muslims at the end of the century.

The soldiers depicted on the Tapestry are of three basic types. The first, the greater majority, are shown fighting on horseback and wear mail shirts and helmets. Most carry kite-shaped shields and are armed with swords and lances while a few carry some form of club or mace. A second group also wears mail and helmets but fight on foot with swords. The last group, who also fight on foot, are armed with bows and arrows and are shown without any protective armor, mail, or helmets. Each will be discussed in detail.

The mail shirts, called hauberks, shown in the Tapestry cover the torso and arms extending to just above the elbow. The upper parts of the legs of the soldiers are also protected with mail though whether these are legs in the same manner as the arms and completely enclose the thighs is not easy to determine. However in the margins of the battle scenes dead soldiers are shown being stripped of their armor and these would confirm that the mail was just a long shirt reaching down to just above the knee, split at front and back to enable enough movement to walk and ride a horse. The way the legs are shown covered in mail is probably just a convention of the Tapestry makers.

The helmets worn in the Tapestry are all very much alike and are the type known as spangenhelm, consisting of a wide band that encircles the head attached to which are two narrow bands—one from front to back, the other from side to side—which go over the head. The resulting triangular-shaped spaces are then filled with iron plates though the example from Benty Grange, admittedly much earlier in date, is thought to have been filled with horn. A projection, called the nasal, extends down from the front of the encircling band to cover the nose. This form of helmet shows some similarities to those found at Benty Grange and the Coppergate site in York,

England, as well as helmets from Scandinavia, and appears to have been widespread throughout Europe from the late Roman period. Unfortunately, the haphazard way colors are used in the Tapestry means it is not possible to be clear about the materials used in their manufacture. Unlike the helmets mentioned earlier, those shown in the Tapestry are less rounded and come to a point at the top of the head.

Many of the soldiers are also wearing mail beneath their helmets as an additional protection. Though it has been claimed that this mail may be attached to the lower rear of the helmet and act solely as a neck defender, it is clear that this was separate from the helmet. This is confirmed by the fact that where a helmet has been displaced to one side or where a helmet is not being worn the mail is shown covering the head as well as protecting both the front and back of the neck—essentially a mail "helmet" or coif. Whether the coif was part of the main body of the shirt or is separate is not at all clear, though later evidence would suggest that the coif was attached to the shirt. An unusual feature on many of the mail shirts is a rectangular piece, outlined with a different color, in the top front of the shirt. This has not been satisfactorily explained but may be additional protection for the opening at the neck.

The mail shirt, coif, and helmet are usually the only pieces of armor worn—the lower legs, feet, and hands are not normally protected in any way—just one or two figures, usually that of the Duke, are shown with mail protecting the lower limbs. However, most of the mounted soldiers are also carrying a distinctive kite-shaped shield—rounded at the top and extending down to a point—which also served as an effective additional defense. Made of wood, and probably covered with leather, all appear to have a binding, possibly of iron though this cannot be proved, round the edges. Though many are plain some are decorated with small discs, possibly rivet heads, around a central boss. A small number have very simple designs that may have acted as an identifier of some kind—the function of heraldry at a later date—though this is pure conjecture. Each shield is fitted with three straps at the rear. In action the left arm was inserted through two shorter straps and rested against a small internal pad. The shield could then be maneuvered effectively as a defense against both sword blows and arrows. A longer strap was used to sling the shield over the left shoulder when not in use. Although this type of shield is mostly shown being used by the mounted soldiers, some were also used by foot soldiers who could hold them side by side to form a "shield wall" for additional protection.

Though the kite shape is ubiquitous there are a few examples of the round shield with a central boss. These appear to have been used exclusively by the English foot soldiers and, like the kite-shaped shield, they also appear to have their edges bound with iron. They have very prominent bosses—probably of iron as in many excavated examples. It is possible that the English were using the older form of shield and that the kite shield was fairly new at this period.

The offensive weapons of the mounted soldiers were the sword, spear, and a variety of clubs or maces. The swords are all very similar to one another and of a simple shape. The broad blade, in the region of 3 feet (90 centimeters) long, is parallel for much of its length with a rounded, blunt point used primarily for slashing and cutting rather than for thrusting. The hand is protected by a very simple short cross guard, occasionally slightly curved toward the hand, and the pommel is usually of simple globular form. The scabbard appears to be attached to a simple waist belt at the left side; most seem to be plain, with no chape or locket, but occasionally a binding can be seen. No daggers are visible.

The spear, apparently about 6–7 feet (2–2.3 meters) long, was fitted with a simple, sometimes barbed, leaf-shaped head. Where they are being used in attack the spear is more often than not shown in such a way that it is clear that it was thrown and not used as a couched lance, held under the arm, as would later become the norm. Only in one or two cases is the spear shown in a "couched" position. It seems likely that this was probably not the normal method of fighting at the time and that throwing the spear was the preferred way. Occasionally, too, the spear appears to have been used as a thrusting weapon with the soldier leaning forward in his saddle to extend his reach.

The final weapon used by the mounted soldiers is some form of club or mace, though these are not common. Though some have a very definite mace-like head, others are just simple clubs that just thicken toward the end.

The foot soldiers can be divided, as already mentioned, into two types—those with and those without armor. Those wearing armor are dressed in exactly the same manner as those on horseback in a long mail shirt, helmet, and mail coif and again are not wearing defenses on their lower legs, feet, or hands. Many carry the same kite-shaped shield, although some of the English soldiers are using the round shield noted above. The armored foot soldiers are carrying swords of the same type as those on horseback, and some are shown wielding spears, again using them both as a throwing or thrusting weapon. Just one armored soldier is shown wielding a bow and arrow—the stave of which is approximately 5 feet (1.5 meters) long while the arrows are in the order of 30–36 inches (75–90 centimeters) long with barbed heads and flights. He has a sheaf, a cylindrical bag or container, of arrows secured to his waist belt and, rather strangely, is holding an additional four arrows in his left hand while actually appearing to be shooting!

The final weapon depicted on the Tapestry is the battle-axe, which is shown being wielded by the English armored foot soldiers. Two types are evident. A smaller one-handed axe that could also be used as a club and that, in one or two cases, may be being thrown. The larger axe is usually wielded with both hands.

Finally, there are completely unarmored foot soldiers. Most of these are shown armed with bows and arrows much like that of the armored soldier noted above—a bow about 5 feet (1.5 meters) long with arrows with barbed heads and flights. All have a sheaf of arrows at their right hip slung on either a waist or a shoulder strap. Unlike the later longbow, which was drawn so that the rear of the arrow came to the side of the face, these archers appear to be drawing the arrow back to their chest. Though unarmored, many of the archers are shown wearing a headpiece of some kind, although these appear to be more like caps or soft hats than helmets. Toward the end of the Tapestry a number of unarmored foot soldiers are also shown with kite-shaped shields and spears or else armed with a two-handed axe.

The horses depicted in the Tapestry are not protected with any form of armor. Bridles, bits, and reins appear to be well developed and similar to those used right down to the modern day. Saddles are very distinctive and appear to be very "box-like" with high fronts and backs (though not as high as they were later to become). Stirrups are universally used and are worn very long—the legs of the riders being straight, or very nearly so, in all cases. Almost all riders wear simple prick spurs. It is also clear that almost all the horses were male.

The evidence from the Tapestry gives us not only a snapshot of the weapons used and the ways that each type of soldier was armed at the time but it also gives us some clues as to fighting tactics. Many soldiers, especially the Normans, fought on horseback and were protected with mail armor and helmets. They almost all carried a shield and fought primarily with the spear and the sword. The former was used mainly as a throwing weapon. Tactics appear to have been an initial charge with the spear, which was then thrown, and this was followed up by the use of the sword as a slashing and cutting weapon. The foot soldiers were divided into two types. The first, armored in exactly the same way as those on horseback, fought with a spear and sword. They too carried shields that could, when need arose, be held side by side to form a protective shield wall. Although some armored foot soldiers fought with bows, unarmored archers were widely used. What the Tapestry does tend to show is that the armor and weapons used by both the Normans and English were very similar so that it is clear that the victory of the Normans was not due to their technical superiority. Victory or defeat in battle was rarely if ever dictated by the actual hardware used but was more a consequence of a complex combination of factors—not least training, leadership, morale, and luck.

The wealth of artistic information in the *Bayeux Tapestry*, which is virtually unsurpassed until the early modern period, offers us a rare glimpse at the breadth and depth of the arms, armor, and tactics of Western Europe at the turn of the first millennium. When the armies of the First Crusade made their way to the Holy Land in 1096 they were essentially armed in the same way as the soldiers who took part in the battle of Hastings in 1066. Mounted soldiers wearing a long mail shirt and helmet and carrying a spear and sword formed the backbone of the forces that set out to free Jerusalem from the Muslims. And indeed there were few significant changes in arms and armor through the first half of the twelfth century. Among the small changes that are apparent, extending the sleeves to cover the arm down to the wrist is perhaps the most significant. What is also clear from other pictorial evidence, illustrations and sculpture, is that the forms of arms and armor depicted on the Tapestry were used throughout Europe.

ARMOR

The period from around 1050 to the end of the thirteenth century is one in which there are surprisingly few changes to armor. Mail armor was used to protect the body from the head to the thighs. This was augmented by quilted garments, the aketon and the gambeson, and by the end of this period the whole was covered with a flowing surcoat. A simple conical helmet was still being used, though the more rounded form, the *cervelliére*, was perhaps more common by 1300. In addition there was the great helm and the kettle hat. Armor for the hands, basically just simple mail extensions of the sleeves, and for the legs was also introduced.

From the middle of the twelfth century the wearing of a long textile garment, called a surcoat or coat armor, over the armor was adopted. The reasons for this are still debated. Its use to display heraldry to enable the identification of the wearer cannot be sustained as surcoats bearing arms do not appear till the early fourteenth century. It may be that their use was the result of copying the fashion of the crusaders' Muslim enemies in the Holy Land. Whatever the reason, the surcoat, rare till the end of the twelfth century, became increasingly common after about 1210 when it developed into a loose sleeveless garment with a deeply slit skirt reaching to around the mid calf. It was widely used throughout the thirteenth century, eventually disappearing at the beginning of the fourteenth. Its widespread use and depiction in illustrations and sculpture obscures the detail of the armor worn beneath with the result that it is often difficult for us to see the changes going on.

The lengthening of the sleeves of the mail shirt down to the wrist that occurred from about 1100 was followed toward the end of the twelfth century by their extension to cover the backs of the hands, to form so-called mufflers, a fashion which lasted till the early years of the fourteenth century. The mail just protected the back of the hand and the palm was covered with cloth or leather. Occasionally separate fingers are shown but this is rare. To hold the sleeve tightly in position, cords or thongs at the wrist were also common.

The ubiquitous conical helmet with a nasal depicted in the *Bayeux Tapestry* also continued to be used throughout the twelfth century and well into the next. A slightly more rounded form appeared toward the end of the twelfth century and the two were used side by side. From about 1220 a simple rounded skull-like helmet, called a *cervelliére* or, later, a bascinet, often worn under the mail coif, became very common. From the early years of the thirteenth century a guard covering the face was also sometimes fitted to the helmet and this was then extended round the head to form perhaps the most recognizable piece of armor today, the helm or great helm. Of fairly simple cylindrical shape with a flat top and with sight and breath holes cut into the front, it was worn over the mail coif and arming cap, though it had its own padded lining, and secured with a chin strap.

The last helmet to be introduced in this period was the so-called kettle hat. It consisted of a close-fitting bowl with a wide, flat brim. This style of helmet had been common in the classical world and in fact a very similar helmet was used by the Carolingians as already noted. It had fallen out of use in Europe, though, and was not reintroduced till the end of the twelfth century, but it then had a very long life—similarly shaped helmets were still being made and used in seventeenth-century Europe. The earlier examples, at least till well into the fourteenth century, were constructed like the spangenhelm—from an iron framework in which the spaces were filled with separate triangular-shaped plates—though later examples were made from either a single piece of iron or from two plates joined down a central ridge. The kettle hat was, like the spangenhelm, relatively easy and cheap to produce and was the helmet used by the common soldier though it was sometimes also worn by the knightly and upper classes.

Alongside the use of mail armor there developed from the second half of the twelfth century various quilted textile defenses, the pourpoint, the aketon, and the gambeson, though their exact purpose and use are somewhat difficult to differentiate. Trying to pin down just what a gambeson was is confusing as both it and the term *aketon* seem to have been used indiscriminately for garments worn both over and under the hauberk. However, for our purposes it is likely that it refers to a garment worn over the mail shirt, rather like the surcoat. The aketon was probably a plain, quilted coat worn underneath the mail armor though it was also worn by common soldiers as their only defense. Pourpoint is probably the more generic name used for all types of soft, quilted defenses. Unfortunately, none of these garments survive and all our information on them is derived from written sources, which are often difficult to interpret, or from illustrations, sculptures, or brasses. Of course by their very nature they are not prominent as they were worn beneath other defenses so that we can only catch glimpses of them at best. Before leaving the discussion of armor, mention must be made of gamboised cuisses, essentially padded thigh defenses, which started to appear in the later thirteenth century.

From the middle of the thirteenth century began the long development of plate armor. At first this was quite limited with the addition of small plates to vulnerable parts of the body, particularly the elbows and knees, but these gradually extended till plate armor covered almost the entire body. These developments are more fully dealt with in Chapter 4.

Horse Armor

As already noted no horse armor is shown in the *Bayeux Tapestry*, and it would appear that horses were not protected till perhaps the later twelfth century, though the early evidence is rather confusing. From the later twelfth century, too, it was common to cover the horse in a large flowing cloth called a caparison, which was emblazoned with the rider's colors or arms, especially later on. Defenses in the form of a mail trapper, which covered the horse from the head down to its knees, appear from about the middle of the thirteenth century, though the caparison often obscures it in contemporary illustrations.

Plate armor for the horse was developed at much the same time as plate defenses for the rider—around 1250, though early references are rare. Certainly armor to protect the head, the shaffron, was common from about 1275, as are defenses made from hardened leather, *cuir boulli,* to protect the sides and rear of the horse. The development of horse armor in the later thirteenth century is discussed in greater detail in Chapter 4.

Shields

As we saw in the discussion of the arms and armor of the *Bayeux Tapestry* the common shield in use in the later eleventh century was kite-shaped with a distinctive curved top and long tapering form. It remained in use until about 1200, although the top became flatter and the overall shape more triangular. Through the first half of the thirteenth century it was then reduced in size while the sides became slightly convex. This smaller triangular-shaped shield, sometimes today called the "heater" shield from its similarity in shape to the bottom of a flat iron, remained in use throughout the rest of this period.

Lances

A major change in this period, and one that was eventually to have a far-reaching effect, was the introduction of the lance and its use as an offensive weapon from around 1150. This important change was to influence the way armies fought for the next four centuries. Essentially, there was a change from using the spear as a throwing weapon to using the lance as a thrusting weapon and the parallel development of what is frequently referred to as the use of mounted shock tactics. It is, perhaps, worthwhile to look at this important development and this weapon and its use in more detail. In the *Bayeux*

Tapestry the spear is a weapon made of wood of perhaps 6–7 feet (1.8–2.1 meters) long with a leaf-shaped head that was sometimes barbed. It was held either at the side of the body or in an over arm position and was essentially thrown at the enemy at a suitable close range. The rider would then draw his sword and continue the attack. The lance was a little longer—around 9–10 feet (2.7–3 meters)—and sturdier and was held under the arm, couched, and gripped in such a way that it could be used to thrust and charge at the enemy, keeping hold of the lance the whole time. Using the throwing spear the horse troops rode up to the enemy's lines, threw their spears, and then continued the attack with swords. Armed with the couched lance the rider rode right at the formation of foot soldiers hoping to be able to sweep all before him. What was important was the "shock" element of the attack. And here perhaps is the crucial part of the lance attack—what the cavalry were trying to accomplish was to so overawe the enemy that they turned and ran—and who would not with a formation of horsemen coming directly at you. And many battles and skirmishes must have been won in this manner—a close-knit and disciplined unit of cavalry riding down on you was enough to put fear into most hearts. However, with experience and training it was clear that this sort of attack could be "adsorbed" and deflected; for example, letting the cavalry through the lines of foot soldiers and then attacking them from behind—a tactic that was to be seen in its final form in the early fourteenth century.

And here is the second crucial change in warfare—training. Soldiers must always have undertaken some form of training and practice in fighting—most especially those on horses. Acting together as a unit and performing the same maneuvers in unison was essential. And at about this time, the beginning of the twelfth century, we see the beginnings of the training for battle in the development of the tournament. Tournaments emerged as a distinct feature of martial games from about the end of the eleventh century, possibly in northern France. It is probable that their rise was linked to the development of the use of the couched lance in war, which necessitated practice and training, especially as part of a team or group of knights. Tournaments enabled individuals to gain experience both with the new weapon and with fighting as part of a "team" or group of other knights.

At first tournaments were basically contests between large groups of knights, called melees, and usually involved several companies of combatants, each of which could consist of up to 200 knights. They took place over very large areas—many square miles—and there were few, if any, rules or regulations—largely because there was no enforcement. Considerable damage was done to land, crops, and buildings by those taking part, and this was much resented though there was often little that could be done to stop them. In England there was some attempt to designate parts of the countryside as places where tournaments could take place, but this was not adopted elsewhere. Injuries were frequent and deaths not at all unusual among the participants. Not surprisingly perhaps, the church did not view these activities very favorably and from the 1130s tried to ban them. Failing this they excommunicated participants and prevented those who were killed during a tournament, not an unusual occurrence at this period, from being buried in consecrated ground. The church, though, never succeeded in having them stopped altogether—they were just too useful and were obviously such an essential part of the life of the mounted soldier.

Training for battle meant that not only were you able to fight as a unit or group and carry out the same maneuvers and movements as your fellow soldiers but, when it did come, you were prepared for the harsh realities of combat. And it was probably this combination, more than anything, that was important—developing fighting methods and techniques as well as gaining experience that was crucial. And this helps to explain, perhaps, why early tournaments were so violent—they needed to replicate as closely as possible the actual conditions of battle. For of course training and experience could significantly raise the chances of success on the battlefield and, though it is clear that it did not guarantee victory, might tip the balance from a possible defeat to victory much like the morale-boosting effect of showing your leader's presence—much as William of Normandy did in the closing stages of the Battle of Hastings. And indeed it is worth noting that creating an impression of power and force so that your opponent was overwhelmed and fled was just as important, perhaps more so, than actually killing the enemy.

Swords

As we saw in the discussion of the *Bayeux Tapestry*, the sword in use in the later decades of the eleventh centuries was quite simple—consisting of a wide, double-edged blade with a somewhat rounded end, a simple cross guard, and pommel. Essentially, this was a cutting and thrusting weapon well suited to the hand-to-hand combat and the mail armor in use at the time. It was kept in a scabbard that was secured to a simple waist belt. And basically this was the type of sword that was used throughout the next two centuries—a weapon with a broad blade and simple hilt. However, it is not true to say that all swords in this period were identical. There was considerable variation in length, for example, from as short as 26 inches (66 centimeters) to as long as 38 inches (96 centimeters). The cross guard, though usually of quite simple form, often just a plain straight bar of iron, could also be more elaborate. For example, the ends might curve either away from or toward the hand, it might be more highly shaped, and it might be decorated. The pommel too tended to be relatively simple—many swords just having a plain disc pommel—though earlier examples were often of the so-called "brazil nut" form common in the earlier period. These early examples frequently have inscriptions or inscribed decoration on the blade itself.

The grip was usually short, fitting just one hand, though longer grips, which could accommodate a second hand to increase the power of attack, were not unknown. Grips themselves ranged from the simple wood bound with leather to the very elaborate decorated high-status examples made for kings and princes.

Daggers

Despite the fact that no daggers are depicted on the *Bayeux Tapestry*, their use must have been widespread at the time and indeed for all this period, though they do not figure greatly as a fighting weapon until the later thirteenth century (see Chapter 4). The seax seems to have been the common and widespread form of dagger from before this period (see Chapter 2) until around 1300.

Clubs, Cudgels, and Irregular Weapons

The *Bayeux Tapestry* includes among the weapons used what appears to be a simple club—a simple handheld weapon that swells toward the end and that could obviously be used to deliver an effective and disabling blow, especially to lightly armored or unarmored soldiers. The very nature of warfare means that sometimes quite crude and simple weapons were used that, by their very nature, do not survive. This has lead to the erroneous view that they were not used at all or, more commonly, they are completely ignored in studies of arms and armor. However, it must have always been the case that simple weapons, farm implements and clubs for example, were used in warfare, especially of course by the poorer soldiers of low social standing but also perhaps by "irregular" combatants.

And here perhaps we should consider the weapon that consists of a wooden handle to one end of which is attached a length of chain ending with an iron ball, often spiked. Opinions about whether this seemingly "quintessential medieval weapon" of cartoon and movie fame really existed are severely divided. However, it just does not appear in the medieval record in Western Europe—though something similar is occasionally shown in non-Western sources. Indeed from a practical point of view it would make a very problematic weapon for the wielder, as, should the blow fail to meet its attacker, the momentum of the ball end would bring it back to injure the user!

What was sometimes used, however, was the agricultural flail or a weapon based on it. This consisted of a long wooden shaft to which a second, and shorter, piece of wood was attached by means of a simple iron ring. This was certainly used by the common soldier, though surviving examples date from the late modern period and into the seventeenth century.

Staff Weapons

Evidence for the types and use of staff weapons before the end of the thirteenth century is somewhat patchy. They were always the weapons of the foot soldiers and it appears that in this period were, on the whole, somewhat idiosyncratic.

The staff weapons of the later middle ages, described in detail in Chapter 4, appear to have been introduced from the end of the thirteenth century. There is little evidence for their use before then, though there are occasional references to some form of long-hafted weapon, some of which may be referring to axes rather than the polearm of the later medieval period. For example, in 977 a Catalan document refers to a *guisarme*, described as a long-hafted weapon with an extremely long, axe-shaped head. Similarly, a capital of the Church of St. Nectaire in France, carved in the late eleventh or early twelfth century, depicts two Roman soldiers carrying long-hafted weapons, one of which is fitted with an axe head and the other with what appears might be a broad blade like the later glaive.

Slings

Though hardly considered today, the sling was used throughout the medieval period to throw projectiles of stone or lead. Extremely simple, slings were made from knotted string and leather and were used exclusively by the common soldier. Unfortunately, their very nature means no examples have survived, and they are frequently overlooked as a weapon even though there are illustrations of their use.

Crossbows

The crossbow probably descended from the ancient Greek *gastraphretes* (or "belly-bow"), and was also used both in Rome and China. However, it does not seem to have become popular in Western Europe until the eleventh century, though some historians have argued that the crossbow was used, albeit infrequently, by the Franks throughout the early Middle Ages. It seems certain that it was not known to the Muslims nor the Byzantines. Anna Comnena, the daughter of the Byzantine emperor, seemed completely overwhelmed by the weapon, which was carried by the first crusaders. This is her intricate description of the crossbow:

> The crossbow is a weapon of the barbarians, absolutely unknown to the Greeks. In order to stretch it one does not pull the string with the right hand while pushing the bow with the left away from the body; this instrument of war, which shoots missiles to an enormous distance, has to be stretched by lying almost on one's back; each foot is pressed forcibly against the half-circles of the bow and the two hands tug at the bow, pulling it with all one's strength towards the body. At the mid-point of the string is a groove, shaped like a cylinder cut in half and fitted to the string itself; it is about the length of a fair-sized arrow, extending from the string to the centre of the bow. Along this groove, arrows of all kinds are shot. They are very short, but extremely thick with a heavy iron tip. In the shooting the string exerts tremendous violence and force, so that the missiles wherever they strike do not rebound; in fact they transfix a shield, cut through a heavy iron breastplate and resume their flight on the far side, so irresistible and violent is the discharge. An arrow of this type has been known to make its way right through a bronze statue, and when shot at the wall of a very great town its point either protruded from the inner side or buried itself in the wall and disappeared altogether. Such

is the crossbow, a truly diabolical machine. The unfortunate man who is struck by it dies without feeling the blow; however strong the impact he knows nothing of it (Comnena [1969]:316–317).

Essentially then the crossbow consisted of a tiller, made of wood and often decorated with horn ivory or bone, to one end of which was attached a short bow. At first this was just made from wood, like the ordinary bow, but was replaced by stronger and more powerful composite bows made from layers of horn and sinew glued together. The string, stretched between the ends of the bow, was pulled back, either by hand or by means of a mechanical device, and fitted into a groove cut into the edge of a disc, the nut, made of horn or other hard material, set into the stock and which was held in the firing position by a trigger mechanism. A short-flighted arrow, called a quarrel, was then placed in a groove cut in the top of the tiller and set against the string. Squeezing the trigger released the nut, which turned about its center, releasing the string and shooting off the quarrel. At first they were not so very powerful, despite perhaps Anna Comnena's description, which exaggerates their effectiveness, and the string could be pulled back by hand, the crossbow being held securely by inserting a foot through a loop fastened to the end of the tiller. A simple hook, attached to a waist belt, was also frequently used. Again the crossbow was held by one foot and the user bent down and caught the string in the hook. The act of standing up pulled the string back to the firing position. For more powerful bows the so-called "goats-foot" lever was used. This simple lever device consisted of two interlocking frames pivoted about their ends. It was laid onto the stock folded over. The string was then hooked on to one end and the action of unfolding the two ends and pulling the frames back into the straight position drew the string back to the nut.

The quarrel was normally short—in the region of 12 inches (30 centimeters) long—and thicker than the arrows used with ordinary bows, around 1/2 inch (12.5 mm) in diameter and fitted with a substantial iron head often of pyramidal form.

The crossbow offered a number of advantages over the bow. First, it could be prepared and be ready to let off ahead of the time needed—unlike a longbow which has to be released as soon as it is drawn. Second was the fact that its effective use did not depend on an enormous amount of training and practice as did the longbow. On the negative side, it could take some considerable time to prepare for shooting.

Just how effective a weapon it was is difficult, well nigh impossible, to ascertain with any confidence. Though it has been said to be a very powerful weapon, as Anna Comnena, for example, states, its use never seems to have conferred any significant advantage to either side. However, it must have been useful after the twelfth century as its use increased markedly across continental Europe. Commanders frequently employed mercenary crossbowmen—primarily from Gascony or Genoa. They were used tactically at the beginning of a battle and on the flanks as a means to harass opposing forces and prevent flanking actions.

Of all the weapons used in the Middle Ages the crossbow was singled out for particular condemnation by the church, which proscribed its use on the grounds of its violence and power, first in 1096–1097 and again by the Second Lateran Council in 1139. The fact that these prohibitions had a very limited effect is perhaps surprising but does show that no military leader or commander could afford not to use them.

Longbows

The longbow, as we have seen above, is featured on the *Bayeux Tapestry* and was used throughout the period. It required a great deal of skill, experience, and training and, probably for this reason, it was a specialty weapon of particular regions of Europe, most notably the Welsh Marches. Archers in the *Bayeux Tapestry* are shown pulling the string back to the chest while later the bow was pulled back to the side of the face. Whether this resulted in greater power, needed more skill, or was just a different fashion is impossible to ascertain. It became the weapon, par excellence, of the series of wars known today as the Hundred Years War, and is dealt with in detail in the final section below.

Siege Weapons

In a period that saw little change in many weapons and few new ones, perhaps the greatest developments were in siege engines—the trebuchet, the great crossbow, and the springald.

Like several other important and significant innovations, gunpowder and Greek fire for example, the origins of the trebuchet are much discussed and disputed. It is likely that it is very ancient, originating probably in China between the fifth and third centuries BC, and from there diffused westward to the Islamic lands by the end of the seventh century AD. It then spread to the Mediterranean, where it is possible to follow it via Byzantium to Sicily and southern Italy, where it might have arrived as early as the ninth century, but it was always rare and unusual till the middle of the twelfth century. However, it is impossible to track its progress with any certainty, and there will probably always be controversy about its development before the twelfth century.

What is clear though is that there were two different types of machines. The first and simpler version, called a traction trebuchet or possibly a *perrière,* consisted of an arm set unequally on two upright supports. To the shorter end were secured many short lengths of rope while to the other was attached a sling containing the projectile. A man was assigned to each of the short lengths of rope and at a given signal all pulled down in unison—the arm swung about its pivot launching the projectile on its way. The second version was very similar to the *perrière* but was usually larger and instead of the force being generated by manpower it was powered by means of a large counterweight—hence the common modern name, the counterweight trebuchet.

The first accounts of the use of both types of trebuchet in Western Europe are from the middle years of the twelfth century. Perhaps the first is in 1147 when two traction trebuchets were reportedly used by the crusaders to capture Muslim Lisbon, while one of the first mentions of the counterweight trebuchet was in 1165 at the Byzantine siege of Zevgminon. From then on there are frequent mentions of their use in both narrative and pictorial sources, and it is clear that they spread throughout Europe. The traction trebuchet probably went out of use around the middle of the thirteenth century, possibly as a consequence of the superiority and improved accuracy of the counterweight trebuchet, which continued in use down to the middle of the fifteenth century, though its use after 1400 was very limited.

The ammunition for both types of trebuchet was primarily stone and only by using balls of a consistent weight was any accuracy achievable. However, it is clear that almost anything that could be used as a projectile was used at one time or another—including animal carcasses (possibly to spread disease) and incendiaries. Just what weight of projectile was common is difficult to ascertain with any certainty. There are claims that stones up to several hundred pounds were used, though modern experiment has shown that the counterweight to throw such weights would have been astronomical.

A weight of around 110 pounds (50 kilograms) is perhaps the upper limit, though it has been found that 35 pounds (15 kilograms) is probably the most effective size to achieve a reasonable range, in the region of 330 yards (300 meters). The ammunition for traction trebuchets would have been less as the force available to throw the projectiles was limited. Caches of stone reputedly to be used by traction trebuchets for the defense of Damascus during the crusades show a general uniformity in weight of around 11 pounds (5 kilograms).

The great crossbow was essentially the same as the weapon described earlier but of greatly increased size—larger than can actually be held by hand. The bows of these large crossbows were of composite construction, made from horn and sinew, and were in the order of 5–6 1/2 feet (1.6–2 meters) long and were mounted on a wooden stand. They were spanned by means of a windlass arrangement or by means of a screw-threaded mechanism. One modern estimate for the force required to draw the string back is in the region of 2,800 pounds (1,300 kilograms) though this seems a very high figure. They shot large quarrels of perhaps 1 1/2–2 1/2 feet (50–80 centimeters) long and weighing about 1 pound (500 g). They were too large to move around easily and were set up on castle or fortification walls or else brought to the site of a siege when needed.

The springald is a somewhat more problematic weapon as it is completely unclear whether it was the same weapon as the Roman ballista which some historians believe never disappeared from the battlefield and remained in use throughout the intervening period or whether the Roman weapon died out and the later springald was a reinvention. On balance it is difficult to support the position that the Roman machine continued in use and it would appear that the springald was reinvented and probably first used in the middle of the thirteenth century. It was somewhat similar to the great crossbow and fired a similar projectile. However, the bow was made in two halves, each about 2–3 feet (70–80 centimeters) long, one end of each was attached to either side of a wooden frame by means of a twisted and tensioned skein of horse hair. The string was attached to the outer ends of the two bows and a windlass was used to pull it back to the firing position against the tension of the securing skeins. A modern estimate of the force needed to pull the arms back is 3,900 pounds (1,800 kilograms). Evidence for their use is rare and what is there is difficult to evaluate, but by the end of the fourteenth century they had largely disappeared from European arsenals.

Incendiaries

As we saw in Chapter 2, Greek fire, a burning liquid pumped out of some form of machine much like a modern-day flamethrower, was used as a devastating weapon mainly at sea by the Byzantines from the seventh century AD. Its later history is extremely difficult to ascertain as there are few references and what we have are difficult to interpret, though it seems to disappear from the sources from some time in the tenth century.

However, it is clear that the use of fire as a weapon has always been important, especially in a world where everything was made from natural and very flammable materials and the desire to find incendiary mixtures and materials has always been strong. At some time, possibly in the twelfth century, a material that was given the name Greek fire was introduced. However, this was not the liquid of the Byzantines but a mixture of flammable materials such as tar-like substances, gums, and resins mixed with sulfur and other chemicals. It was packed into ceramic pots or small wooden containers and either thrown by hand or from a trebuchet. One of the crucial questions is whether these mixtures contained saltpeter, potassium nitrate, the key ingredient of gunpowder. Though it is unlikely, at least before the later decades of the thirteenth century, it is not inconceivable and much remains to be done on the history of incendiaries in the twelfth and thirteenth centuries before we can answer this question with any certainty.

THE ENEMY: THE ARMY OF SALADIN

For a little under two centuries, from 1099 to 1291, Europe fought a series of wars and battles for control of the Holy places in the Middle East—the campaigns that today we call the crusades. Although the forces against which they fought over this period were many and varied, it is perhaps those of the great Muslim leader Saladin in the later twelfth century that had probably the greatest effect on the armies and tactics of Western Europe.

Much like the armies of Western European, those of Saladin were composed of both horse and foot soldiers in which the cavalry, though fewer in number, were again dominant—not only in the tactics and strategy adopted but also in the minds and hearts of those that fought—it is the mounted soldiers who were remembered both then and today. And again though very different in detail, the arms and armor worn by the Middle Eastern troops was broadly similar to those used in the West—the mail shirt, helmet, sword, lance, and bow, for example.

Mail armor was the usual form of defense for the body as in the West but was often augmented by large iron plates over the chest area or by panels made from small rectangular plates of iron that were interwoven with the mail—sometimes called "mail and plate" construction. This type of defense was extensively used and continued far longer than in the West and can, probably, be explained by the desire for more flexible armor that reflected the tactical use of speed on the battlefield. The armor was very like the hauberk and covered the torso from the neck to the upper thighs and usually had integral short sleeves. A mail coif might also be worn, again sometimes augmented with small rectangular iron plates. Fabric armor, or quilted defenses, was also known, as was armor made where the plates were made from leather. Armor of a similar type, mail and plate, was also made for the arms and legs.

A number of helmet types were used. The first was made from "mail and plate" as already described and covered the head and the back of the neck. The second type consisted of a simple one-piece iron helmet that just covered the top of the head with a simple mail defense hanging down to cover the sides and back of the head and neck. In more developed forms the helmet "bowl" was enlarged and covered the head down to the level of the ears. The sides of the face were protected with cheek-pieces and the back of the head with mail. On some examples a separate nose guard, a nasal, which could be raised and lowered was fitted to the front of the helmet.

Muslim troops also carried circular shields, though the kite-shaped shield was also known as was a tall infantry type with a flat base.

The characteristic sword of the late-twelfth-century Muslim warrior was, like the older Arabic swords, straight and either single or double edged. It had a relatively simple cross guard and hilt, though highly decorated and ornate pieces were always produced for those who could afford them. At some stage, and just when is hard to pin down, the curved saber or scimitar was introduced from the East. Both, though especially the saber, were designed as cutting and slashing weapons and not thrusting weapons. Swords of both types were kept in a sheath attached to a waist belt or slung over one or other shoulder. The myth of the quality of Muslim swords and the confusion over the use of the terms "Damascus" or "damascene blade" has often confused writers. The confusion has arisen, per-haps, because the phrase is used to describe blades that have a sur-face pattern sometimes called a watered surface. There are, in fact, four ways patterns can be produced and four varieties of swords or, rather, steel to which this word has been applied. These are, using their modern terminology: pattern welded, inlaied, preferentially etched, and crucible. Pattern-welded blades are, as we have already seen, made by welding together several rods or bars of iron and these are forged into a blade which, when the surface is lightly etched, re-veals a surface pattern. Inlayed steel, where different metals are in-layed into the surface, and preferentially etched steel, where a pat-tern is etched into the surface, are frequently referred to as "false damascene" or "artificial damascene." True Damascus is made from crucible steel and is a much superior material from which to make blades. In the twelfth century this material was imported from India and much prized—for example, when Saladin wanted to secure the help of the Muslim West he sent them, among other things, a present of Indian sword blades. It should be noted that though the word "Damascus" or "damascene" is used, there is no evidence that swords were ever made in Damascus!

Whereas in the West the mace was not ever a popular weapon it was very common among the Muslim soldiers of Saladin's army. It was described as an armor-breaking weapon and was usually short and often had a flanged or globular iron head.

The Muslim soldier's primary weapon was, as in Western Europe, the lance, although it was used in a more flexible way—not just as a shock weapon. It is also clear that they used both the lance, couched under the right arm, and the spear, which was thrown. Other forms of polearms were also certainly used by Muslim infantry but, though it is clear that they were used, they are not easily identifiable.

The bow, the recurved or composite type, was also used, though to what extent is uncertain. It may have been used by the infantry, pos-sibly in place of the throwing spear, but the evidence is somewhat contradictory. The axe, with a characteristic semicircular head, was also used by some sections of the army.

The two armies that faced each other, Muslim and Christian, dur-ing the late twelfth century were not, as is evident, armed or equipped that differently from each other. Although there were dif-ferences, these were in no way decisive. What was different were the strategy, tactics, leadership, morale, and discipline of the soldiers. Even before the first blow was delivered, Saladin and his army had a very positive advantage.

CHAPTER FOUR

The Late Middle Ages, 1300–1550

HISTORY

After the fall of Acre and the effective end of the Crusading Era in 1291, the fourteenth and fifteenth centuries were a period dominated by conflicts both within and between European countries and states. The English fought the Scots, the French, the Burgundians, and the Spanish and endured a brutal civil war, the War of the Roses. The French waged war against the Burgundians, the Italians, and the Portuguese. The Burgundians campaigned against the Swiss and the Germans. The Germans went to war with the Italians and they also fought among themselves, as did the Italians. The various Iberian kingdoms attacked one other and waged war against the Muslims. The Danes clashed with the Swedes, and both fought the Norwegians. The Teutonic Knights battled with the Prussians, Livonians, and Russians; and everyone tried—vainly—to fight against the Ottoman Turks.

However, the most enduring and sizeable conflict of this whole period was the series of wars and battles that lasted from 1337 to 1453 and came to be known as the Hundred Years War. When King Edward III of England launched his first major invasion of the continent in 1339, it was ostensibly to recover the crown of France, which in his view had been "stolen" from him in 1328. Despite being the closest genealogical heir to Charles IV, he was declared ineligible to be king of France because his descent was through a woman, his mother, Isabella, the sister of the deceased king. The throne instead was given to a cousin, Philip of Valois, who was crowned as King Philip VI of France.

At the time the French had a strong and renowned army and Edward's move was thought by many in England and in France to be foolish. During the thirteenth century, under able warrior kings such as Philip II Augustus and Philip IV the Fair, France had won many wars and strengthened its borders against the Spanish kingdoms, Italy, and the Holy Roman Empire, while at the same time regaining almost all of the English lands in France. Rebellious lords and heretical sects also felt the strength of France's military might. The former were imprisoned or, more often, executed while the latter had their power and authority challenged. Philip IV was so confident of his military, political, and ecclesiastical power that in 1307 he was able to challenge the Knights Templar, the largest military monastic order. He declared this remnant of the crusading past to be heretical and confiscated its treasures and lands. Though it is true that during the thirteenth and early fourteenth centuries, the French had suffered some defeats, most notably that by King Louis IX on crusade in Egypt and North Africa and by French noble armies who fought against Flemish townspeople at the battles of Courtrai in 1302 and Arques in 1303, these were quickly forgotten and whatever setbacks that resulted were quickly reclaimed.

At first Edward III's campaign in 1339 gained him very little. Though buoyed up by alliances with several Low Countries principalities—which were dependent on English wool for their economic prosperity—he sailed back across the Channel only to find his landing blocked by a large French and Genoese fleet at Sluys. The resulting naval battle, which took place on 24 June 1340, was the first major engagement of the Hundred Years War. By the end of the day, the English navy had won, ably assisted by their allies, principally Flemings from Sluys and nearby Bruges who watched the fight from the shore and kept any French sailors from escaping. In doing so, the English almost completely destroyed the French navy. Edward III followed this with a siege of the town of Tournai, the largest northern town that had declared its allegiance to the French. Initially, at least, the siege went the way the English king had planned. His army and allies destroyed French-allied lands and villages nearby and, though Philip VI and the French army camped within sight of the besieged town, they refused to do battle. The town seemed on the verge of surrendering. However, the alliance that Edward III depended on broke up because of internal bickering, and his own parliament held up much-needed funds for him to carry on the war. He was, therefore, forced to sign the Truce of Espléchin with the French and to return with his army to England.

Although Philip VI appeared to have won a great victory by raising the siege of Tournai, it quickly proved to have gained him little more than a brief respite. Edward III removed opponents to the war from his government, built up his war finances, and planned his return. According to the Truce of Espléchin, the English could not attack France for five years. Before that time had passed, however, civil war broke out in Brittany between two heirs to the vacant ducal throne. Supporting one Breton candidate while Philip supported the other, Edward used this excuse to restart hostilities with France. But this proved to be but a sideshow to the main war. In 1346, after the Truce of Espléchin had officially expired, the English attacked France proper. With a large army, numbering probably as many as 15,000, Edward landed in Normandy—a duchy lost in 1214 by his great-great-grandfather, John—and began a march toward the Low Countries. He stopped at Crécy, in the county of Ponthieu. The French army, still under the leadership of Philip VI, which was following the English, decided this time to give battle, and on 26 August 1346, the two sides fought the first great land battle of the Hundred Years War. As was to be repeated throughout the next century, the French soldiers greatly outnumbered their opponents, but lost. Philip was able to escape the carnage, fleeing to Paris under the cover of darkness, but many of his lords and captains were killed. Edward moved victoriously to the town of Calais, and, after a year-long siege, again with the French king camping idly by, the burghers could no longer withstand their forced hunger and the town fell. The English were to use Calais as their continental "beachhead" for the next two centuries.

While the French seemed incapable of slowing English military progress, a plague of unprecedented scale and mortality did. The Black Death, as it became known, swept through Europe in 1348–1349 and effectively halted further campaigning by Edward and the English army. The effects of this pestilence on the Hundred Years War—on manpower, leadership, finances, as well as strategy and tactics—were major. Not only was there a cessation of hostilities for nearly a decade, but when they began anew, in 1355–1356, the sizes of armies were dramatically reduced. Because of this, the English adopted a new tactic of warfare that they would practice with regularity and proficiency for the rest of the Hundred Years War: the *chevauchée*. The *chevauchée* was a quick cavalry campaign with the goal of pillaging unfortified villages and towns, destroying crops and houses, stealing livestock, and generally disrupting and terrorizing rural society.

It was on one of these *chevauchées* in 1356, when Edward III's son, Edward the Black Prince, was raiding through the north-central regions of France, that King John II of France (Philip VI had died in 1350) attacked the smaller forces of the English army outside of the town of Poitiers. The result was the same as a decade before at Crécy: he lost. John was captured and imprisoned in the Tower of London. The incarceration of their king forced French royal representatives to the negotiation table, where, on 8 May 1360, the Treaty of Brétigny was signed between the two warring states. The French promised to pay 3 million golden crowns as a ransom for John and to concede the duchies of Aquitaine and Ponthieu and the town of Calais to the English king. For his part, Edward III, rather surprisingly, promised to renounce his claim to the French throne.

And yet, the imprisonment that kept King John II in London may have been the best thing that could have happened to the French militarily. It was extremely difficult for the French to raise their king's ransom—indeed, it was never completely paid. While he lingered in the Tower of London, the responsibility for protecting France fell on his son and heir, the future Charles V. He was forced to defend his kingdom's borders, not only against the English, who still continued to fight for what was not covered by the Treaty of Brétigny, but also against the Navarrese—whose king, Charles, was making his own claims to French lands and titles—and against roving bands of English and French soldiers left without employment by the treaty, the so-called Free Companies, who were carrying on their own war and plundering the countryside. The dauphin Charles was ably aided in this duty by a rising French military superstar, Bertrand du Guesclin.

Du Guesclin fought many battles. In some he was dreadfully overmatched and unsuccessful. In fact, he was taken prisoner in 1364 after his defeat at Auray, and again in 1367 after the inconclusive battle of Nájera, in Castile. At the latter, sometimes called the War of the Two Pedros, du Guesclin took the side of Enrique of Trastamara in his struggle for succession in Castile against his halfbrother, Pedro the Cruel, who was supported by the Black Prince.

But Bertrand du Guesclin was usually successful and King Charles V—for he had assumed the throne in 1364 on the death of his father in London—saw his military fortunes begin to rise. Slowly, he began to regain lost parts of his kingdom. By 1369, he had taken back Aquitaine; by 1371, he had made peace with Charles of Navarre; in that same year, he again began to exert authority in Brittany and in 1372, his allies, the Castilians, defeated the English fleet off the coast of La Rochelle. By 1377 he had outlived both his chief enemies; Edward the Black Prince died in June 1376 of a disease he had acquired during his campaign in Spain and he was followed less than a year later by his father, Edward III. His successor, Richard II, was a child untrained in the warfare of his father or grandfather, a situation that Charles V, and after his death in 1380, his son, Charles VI, took full advantage of, driving the English back until they could barely hold on to Calais and Gascony.

In 1396 Richard II signed a truce with Charles VI in Paris, dependent on his marriage to Isabella, one of Charles VI's daughters, and a commitment to an Anglo-French Crusade to the east against the Ottoman Turks. Although France and England did not exchange blows during the period between the Treaty of Paris and 1415, when Henry V launched his attack on France, fighting continued. Even without English interference, the military situation in France during this period was far from resolved. Charles VI's mental illness led to unstable kingship, and a number of his cousins and uncles vied for political power to fill the vacuum. The Dukes of Burgundy and Orléans, cousins of both the king and, of course, of each other, both thought they should be the only one helping Charles VI to rule France. As they could not agree to share that responsibility, they fought each other, drawing the rest of France into the conflict. For the rest of the Hundred Years War, these two factions, known as the Burgundians and Armagnacs, used every means, from actual battles and sieges to assassination, to fight one other.

The two parties did little more than exchange bellicose words until 20 November 1407, when Louis, the Duke of Orléans, was assassinated in Paris. John the Fearless was quickly implicated, and the two sides mustered their armies. There seems little doubt among historians that John the Fearless planned this assassination to take advantage of the weak state of the Armagnacs and their supporters to extend his own lands and political power. The plan started to go awry for John when the assassination of a fellow French aristocrat caused many of the other French nobles to oppose him; even his previous allies were now suspicious. But this did not discourage the Duke of Burgundy. Indeed, he decided that this was the time to strengthen his position by military means and began to wage war against anyone who opposed him. He used his large army, together with perhaps the largest, most diverse gunpowder artillery train in Europe, to attack his Armagnac enemies, and by 1419 he had taken a large part of France, including Paris.

When Henry V invaded France, several years into this Franco-Burgundian struggle, he found a France weakened by civil war. The Burgundians either collaborated with his invasion or ignored it, and the Armagnacs seemed unable to decide whether to fight against the English or the Burgundians. When Henry came to the throne of England in March 1413, he seems to have had two goals in mind: the recapture of the formerly English-held lands in France and the reassertion of his claim to the French throne. On 14 August 1415, Henry's invasion force landed at the mouth of the Seine and immediately laid siege to the nearby town of Harfleur. His army was not large, probably numbering no more than 9,000–10,000 soldiers, of which only about a quarter were men-at-arms and the rest longbowmen. But the French appear to have been completely unprepared for this attack and unable to raise a relief army. On 22 September, the town surrendered. Shortly thereafter, Henry began a march to Calais, hoping, it is argued, not to encounter the French army, though willing, it seems from the result, to engage should they catch him. On 25 October 1415, the French finally caught the English outside the village of Agincourt. As at Crécy and Poitiers, the French army should have easily defeated their English foes, if for no other reason than that they outnumbered them by three or four times (around 20,000 to not quite 6,000), and that most of the French were knights and men-at-arms. Yet they did not. In what was certainly one of the greatest and most trumpeted victories of the entire Middle Ages, the English annihilated their opponents. At the end of the day, more than 10,000 French soldiers lay dead, including the Constable and Admiral of France, 3 dukes, 7 counts, and more than 90 other lords and 1,560 knights. Other important French lords had been taken prisoner. On the English side the casualties were light; only a few hundred were killed, including the Duke of York and the Earl of Suffolk.

Immediately following the battle of Agincourt there was little further English military action. Henry V returned to London to his people's acclaim and succeeded in raising more money and troops for a larger invasion of France. He began that invasion late in 1417. By 1420 he had conquered Normandy, giving him complete control of the northeast and southwest of France—the English still held Gascony—while his allies, the Burgundians and Bretons, held the northwest and east of France, including Paris, and the Low Countries. The Armagnacs were pushed south, below the Loire River, where they held on, very tenuously, to a small part of the French kingdom. On 21 May 1420, the Treaty of Troyes was signed between Henry V and Charles VI. This treaty in all its intricacy can be reduced to a single provision: it made Henry V heir to the throne of France. Charles VI was still recognized as king, but should he die, and he was ailing most of the time, Henry V would assume his throne. It effectively disinherited Charles's only remaining son, the dauphin Charles. In addition, Henry V would marry Charles VI's youngest daughter, Catherine, and their eldest son would thus become heir to the crowns of both France and England.

Of course, at the signing of the Treaty of Troyes, no one believed Henry V would die before the frail Charles VI. However, during the siege of Meaux in 1422, Henry V contracted what was probably an intestinal illness, perhaps dysentery, and died a few weeks later, on 31 August 1422. Charles VI still lived, although he followed Henry to the grave later the same year. Also in 1422, Catherine, Henry's wife and Charles's daughter, gave birth to a son, named after his father, who, almost from the moment he was born, was king of France and England. However, the disinherited dauphin, Charles, still had the support of many in France, including the Armagnacs, and they were not prepared to allow this English baby, Henry VI, to sit on the throne of their kingdom. One of these supporters was a young peasant girl named Joan of Arc. During the years between the death of Henry V in 1422 and Joan's rise to leadership in the French army in 1429, the English pushed deep into Armagnac territory, reaching as far as the Loire River and besieging the region's capital, Orléans, although they were unable to capture it. The English had been besieging the city for five months and, despite having too few soldiers even to surround the town, seemed to be on the verge of capturing it. However, Joan—who, following angelic "voices" she said had sent her on a mission of military relief for the French, presented herself to and convinced the heir to the French throne, Charles, to make her a leader of his army—refused to allow Orléans to fall and, after defeating several of their field fortifications, as well as the Tourelles, the stone bridgehead in which they had their headquarters, she forced the English to raise their siege and withdraw. Taking fresh heart the French, with Joan goading them on, chased the English from the rest of their Loire holdings. Following an uneventful march through Burgundian-held territory to Rheims, on 17 July 1429, the man for whom Joan had fought, the dauphin Charles, was crowned King Charles VII. Joan then set out to conquer Paris, which was held at the time by an Anglo-Burgundian alliance, but was unsuccessful, retreating eventually to the town of Compiègne, which was under siege by Burgundian forces. On 23 May 1430, leading a sortie out of Compiègne, Joan was separated from the main body of her force, captured by the Burgundians, and eventually sold to the English. A little more than a year later, on 30 May 1431, she was burned to death as a heretic in the marketplace of Rouen.

After her execution, and perhaps even a little because of it, Joan's influence increased and there were no further major military setbacks for the French or their king, Charles VII. Most importantly, within five years, a peace conference was held at Arras. While failing to stop the war between England and France, the treaty signed at Arras in 1435 forced the Burgundian duke, Philip the Good, who had ascended to the ducal throne in 1419 after the assassination of his father, John the Fearless, to reassess his alliance with England. He decided that it was time to "switch sides" in the Hundred Years War, withdrawing from active support of England, if not completely allying himself with Charles VII. This was a difficult move for Philip, but it was more of a problem for the English, and their war effort in France never quite recovered. It took another seventeen years, but eventually the English king lost all of his lands in France—except for Calais. Maine fell in 1449; Normandy, in 1450; and Gascony, in 1453. The latter had been in English hands since Eleanor of Aquitaine passed it to her son, Richard the Lionheart, in the twelfth century.

The English army's losses in France were devastating for its ineffective king, Henry VI. Unable to sustain, let alone repeat, his father's successes, his throne was threatened when his cousin, Richard, Duke of York, claimed it in 1450. What followed was 35 years of almost constant political upheaval and civil war, what is now called the Wars of the Roses. Burgundy, too, suffered from the consequences of the Hundred Years War. The end of the alliance with England in 1435 led to revolts by the southern Low Countries towns, principally Ghent, Bruges, and Ypres, whose economic prosperity depended on peaceful connections with the English. Moreover, neither Philip the Good nor his son and heir, Charles the Bold, ever completely allied themselves with the French. Thus, when the new king of France, Louis XI—who ascended the French throne at the death of his father, Charles VII, in 1461—fought the Burgundians in the War of the Public Weal, the best they could do was fight to a draw, postponing rather than ending the French acquisition of their lands. Nor did the bellicose Charles the Bold succeed in enlarging his ducal holdings in Lorraine, Germany, or Switzerland. Ultimately, at the battle of Nancy in 1477, Charles was killed. Because he lacked a male heir, the prosperous and powerful domains of the Burgundian dukes were inherited by his daughter, Mary, and after her untimely death in 1482, they were absorbed into the holdings of her husband, the Habsburg ruler of Austria and later Holy Roman Emperor, Maximilian I. But not all of the former Burgundian holdings were inherited by Mary and Maximilian. Louis XI's armies forcibly took a lot of Burgundian territory after Charles the Bold's death—almost the whole of Picardy, Artois, Alsace, Lorraine, and eventually Burgundy itself. The Habsburg response was slow in coming, for Maximilian had more pressing matters at hand. From the end of the War of the Sicilian Vespers (1282–1302), the Italians tried to decide for themselves what government they wanted, resulting in conflict between the Ghibellines—who supported Imperial rule—and the Guelfs—who supported papal rule. The Guelfs were successful in the first decade of the fourteenth century, ironically at much the same time the papacy moved to Avignon in 1308. Suddenly freed from either Imperial or papal influence, the large number of sovereign states in northern and central Italy began to try to exert control over their neighbors. Florence, Milan, and Venice, and to a lesser extent Lucca, Siena, Mantua, and Genoa, all profited from the early-fourteenth-century military situation by exerting their independence. But this independence came at a price. The inhabitants of the north Italian city-states had enough wealth to be able to pay for others to fight for them and they frequently employed soldiers, condottieri in their language (from the *condotte,* the contract hiring these soldiers) and mercenaries in ours. Indeed, the immense wealth of the Italian city-states in the late Middle Ages meant that the number of native soldiers was lower than elsewhere in Europe at the same time, but it meant the cost of waging war was much higher.

One might think that having to add the pay for condottieri to the normal costs of war would have limited the numbers of military conflicts in late medieval Italy. But that was not the case and, in what was an incredibly bellicose time, Italy was one of the most fought over regions in Europe. Most of these wars were small, with one city's mercenary forces facing another's, but they were very frequent. They gave employment to a large number of condottieri, who in turn fought the wars, which in turn employed the condottieri. An obvious self-perpetuating circle developed. It was fueled by a number of factors: the wealth of northern Italy; the greed of wealthier Italians to acquire more wealth by occupying neighboring cities and lands (or to keep these cities from competing by incorporating their economies); their unwillingness themselves to fight the wars; and the availability of a large number of men who were not only willing to do so, but who saw regular employment in their mercenary companies as a means to comfort, wealth, and often titles and offices. In 1416, one condottierie, Braccio da Montone, became lord of Perugia, while a short time later two others, condottieri sons of the condottiere Muccio Attendolo Sforza, Alessandro and Francesco, became the Master of Pesaro and Duke of Milan, respectively. Other condottieri became governors of Urbino, Mantua, Rimini, and Ferrara during the fifteenth century.

Venice and Genoa continued to be the greatest rivals among the northern Italian city-states. Both believed the Mediterranean to be theirs, and they refused to share it with anyone, including Naples and Aragon, nor, of course, with each other. This became a military issue at the end of the fifteenth century. The common practice was a monopoly trading contract. Venice's monopoly with the crusader states ceased when the crusaders were forced from the Middle East in 1291, although they were able to sustain their trade with the victorious Muslim powers. And Venice's contract with Constantinople was abandoned with the fall of the Latin Kingdom in 1261, only to be replaced by a similar contract with Genoa that would last till the city's fall to the Ottoman Turks in 1453.

Frequently during the late Middle Ages, this rivalry turned to warfare, fought primarily on the sea, as was fitting for two naval powers. Venice almost always won these engagements, most notably the War of Chioggia (1376–1381), and there seems little doubt that such defeats led to a weakening of the political independence and economic strength of Genoa. Although Venice never actually conquered Genoa, nor does it appear that the Venetian rulers considered this to be in their city's interest, other principalities did target the once powerful city-state. Florence held Genoa for a period of three years (1353–1356), and Naples, Aragon, and Milan vied for control in the fifteenth century. Seeking defensive assistance, the Republic of Genoa sought alliance with the Kingdom of France, and it is in this context that their most prominent military feature is set, the Genoese mercenary. During the Hundred Years War, Genoa supplied France with naval and, more famously, crossbowmen mercenaries, the latter ironically provided by a city whose experience in land warfare was rather thin.

Before the fifteenth century, the Republic of Venice had also rarely participated in land campaigns—except for leading the forces of the Second Crusade in their attack of Constantinople in 1204.

Seeing the sea not only as a provider of economic security but also as defense for the city, Venetian doges and other city officials had rarely pursued campaigns against their neighbors. However, in 1404–1405, a Venetian army, once again almost entirely mercenaries, attacked to the west and captured Vicenza, Verona, and Padua. In 1411–1412 and again in 1418–1420, they attacked to the northeast, against Hungary, and captured Dalmatia, Fruili, and Istria. So far it had been easy—simply pay for enough condottieri to fight the wars, and reap the profits of conquest. But in 1424 Venice ran into two Italian city-states that had the same military philosophy they did, and both were as wealthy: Milan and Florence. The result was thirty years of protracted warfare.

The strategy of all three of these city-states during this conflict was to employ more and more mercenaries. At the start, the Venetian army numbered 10,000–12,000; by 1432 this figure had grown to 18,000; and by 1439 it was 25,000, although it declined to 20,000 during the 1440s and 1450s. The other two city-states kept pace. At almost any time after 1430 more than 50,000 soldiers were fighting in northern Italy. The economy and society of the whole region were damaged, with little gain by any of the protagonists during the war. At its end, a negotiated settlement, Venice gained little, but it also lost very little. The city went back to war in 1478–1479, the Pazzi War, and again in 1482–1484, the War of Ferrara. The Florentines and Milanese participated in both as well.

After the acquisition of Vicenza, Verona, and Padua in 1405 Venice shared a land frontier with Milan. From that time forward Milan was the greatest threat to Venice and her allies, and to practically any other city-state, town, or village in northern Italy. Milan also shared a land frontier with Florence, and if Milanese armies were not fighting Venetian armies, they were fighting Florentine armies, sometimes taking on both at the same time.

Their animosity predates the later Middle Ages, but it intensified with the wealth and ability of both sides to hire condottieri. This led to wars with Florence in 1351–1354 and 1390–1402, and with Florence and Venice (in league together) in 1423–1454, 1478–1479, and 1482–1484. In those rare times when not at war with Florence or Venice, Milanese armies often turned on other neighboring towns, for example, capturing Pavia and Monza among other places.

Perhaps the most telling sign of Milan's bellicosity is the rise to power of its condottiere ruler, Francesco Sforza, in 1450. Sforza had been one of Milan's condottieri captains for a number of years, following in the footsteps of his father, Muccio, who had been in the city-state's employ off and on since about 1400. Both had performed diligently, successfully, and, at least for condottieri, loyally, and they had become wealthy because of it. Francesco had even married the illegitimate daughter of the reigning Duke of Milan, Filippo Maria Visconti. But during the most recent wars, after he had assumed the lordship of Pavia, and in the wake of Filippo's death in 1447, the Milanese decided not to renew Francesco's contract. In response, the condottiere used his army to besiege the city, which capitulated in less than a year. Within a very short time, Francesco Sforza had insinuated himself into all facets of Milanese rule; his brother even became the city's archbishop in 1454, and his descendants continued to hold power in the sixteenth century.

Genoa, Venice, and Milan all fought extensively throughout the fourteenth and fifteenth centuries, but Florence played the most active role in Italian warfare of the later Middle Ages. A republican city-state, although in the fifteenth century controlled almost exclusively by the Medici family, Florence had been deeply involved in the Guelf and Ghibelline conflicts of the thirteenth century, serving as the center of the Guelf party. But though the Guelfs were successful this did not bring peace to Florence and when, in 1301, they split into two parties—the blacks and the whites—the fighting continued until 1307. Before this feud was even concluded, however, the Florentine army, numbering 7,000, mostly condottieri, attacked Pistoia, capturing the city in 1307. In 1315 in league with Naples, Florentine forces attempted to take Pisa, but were defeated. In 1325, they were again defeated while trying to take Pisa and Lucca. Between 1351 and 1354 they fought the Milanese. From 1376 to 1378 they fought against papal forces hired at and drawn from Rome in what was known as the War of the Eight Saints, but the Florentines lost more than they gained. Forming the League of Bologna with Bologna, Padua, Ferrara, and other northern Italian cities, they warred against Milan from 1390 to 1402. While they were initially successful against the Milanese, Gian Galeazzo, Duke of Milan, was eventually able to bring Pisa, Lucca, and Venice onto his city's side, and once again Florence was defeated. In 1406 Florence annexed Pisa without armed resistance. But war broke out with Milan again in 1423 lasting until 1454; Florence would ally with Venice in 1425, and with the papacy in 1440. Battles were lost on the Serchio in 1450 and at Imola in 1434, but won at Anghiara in 1440. Finally, after the Peace of Lodi was signed in 1454 ending the conflict, a league was formed between Florence, Venice, and Milan that lasted for 25 years. But, after the murder of Giuliano de' Medici and the attempted murder of his brother, Lorenzo—Pope Sixtus IV was complicit in the affair—war broke out in 1478 with the papacy and lasted until the death of Sixtus in 1484. In addition, interspersed with these external wars were numerous rebellions within Florence itself. In 1345 a revolt broke out at the announcement of the bankruptcy of the Bardi and Peruzzi banking firms; in 1368 the dyers revolted; in 1378 there was the Ciompi Revolt; and in 1382 the *popolo grasso* revolt. None of these were extensive or successful, but they did disrupt social, economic, and political life in the city until permanently put to rest by the rise to power of the Medicis.

Why Florence continued to wage so many wars in the face of so many defeats and revolts is simple to understand. Again one must see the role of the condottieri in Florentine military strategy; as long as the governors of the city-state were willing to pay for military activity and as long as there were soldiers willing to take this pay, wars would continue until the wealth of the town ran out. In Renaissance Florence this did not happen. Take, for example, the employment of perhaps the most famous condottiere, Sir John Hawkwood. Coming south in 1361, during one of the lulls in fighting in the Hundred Years War, the Englishman Hawkwood joined the White Company, a unit of condottieri already fighting in Italy. In 1364, while in the pay of Pisa, the White Company had its first encounter with Florence when, unable to effectively besiege the city, they sacked and pillaged its rich suburbs. In 1375, now under the leadership of Hawkwood, the White Company made an agreement with the Florentines not to attack them, only to discover later that year, now in the pay of the papacy, that they were required to fight in the Florentine-controlled Romagna. Hawkwood decided that he was not actually attacking Florence, and the White Company conquered Faenza in 1376 and Cesena in 1377. However, perhaps because the papacy ordered the massacres of the people of both towns, a short time later Hawkwood and his condottieri left their papal employment. They did not stay unemployed for long, however; Florence hired them almost immediately, and for the next seventeen years, John Hawkwood and the White Company fought diligently, although not always successfully, for the city. All of the company's condottieri became quite wealthy, but Hawkwood especially prospered. He was granted three castles outside the city, a house in Florence, a life pension of 2,000 florins, a pension for his wife, Donnina Visconti, payable after his death, and dowries for his three daughters, above his contracted pay. Florentines, it seems, loved to lavish their wealth on those whom they employed to carry out their wars, whether they were successful or not.

In comparison to the north, the south of Italy was positively peaceful. Much of this came from the fact that there were only two powers in southern Italy. The Papal States, with Rome as their capital, did not have the prosperity of the northern city-states, and in fact for most of the later Middle Ages they were, essentially, bankrupt. But economic problems were not the only matter that disrupted Roman life. From 1308 to 1378 there was no pope in Rome and from then until 1417 the Roman pontiff was one of two (and sometimes three) popes sitting on the papal throne at the same time. But even after 1417 the papacy was weak, kept that way by a Roman populace not willing to see a theocracy return to power. Perhaps this is the reason why the Papal States suffered so many insurrections. In 1347 Cola di Rienzo defeated the Roman nobles and was named Tribune by the Roman people. He governed until those same people overthrew and executed him in 1354. In 1434 the Columna family established a republican government in the Papal States, forcing the ruling pope, Eugenius IV, to flee to Florence. He did not return and reestablish his government until 1343. Finally, in 1453, a plot to put another republican government in place was halted only by the general dislike for its leader, Stefano Porcaro, who was executed for treason.

One might think that such political and economic turmoil would not breed much military confidence, yet it did not seem to keep the governors of the Papal States from hiring mercenaries, making alliances with other Italian states, or pursuing an active military role, especially in the central parts of Italy. Usually small papal armies were pitted against much larger northern city-state forces, yet often these small numbers carried the day, perhaps not winning many battles, but often winning the wars, certainly as much because of the Papal States alliances as its military prowess. This meant that despite all the obvious upheaval in the Papal States during the later Middle Ages, at the beginning of the 1490s it was much larger and more powerful than it had ever been previously.

The Kingdom of Naples, encompassing both the southern third of the Italian peninsula and Sicily, seemingly had none of the political or economic problems of its nearest neighbor, the Papal States. Coming out of the War of Sicilian Vespers in 1302, it had both a prosperous economy and a stable government under its kings, Charles II of Anjou and Robert of Anjou, until the middle of the fourteenth century. But the Angevins were a large family and many of its members lusted for power, no matter how they obtained it, and when Robert died in 1343, a succession crisis developed.

Robert's daughter, Joanna I, was named queen, but this did not satisfy her Angevin cousin, King Lewis of Hungary. He invaded Naples in 1348, only to be driven out by the Black Death, but he returned in 1350 and captured Naples. He left, however, in less than a year, and Joanna resumed control. When she died without children in 1382, and her cousin, Charles III, was crowned in her place, another cousin, Louis of Anjou, led an army into Naples to claim the throne. Although Louis died in the attempt to capture the southern Italian kingdom, his son, Louis II, did so in 1390. He, in turn, was removed by yet another cousin, Ladislas, who ruled until 1411 when Louis II, in yet another attempt to gain the throne, defeated him at the Battle of Roccasecca. But Louis returned to France, leaving Ladislas as king. At his death in 1414, Ladislas was succeeded by his sister, Joanna II. She ruled until 1420 when invasions, by both her cousin Louis III and Alfonso V of Aragon, resulted in the kingdom coming under Alfonso's control. To preserve her reign, Joanna was forced to name Alfonso as her successor. But when she died in 1435, the Aragonese had been thrown out of Naples, and Joanna's cousin, René II of Anjou, was recognized as king of Naples. René ruled, although almost always absent from the kingdom because of threats against his lands in Anjou and Lorraine, until Alfonso returned to Naples in 1443. Alfonso, known as Alfonso the Magnificent, and his son, Ferrante, governed Naples relatively peacefully from then until 1494.

The struggles over Naples by various branches of the Angevin family meant two very important things: the economy went from robust to ruin, and their armies were always in the field. Of course, the second no doubt added to the first, for the cost of paying troops—although it appears that most of these were Neapolitans and not condottieri—and the destruction caused by the constant warring on an agricultural society was immense.

The various states that made up the Holy Roman Empire entered the fourteenth century in chaos. There had been little continuity in Imperial government, and the electoral process of choosing an emperor produced confusion and turmoil. Since the end of the reign of Frederick II in 1250, there was rarely a smooth transfer of power from one ruler to the next. Nor did military success guarantee hereditary succession, as it had earlier in the Middle Ages. Ego and jealousy determined far more than did competence. So, although Rudolf of Habsburg, in his wars in Bohemia, had done much to add to the Empire and to increase the security of its borders—which earlier would have ensured patrilineal succession—when he died in 1291, the electors did not choose his son, Rudolf, but crowned Adolf of Nassau in his stead. Civil war ensued until 1298 when Albert I of Habsburg, one of Rudolf's sons, defeated and killed Adolf at the battle of Göllheim. But as many of the Imperial electors and nobles continued to reject his rule, Albert's reign was anything but peaceful, and at his death in 1308 the electors passed over his son, also named Albert, to choose Henry of Luxembourg, who reigned until 1313. Thus, the two most important families for the later history of the Holy Roman Empire gained power and although it transferred back and forth between them, they did not lose it until 1918.

But it was an insecure beginning. Once again, in 1313, there was no smooth election. John of Bohemia, Henry of Luxembourg's son, was challenged by Frederick of Habsburg and Lewis of Bavaria. As had been done so many times before in these situations, armies were mustered and a civil war was fought. Lewis, who had too little power to be elected emperor in his own right, quickly supported John of Bohemia's claim, and when the two sides finally met in battle, at Mühldorf in 1322, it was they who won, capturing Frederick in the encounter. A shaky agreement for coemperorship between the three claimants was bought with the victory, but after Lewis declared himself sole emperor in 1328, being crowned as such in Rome, and the death of Frederick in 1330, the Holy Roman Empire was once more embroiled in civil war. This was given even more significance when Pope John XXII excommunicated Lewis for his presumptive actions, and John of Bohemia responded by declaring that this war had become a crusade.

By 1346 nothing had been decided by military means, so when John died, the German princes, refusing to recognize the excommunicated Lewis, chose John's son, Charles of Bohemia, a man who had Pope Clement VI's blessing and who they hoped would be able to restore peace to the Empire. After Lewis died the following year there was no further opposition to Emperor Charles IV's rule and, until 1378, there was peace for the most part in the Holy Roman Empire. Charles even had the confidence to regulate the process of electing new rulers by proclaiming the Golden Bull in 1356. From then on there would be a college of no more than seven electors who would elect a new emperor, hopefully instilling peace to a process that had seen little since its initiation.

This might have worked, too, if Charles's successors had been anything like him. His son, Wenceslas II of Bohemia, spent his reign (1378–1400) for the most part in a drunken and incompetent stupor. Rupert III of the Palatinate (also known as Rupert of Wittelsbach) deposed Wenceslas in 1400, and, when he died in 1410, another of Charles' sons, Sigismund of Luxembourg, king of Hungary, was elected, For the rest of the fifteenth century—in 1438 Sigismund was succeeded for a year by his son-in-law, Albert of Austria, and then by Frederick III of Habsburg until 1493—Germany remained free from civil war, but had little peace on its borders, as her neighbors preyed on what they perceived as weak government and disunity among the various princes to gain land and sovereignty.

Two groups are especially important to the military history of the region during the late Middle Ages. The more successful of the two, the Swiss, began seeking independence from their German overlords in the late thirteenth and early fourteenth centuries. The Holy Roman Empire had ruled the Swiss since the time of Charlemagne, but in times of governmental instability, the thinly populated Switzerland was usually overlooked. To survive, Swiss towns—far smaller than most German, Flemish, or Italian ones—formed independent political organizations with their neighboring rural enclaves, known as cantons. In 1291, three of these cantons, Uri, Schwyz, and Unterwalden, allied to form a union, the first Swiss Confederation.

This new Confederation did not generate much interest in the Holy Roman Empire as a whole, but it caused some consternation in the Austrian Habsburg family whose holdings included Switzerland. This concern increased further in 1292 when the Confederation united with Zurich and Bern to form an anti-Habsburg league. However, Albert I of Habsburg was at that time concerned more with his struggle to gain the Imperial throne, and neither he nor his sons paid them much attention until 1315, when Leopold I of Habsburg, Duke of Austria, mounted a major campaign against them.

In their twenty-four years of independence the Swiss Confederation had always prepared for an invasion, and when Leopold attacked he found that many of the easy mountain passes were barred to him by well-maintained fortifications, forcing him to take more dangerous routes. He also found a population that was unwilling to either give up their independence or fight by conventional means. At the Battle of Morgarten, on 14 November 1315, the Austrian army was ambushed and massacred while traveling through one of these more dangerous passes.

Following their unanticipated success the Swiss Confederation initiated a peace treaty that Leopold was forced to sign in 1318. Problems elsewhere in the Holy Roman Empire allowed them to remain independent for another sixty-eight years, until 1386, when another largely Austrian force decided to take them on. The Battle of Sempach that followed had the same result as Morgarten, except that this conflict also cost the Duke of Austria, Leopold III, his life. Two years later, his successor, Albert III, lost yet again to the Swiss at the battle of Näfels.

In all of these conflicts the Swiss displayed a talent for strategy and tactics. Greatly outnumbered each time and fighting more noble armies, they nevertheless won. The Holy Roman Empire eventually saw the futility of trying to regain their lost Alpine lands and in 1446 signed the Treaty of Constance, formalizing what everyone already knew to be a reality, the Swiss Confederation's right to self-governance. Not learning the Germans' lesson, in the 1470s Charles the Bold, Duke of Burgundy, tried again to capture a part of Switzerland. Once more Swiss soldiers rose to the occasion, soundly defeating the Burgundians at the battles of Grandson and Murten in 1476 and Nancy in 1477, where Charles the Bold was killed. The following year, Charles's heir, Mary, made peace with the Swiss Confederation at Zurich. Her cosigner was her husband, Maximilian, the Duke of Austria.

All during this period the Swiss Confederation grew ever larger. Lucerne joined it in 1332; Zurich in 1351; Bern, Glarus, and Zug in 1352; and Valais in 1403. However, the Confederation was not without its problems and the cantons frequently fought among themselves, mostly because the larger Swiss towns desired territorial expansion. Yet when there was a common enemy, for example the Austrians or the Burgundians, these same rivals united in defiance of the foreigners. And they usually won. In Early Modern Europe the reputation of the Swiss soldiers' ability in warfare had grown to such heights that they became the most sought after and highly paid mercenaries.

For twenty-five years, between 1415 and 1440, a second group, the Hussites, also gained numerous victories against Holy Roman Imperial forces. Originally formed by Bohemian and Moravian nobility protesting the theologian Jan Hus's execution for heresy at the Council of Constance in 1415, the Hussites became a military target both for their religious differences and their nationalistic presumptions. Because of their association with the executed heretic, on 1 March 1420 Pope Martin V declared that all Catholic princes should lead crusades against them. The first crusade was launched that same year by Emperor Sigismund and surprisingly met with disaster at the battles of Sudomer (25 March), Vitkow Hill (21 July), and the Heights of Vyšenrad (1 November). A second crusade failed when the Hussites defeated a combined army of several German princes at the Battle of Saaz in November 1421, and then, in January 1422, the army of Sigismund at the battles of Kutná Hora and Německý Brod. Four years later a third crusader army, led by Albert, Duke of Austria, was defeated first at Zwettl in March and then at Ústi in June. The next year a crusading army of the English cardinal Henry Beaufort fled as the Hussites approached them at Střibo. A crusading army led by the Italian cardinal Juliano Cesarini had a similar experience at Domažlice in 1431.

In the first sixteen years of their rebellion, the Hussites were only defeated in minor skirmishes, winning every other military engagement against any forces sent against them. Sometimes, as in the last two battles, their opponents refused even to fight them. Credit must certainly be given to the Hussite generals Jan Žižka and Andrew Prokop the Great for their leadership, as well as blame to Sigismund, Albert of Austria, cardinals Beaufort and Cesarini, and various German princes for their ineffective military command. The Hussites were helped too by their novel tactics, chiefly their use of *wagenburgs*, fortified wagon formations from which gunpowder weapons were fired. That their families traveled with them and were present at their battles also gave an undoubted morale boost to the Hussite soldiers.

Defeat eventually came from within the Hussites themselves. From the very beginning they had divided into two factions. The Utraquists, a more moderate group, was less impressed by Hus's theology than they were by the idea of Bohemian nationalism. The second faction, which was more fanatically attached to Hus's reforming ideas, was called the Taborites after 1420 when they seized Austi in Bohemia and founded the community of Tabor. The Taborites always united with their more moderate coreligionists when there was a common enemy to defeat, but in times of peace, especially after the Council of Basel agreed in principle to the Hussite-initiated Compacts of Prague in 1433, the Taborites clashed with the Utraquists. Eventually, in 1434, the Utraquists, allied with Catholic contingents of their former enemies, met and defeated the Taborites at the Battle of Lipany, killing their leader Prokop. This marked the beginning of the end. Despite Sigismund's acceptance of the Compacts of Prague in 1436, the Hussites began to lose support. By the middle of the century, unable to recover their former military glory or even to mount much of an armed resistance to further invasions, the leading members were hunted down and killed.

By the middle of the thirteenth century, the Spanish *reconquista* had stalled. The kingdoms of Castile, Aragon, and Portugal had all gained much land by pushing the frontier between Muslim and

Christian southward, but around 1250 this advance stalled. Fortifications went up on both sides, and a tenuous peace set in. Warfare between the two religions was quickly replaced by wars among the Muslims and the Christians. Most often, these wars were fought over questions of succession at the death of a previous ruler. Wars to decide the succession in Castile (and early on Castile and Leon) were fought in 1284, 1295, 1312, and from 1366 to 1369. This last, the War of the Two Pedros, was fought between Pedro the Cruel and his half-brother, Enrique of Trastamara, and led eventually to the 1367 Battle of Nájera, which included the Black Prince and an English army fighting on the side of Pedro and Bertrand du Guesclin and a French army fighting with Henry. Further wars of succession were fought in 1386, 1390, and 1465–1467. The succession in Aragon provoked conflicts in 1410–1412 and 1461–1462. Portugal suffered too with succession wars in 1372–1385, 1449, 1475–1480, and 1483. This included the Battle of Aljubarrota, fought in 1385, where João of Portugal, with English assistance, defeated Juan of Castile to gain the throne. Ultimately, it was the marriage of Ferdinand of Aragon and Isabella of Castile in 1469 and the later combination of their two kingdoms that brought peace to the Iberian peninsula, especially after peace was made with Portugal in 1480.

Sometimes the problems of succession were hastened by the forcible overthrow of rulers and, on occasion, murder. This was especially true in the Caliphate of Granada. In 1309, the caliph Muhammed III was deposed by his brother Nasr. In 1354, Yusuf I was murdered and succeeded by his son, Muhammed V, and in 1359, he was deposed in favor of his brother, Isma'il II, who a year later was murdered and replaced by Muhammed VI. Two years after that, Muhammed VI was murdered at the behest of the king of Castile, Pedro I "the Cruel," who placed Muhammed V back on the Grenadian throne. In 1427, a revolution deposed Muhammed VIII and put Muhammed IX in control, only for him to be murdered two years later and Muhammed VIII returned to power. In 1431 Muhammed VIII was again deposed, this time replaced by Yusuf I, who the next year was replaced by Muhammed VIII and then executed. In 1445, Muhammed VIII was deposed for a third and final time by his nephew, Muhammed X, who later in the year was deposed and replaced by Sa'd al-Musta'īn, only to return to Granada one year later. In 1454, Sa'd once again deposed Muhammed X. In 1482, Boabdil deposed his father, 'Abū l-al-Hasan, becoming Caliph Muhammed XI, but after he was captured at the siege of Lucena by a Castilian army, 'Abū l-al-Hasan returned to the throne. In 1485 he abdicated in favor of his brother, Muhammed XII, only to have Boabdil released from prison by Ferdinand and Isabella in order to cause further succession problems for the Islamic state. In 1489, the king and queen of Spain captured Muhammed XII at the Battle of Baza, and he was replaced by Boabdil.

Until the rule of Ferdinand and Isabella at the end of the fifteenth century, the Spanish Christian kings made very few attempts to capture more Muslim territory during the later Middle Ages. In fact, in many of the numerous conflicts the Muslims were seen as allies by the various Christian heirs who were fighting for succession to their respective thrones, and vice versa. Muslims also fought as mercenaries in Christian-Christian conflicts, and Christians were hired to fight in the Muslim-Muslim wars. There were some successes— Guzmán el Bueno captured Gibraltar from Grenada in 1309, but it was lost again in 1323. Alfonso XI, king of Castile, tried to take Gibraltar in 1349, but he died of the Black Death in the process and his armies withdrew. João I of Portugal captured Ceuta on the Moroccan coast in 1415. Juan I of Castile defeated a Granadian army at the Battle of La Higuera in 1437. Enrique IV of Castile recaptured Gibraltar in 1462. And the Portuguese took Tangier in 1471.

But it was the combined efforts of Ferdinand and Isabella that eventually drove the Muslims from Spain. Beginning almost immediately after their accession to the thrones of Castile in 1474 and Aragon in 1479, the two *reyes catolicos* (Catholic kings) revived the *reconquista* and almost immediately met with success. As mentioned, in 1483 they defeated and captured the caliph of Granada, Boabdil; at Luana, in 1489 they defeated his replacement, Muhammed XII, at Baza; and in 1492, they defeated Boabdil again after a year-long siege of the city of Granada after which the Muslim occupation of the Iberian peninsula, which had begun in 711, ended entirely.

MILITARY ORGANIZATION

By the beginning of the fourteenth century it had become evident that the traditional system for military recruitment was failing to call up sufficient troops to fight a major campaign or even to defend the borders of a state under attack. The result was an increased use of paid troops. At first this was simply the payment for service to the traditional leaders of forces. Taking as a model an earlier provision, called a *fief-rente*—monetary compensation of an annual payment to cover some of the costs of military service—which had been more and more frequently used during the thirteenth century, kings and princes began to institute a system whereby they paid a pension, rather like a retainer, to the leaders of their armies. By the end of the fourteenth century, such pensions were in place throughout Europe, and most major military leaders were well paid for their service. By this time traditional levy summonses had also been suspended.

A second way of augmenting the traditional means of acquiring military service was the war indenture. This was a slight variation on the pension, usually on a smaller scale, and was a contract between a lord and a retainer (or captain), the latter to serve the former, or between two minor military leaders, dukes, counts, earls, and so on, of mutual military support when required. In return for the service of a certain number of cavalry, infantry, and missile troops, they were given an annual payment, as well as reimbursement for transportation costs and any losses of warhorses. Booty and ransoms were divided into three equal shares: a third for the lord, a third for the captain, and a third for the men. War indentures could also be subcontracted out to leaders of smaller, often more specialized, forces.

Military leaders might agree to serve a lord for life, such as Sir Hugh Hastings who in 1366 contracted by indenture to fight with John of Gaunt until either he or Gaunt died. At other times, the indentures were of much shorter duration. Almost all of the leaders who answered Henry V's summons to fight in France in 1415 contracted with him only for the length of the campaign. Many of these fought for promised, future compensation, as Henry had not been allocated money from Parliament to pay for the expedition. However, this was rare. Normally, ordinary soldiers were paid quite well for their service, and captains, of course, were paid even better. The latter were also often able to siphon off some of the money meant for other soldiers into their own pockets. Still, they were responsible for any extra costs incurred, and they were always accountable for prompt payment to their own men, even if the lord who hired him was late with his payment.

By the end of the Middle Ages, military recruitment relied heavily on indentures and many contractors and subcontractors were hired for each military campaign. These provided many different types of soldiers, and all were paid for their skills and experience, as well as for the tasks they performed in battles and at sieges. Knights were paid the most; esquires (or squires) and men-at-arms were next—

although often depending on whether they fought on horse or foot—and crossbowmen and archers were paid the lowest wages. Gunners were paid as much as knights.

But even pensions and war indentures did not satisfy the need for the large numbers of soldiers required to fill the ranks of many armies in Europe during the late Middle Ages. Thus, many sovereigns began to look for nonnoble military leaders willing to fight with their retinues for similar payments to those offered to their more noble counterparts, generally with the addition of unregulated booty. These groups of mercenaries became known by the names free companies or, in Italy, condottieri.

The problem was, however, whom to hire and how to hire them. Actually, this turned out to be relatively easy. Mercenaries have always existed, mostly veterans of military service who, in times of peace, could not find employment in the armies or at the garrisons of their previous leaders and who did not feel inclined to return to a nonmilitary life. Often, groups of these soldiers, sometimes former enemies, gathered around leaders who had gained a good reputation for fighting. They were led by captains who were usually not nobles, certainly not nobles of high rank, but who had leadership and organizational qualities that appealed to men whose lives depended on them. Captains would present their mercenary companies for hire, and they would agree with a potential employer to serve for a set amount of time for an agreed amount of money—almost always paid in advance—negotiating also their supply of food, housing when not on campaign, and the taking and distribution of booty. Arms, armor, and horses were supplied by the mercenaries themselves, although replacements for losses as a result of military action could also be part of their contracts.

Periods of employment varied of course, and depended on the threat perceived by their employer as well as, crucially, on how much money they had available and were willing to spend.

Many of their leaders, or captains, became well known. Men such as John Hawkwood, Montreal d'Albarno, Robert Knolles, Albergio da Barbiano, Werner of Urslingen, Albert Sterz, Ettore Manfredi, Bertrand du Guesclin, Conrad of Landau, Castruccio Castracane, Sylvestre Budes, Hannekin Bongarten, Bertrand de la Salle, Ambrogio Visconti, and many others led armies of mercenaries during this time. Generally, captains only stayed leaders until they could no longer bring in the desired payment or began to be less successful—sometimes these two were interrelated—and then their troops sought new leadership. They were also not so bound by the traditional codes of chivalry, and their practice of war was generally accompanied by unlimited pillaging and vicious brutality.

Often it is difficult to judge from the extant sources what percentage of a late medieval army was hired. During the Hundred Years War, there were campaigns where few, if any, soldiers were mercenaries—for example, Edward III's Crécy/Calais campaign of 1346 and Henry V's conquest of Normandy from 1417 to 1420. In contrast, in Italy during the fourteenth, fifteenth, and sixteenth centuries, mercenaries could number in the thousands. Indeed, the extensive warfare of the region during this period and the wealth of the towns that employed them may have stimulated a market for this type of warrior with few comparable historical examples. Most mercenaries were infantry soldiers, but many others made their living as archers—both longbowmen and crossbowmen—gunners, and even cavalry.

For most of the fourteenth century, there was no national unity to the groups for hire, other than most came from outside the Italian peninsula. For example, William de la Torre, a Catalan mercenary, whose company was hired first by Bologna and then by Florence at the very end of the thirteenth and beginning of the fourteenth centuries. From pay rosters that remain, the nationality of 53 of his 100 men can be ascertained: 28 from Provençe, 8 from northern France, 7 from Italy, 7 from Iberia, 2 from Flanders, and 1 from England.

As already outlined, the Italian city-states provide the best example for the use of mercenaries in the later Middle Ages, though they were by no means the only ones. By the end of the fifteenth century, every kingdom and principality was employing paid soldiers of one kind or another. For example, throughout the Hundred Years War, the French kings employed Scottish soldiers, Genoese crossbowmen, and Genoese and Castilian sailors. In the 1475–1477 Swiss-Burgundian War, Charles the Bold, Duke of Burgundy, hired Italian and English mercenaries—especially English longbowmen. In the 1480s and 1490s, Liége paid mercenaries from the Holy Roman Empire, Switzerland, and France, and in the Aragonese-Castilian War against Granada of 1486–1492, Ferdinand and Isabella hired French, German, Flemish, and English troops. The town of Metz, fighting against the Duke of Lorraine in 1490, employed French, Germans, Burgundians, Spaniards, Italians, Slavs, and Albanians. By the end of the fifteenth century, Swiss mercenaries had become the most desired professional soldiers for hire, and they would remain so well into the seventeenth century.

During the fourteenth century, there was usually a mixture of forces in an army, some traditionally recruited, some paid by pension, some indentured, and some mercenaries. By the beginning of the fifteenth century, however, most military organizations were made up of only two types: mercenaries and permanent "standing" armies. Though the latter eventually became the norm, throughout the sixteenth and into the seventeenth century, mercenaries continued to play a leading role in armies throughout Europe.

Between 1000 and 1300 a new middle class began to develop in towns and urban centers. The middle class was wealthy and locally powerful but was not represented in the traditional agricultural socioeconomic structures of government. This frequently led to rebellions, actions that did not necessarily begin but often ended with military conflict. Before 1300 there had been some popular rebellions, but these had most often been short-lived and violently suppressed, such as those in Laon, Vezelay, and Bruges during the twelfth century. However, during the last quarter of the thirteenth century, as towns continued to grow and gain in importance, popular urban uprisings increased considerably, and the largest urban concentrations produced the largest popular rebellions. By the end of the century, the citizens of both Bruges and Laon had openly rebelled, and citizens in other towns in the southern Low Countries and northern Italy threatened similar uprisings.

But while some towns checked their rebellions during the thirteenth century, it appears as if nothing could be done to stop the large numbers of popular revolts that occurred throughout Europe during the fourteenth, fifteenth, and sixteenth centuries. These were mostly urban affairs. These rebellions were especially prevalent in the towns of northern and central Italy, the southern Low Countries, the Swiss cantons, and the towns of the Hanseatic League. For example, during the later Middle Ages not only was the County of Flanders as a whole involved in uprisings from 1302 to 1305, 1323 to 1328, 1339 to 1346, 1379 to 1385, and 1449 to 1453, but there were smaller local rebellions almost every year. During the reign of one count, Louis of Male, who ruled from 1346 to 1384, not only was there a large rebellion that lasted from 1379 to 1385, but also several uprisings in all three of the county's large towns—in Ypres in 1359–1361, 1367, 1371, and 1377; in Bruges in 1351, 1367, and 1369; and in Ghent in 1359–1360—as well as numerous uprisings in several of the smaller towns of the county. There were also more than 200 rebellions in more than one hundred towns in the Holy Roman Empire between 1301 and 1540.

Those facing late medieval urban rebellions generally followed only one course: their suppression by the intercession of a strong and decisive military force. The County of Flanders during the fourteenth century is a good example. In 1302, after Brugeois rebels killed more than 300 French soldiers sent to put down a small uprising in the town, the French king, Philip IV (the Fair), sent a large military force north to quell the now, much larger, county wide rebellion. The result was the Battle of Courtrai, and defeat for the French at the hands of the rebels. It took two more bloody battles—Arques, a loss for the French, and Mons-en-Pévèle, a loss for the Flemings—and more than three years before the county of Flanders was forced to submit to the king of France. Before peace was made in 1305, many had died on both sides, including the leading Flemish general, William of Jülich.

Yet the Flemish desire for economic and political self-rule was not quenched by the violence of the French reaction to the 1302–1305 rebellion, and they rebelled once again in 1323–1328. The result this time was the Battle of Cassel, a French victory. Yet again the Flemings revolted in 1338, led by the Ghentenaar weaver, Jacob van Artevelde. On this occasion, the French could not effectively use military force to put down the Flemish rebellion, as the English, allies of the Flemings, posed a greater threat during these early years of the Hundred Years War. It was not until 1346, when an uprising by another faction in Ghent led to Jacob van Artevelde's assassination, that peace would return to the county. However, thirty-three years later, the Flemings revolted again, this time under Philip van Artevelde, the son of the earlier rebel leader. In 1382, a lull in the Hundred Years War fighting allowed the young French king, Charles VI, to send a large army north, which resulted in a French victory at the Battle of Rosebeke, though the citizens of Ghent, leaders among the rebels, held out until 1385.

Peasant revolts were far less frequent and seem to have been put down with far greater violence. The largest of these were the Jacquerie Revolt of the Ile-de-France in 1356–1358, the English Peasants' Revolt of 1381, and the German Peasants' Revolt of 1525. These rural, peasant uprisings seem to have grown out of the same dissatisfaction over economic and political conditions that had led their urban counterparts to rebel, and they may even have been inspired by their success. But without wealth, arms, and fortifications, or even the ability to raise taxes by urban rebels, late medieval peasant rebels could not defend themselves successfully against the large military forces sent against them. They were usually defeated quickly and with much bloodshed, and they rarely rebelled again.

STRATEGY AND TACTICS

Whereas it would be wrong to suggest that the year 1300 marked any sort of dramatic change to the way battles were fought, it is true to say that the trend of an ever-increasing number of battles, which began in the later thirteenth century, continued. Between 1302 and 1347, for example, no fewer than nineteen major encounters were fought in Western Europe, more than during the two previous centuries. What is noticeable about this period too is the greater numbers killed, even of those who would have brought considerable ransoms. At Courtrai in 1302 between forty and fifty percent of the French cavalry were killed; at Bannockburn in 1314, between 154 and 700 English nobles died; at Mons-en-Pévèle in 1304 both the French and the Flemings lost upwards of 4,000 each; at Neville's Cross in 1347, the lowest estimate of Scots killed is 2,000; at Crécy in 1346, nine French princes, more than 1,200 knights, and between 15,000 and 16,000 others were slain; and at Kephissos in 1311, nearly the whole Athenian Frankish force disappeared.

The high number of large-scale battles continued right down to the early modern period, as war after war was decided more on the battlefield than by siege. Three battles, at Grandson, Murten, and Nancy, fought in 1476–1477, decided the final outcome of the Swiss-Burgundian Wars in favor of the Swiss, while no fewer than fifteen major battles were fought during the thirty-two-year span of the Wars of the Roses in England. Finally, the wars between the Holy Roman Empire and France, together with their allies, fought largely in Italy during the late fifteenth and early sixteenth centuries, are characterized more by their battlefield engagements, at Seminara in 1494, Fornovo in 1495, Cerignola in 1503, Garigliano (two battles) in 1503, Agnadello in 1509, Ravenna in 1512, Novara in 1513, Marignano in 1515, Bicocca in 1522, Pavia in 1525, Landriano in 1529, and Ceresole in 1544, than by any other military activity. In all of these battles, casualty rates were also high.

One reason for the increased frequency of battles fought between 1300 and 1544 was the presence of ever-increasing numbers of infantry and their prevalence on the battlefield. Although before this period there had been victories by infantry over cavalry, the predominance of the cavalry was such that many battles were fought essentially by cavalry against cavalry. This started to change in the early fourteenth century when, for example, Flemish, Scottish, Swiss, Frisian, and Liégeois infantry soldiers all began to gain victories over largely cavalry-based French, English, Austrian, and German armies.

The tactics used by these infantry-dominated armies developed quite quickly in the first decades of the fourteenth century. After choosing a suitable site for a battle and preparing the battlefield by digging ditches, constructing wagon fortresses, or flooding already marshy ground, so that their opponents had only one course of attack, the frontal assault, infantry were ordered in a defensive formation in one or more solid lines to await a charge. When it came, the use of missile weapons, combined with the carefully chosen and prepared terrain, caused confusion and disorder in the charging cavalry, with the effect that by the time they reached the infantry they had lost their impetus and hit their target with little force. Well-prepared infantry were then able to pull mounted soldiers from their horses and to finish them off using staff weapons, axes, swords, and daggers. These tactics were effective time and again, no matter who the infantry encountered or how well they were armored. As a consequence, the number of dead, regardless of their rank or status, rose dramatically.

Once established, these tactics proved extremely effective against all opponents. When adopted by the English, at the Battle of Boroughbridge in 1322 and later at Dupplin Moor and Halidon Hill, fought in 1332 and 1333, respectively, the longbow was added on the flanks to replace the need for ditches or woods to prevent flanking attacks. Using longbowmen the English were able to defeat superior forces at such crucial battles of the Hundred Years War as Crécy, Poitiers, Aljubarota, Agincourt, and Verneuil. By the 1440s handheld guns began to appear, augmenting and even supplanting the longbow and the crossbow, although it was not until the early sixteenth century, for example at the Battle of Pavia in 1525, that they can be said to have played a really significant role on the battlefield. Ultimately, cavalry soldiers as main attack troops declined in numbers and importance, and cavalry warfare, so dominant during the Middle Ages, was essentially over by the early sixteenth century.

It was quickly recognized, too, that infantry forces were also more suited to the task of besieging fortifications. Cavalry could perform scavenging and reconnoitering duties, but at the actual siege horsemen were forced to dismount if they wished to participate in capturing the fortification. Castles continued to fall for the same reasons they always had: starvation, negotiation, treachery, or destruction. The only major change at the end of the Middle Ages was the appearance of gunpowder weapons. However, it is a myth that gunpowder artillery brought a quicker end to medieval castles and town walls. While it is often believed that gunpowder artillery could easily breach the flat stone walls of medieval castles, generally this does not seem to have been the case. On some occasions, certainly, gunpowder weapons were very effective in defeating traditional medieval fortifications. In 1453 Philip the Good, Duke of Burgundy, forced the surrender of three small southern Low Country fortifications held by Ghentenaar rebels: Schendelbeke, Poeke, and Gavere. The first two fell to Burgundian gunfire, and the final castle capitulated once a relief force of rebels was defeated in battle against the Burgundians outside the castle's walls. That same year, Constantinople, once the largest city in Europe, fell after a lengthy bombardment by the gunpowder artillery of Mehmed II's Ottoman Turkish army.

On other occasions, the threat of gunpowder artillery in sieges no doubt brought a quicker end to what might have been an otherwise lengthy standoff. This became a strategy practiced especially well by Henry V in his conquest of Normandy from 1417 to 1420. There was little French reaction to Henry's invasion, and the opposing garrisons of the many castles and towns the English captured were small and had little desire to fight or endure a siege against him. They seemed not to have been willing to withstand a concerted English attack using gunpowder weapons. Instead, most often these garrisons would set a date whereby they would surrender if not relieved—usually two weeks. This was done at almost all of Henry's captured sites, all of which surrendered on the agreed date when no relieving force had arrived. Of all the places captured by Henry, only Caen and Rouen resisted the English besiegers; though ultimately, and without French relief, both fell.

Most often, though, gunpowder weaponry did not alter the advantage of the besieged over the besiegers. Should a garrison or the townspeople wish to resist the negotiations of those besieging them, even if facing a large gunpowder artillery train, they were generally able to hold out, at least until defeated in a more traditional way, such as by starvation or treachery. For example, the town of Compiègne, where Joan of Arc was captured, did not fall to Philip the Good in 1430 despite the presence of an extremely large number of gunpowder weapons—contemporary chroniclers report the presence of at least five large bombards, two *veuglaires*, one large and one small, innumerable *couloverines*, and two *engins* among the besieging Burgundian army, and other sources record the transportation of at least 17,000 pounds of gunpowder with the artillery train. A similar situation faced Philip the Good in 1436, when an even larger artillery train—eighteen bombards, twenty *gros veuglaires*, 98 *veuglaires*, 25 *petit veuglaires*, 25 *canons*, 22 *crapaudeaux*, 52 *gros couloverines*, and 245 *couloverines*—was defeated by the English garrison in less than nineteen days. The siege of Neuss, a Burgundian siege, led this time by Philip's son, Charles the Bold, was laid for almost a year, from 30 July 1474 to 13 June 1475, during which time its walls were constantly bombarded by the Burgundian gunpowder artillery. They used bombards, *courtaux, serpentines,* culverins, and *haquebusses* and had, by one account, more than 300 carts of guns, not counting his handheld gunpowder weapons, *couloverines,* and *haquebusses.* Yet Charles was not able to force the inhabitants to surrender. Midway through the siege the gates and walls of the town lay in ruins, but only twice were Burgundian soldiers able to enter Neuss, and on both occasions they were beaten back and their further entry blocked. Finally, in May 1475, with a German relief force approaching, Charles, influenced by the fatigue of his soldiers, dissatisfaction among his subjects paying for the siege at home, and, of course, the rumblings of revolt in the Low Countries, was forced to seek a truce and to raise the siege.

ARMS AND ARMOR

The period 1300–1550 saw a number of developments and changes to weapons and warfare. Although most were merely developments from earlier times rather than revolutionary changes, there were a number of significant advances. A mounted knight still carried a lance and wielded a sword and dagger, although he eventually discarded his shield. Most importantly, his armor developed from the simple mail shirt to the full-plate harness covering almost the entire body. His horse was also increasingly protected and, by the end of the fifteenth century, could also be encased in plate armor like its rider. As noted above this period also saw the rise of the use of infantry, which consisted primarily of the middle and lower classes of society and especially urban militias. Most of these foot soldiers were armed with some form of staff weapon, which also underwent some changes to counter the rise in plate armor. The crossbow continued in use, although it too was improved to increase its power and range with the introduction of the steel bow. Of equal importance, particularly for the English, was the development and tactical use of the longbow. The one really significant change, however, was the development and use of gunpowder weapons, both handguns and artillery, although they did not, at first, completely supplant traditional weapons or non-gunpowder artillery, especially the trebuchet.

Armor

Developments in arms and armor during the Middle Ages did not oc-cur suddenly and change was slow, usually taking decades to become fully implemented. Often, changes in one type of weapon or armor would effect change in another. During the late Middle Ages one of the biggest developments, for those who could afford it (basically the upper classes), was in armor. Although the beginnings of plate ar-mor, leading to the development of the "knight in shining armor," are not fully understood or completely clear, they can be traced to the middle of the thirteenth century. In about 1250 pieces of armor to cover the front and sides of the knees, poleyns, appear in illustra-tions, and disc-shaped couters, armor to protect the elbow, follow soon after in about 1260. Plate armor covering the shins also devel-ops at around the same time but is not common until the early decades of the fourteenth century. Plate armor for the torso also seems to have developed, but the surcoat, a long fabric garment, which was universally worn over it, hides the early developments in illustrations and other depictions. It is clear, too, that the surcoat was itself sometimes reinforced with rows of rectangular plates, set vertically and riveted to the inside of the fabric.

By the late thirteenth century, a new defense had developed, the coat of plates—basically a textile or leather coat to the inside of which iron plates were attached. The exact form and construction of the coat of plates is not always clear as it is hidden, as already noted, by the surcoat that was worn over it. However, the excavation of mass graves from the Battle of Visby, fought in 1361, has provided many examples of coats of plates. The twenty-five recovered all have the same basic characteristics: all cover the torso and consist of overlap-ping iron plates that have been riveted or laced onto the inside of a leather or textile covering. Only two armors have plates attached to the outside of the covering, and in both cases these were only small shoulder plates. There is considerable variation in the size of the plates, from 6 by 20 inches (15 by 50 centimeters) to less than 0.8 by 4 inches (2 by 10 centimeters), and in the number used, from 8 to al-most 600. On some Visby armors the plates are placed vertically, while others are horizontal, and some have combinations of both. While most cover the entire torso with a skirt to the hips, others are more tight-fitting and extend only to the waist. Extra shoulder plates appear to have been added to some, but not all. Most coats of plates cover the front and back, although at least five may have covered only the front and sides, leaving the back without plate protection. Almost all opened at the back, with two opening on one side, two on both sides and one in the front. Some were decorated with bronze mountings in the shape of heraldic shields, fleur-de-lis, or shells.

Plate gauntlets for the hands and gorgets, plates covering the neck and chin, appear at the end of the thirteenth century. From about 1300 poleyns and greaves, the armor for the lower legs, occurred more frequently, and sabatons, armor for the foot often made in the shape of the shoe worn at the period, first emerged around 1320. Full-plate arm defenses appeared about the same time and consisted of two gutter-shaped plates for the upper and lower arms and a central cup-shaped couter over the elbow, all strapped over the sleeve of the hauberk. *Besagews,* small disc-shaped plates, were sometimes fastened with laces at the shoulder and elbow. Rectangular plates, called ailettes, often shown in illustrations from about 1275 to about 1350, were attached to the sides of the shoulders and projected up on either side of the head. These probably filled no defensive purpose, but were only flimsy pieces bearing ornamental or heraldic devices. From about 1250, the mail coif was made separate from the hauberk, which was often shortened at the sides and called a haubergeon. The great helm, worn over the *cervelliére,* deepened until it touched the shoulders. From about 1300 the *cervelliére* was supplanted by the bascinet, a type of helmet that was very common to about 1450 and, though rarer afterward, does not completely disappear until the middle of the sixteenth century. There were three types: a small globular form covering the sides and rear of the head, often with a visor; a deep conical helmet arched over the face and extending down almost to the shoulders at the sides and back and also fitted with a visor; and a tall conical helmet with a straight horizontal lower edge cut off at the level of the ears. All three continued in use until the middle of the fourteenth century. The kettle hat also continued in use, although after about 1320 it is shown with a tall skull, very much like a bascinet.

An up-to-date fully armored knight of the early decades of the fourteenth century would have been better protected than his predecessors of a century earlier. He would have donned a close-fitting shirt, breeches, and hose. On his legs he would then put mail chausses, gamboised cuisses with poleyns attached, greaves, and sabatons. Over his body he would have a hauberk or a haubergeon, probably with the arm defenses, vambraces, attached to the sleeves, and over this a coat of plates. He might have worn *besagews* and ailettes and possibly also a bevor. Over this he would then have donned a surcoat and a sword belt around his waist. When action was imminent he would then have pulled on his bascinet, possibly with a great helm over the top complete with his crest, and gauntlets.

Over the course of the decades after 1320, armorers continued to develop the various pieces of plate armor for the body and limbs. The haubergeon continued to be worn under armor throughout the period as was the aketon. From about 1340, the plates covering the chest were combined to form a rudimentary breastplate, which at first only covered the upper chest area; a series of horizontal plates, riveted to a fabric cover, were added to extend protection to over the hips. By about 1370 the breastplate was extended downward by means of an attached skirt of hoops, a fauld, to cover the whole torso. The evolution of the backplate is more difficult to follow but was probably similar to that of the breastplate.

Toward the end of the fourteenth century two new developments to the breastplate made their appearance. The first was a hinged bracket fastened to the right side of the breastplate, which acted as a stop for the couched lance, the lance rest. The other was an additional bar of iron riveted to the breastplate just below the neck, which acted as a stop if the wearer was hit by a weapon (hence the name stop-rib). These became common on armor until about 1450. Both can be seen on a fine early example of a breastplate now at Churburg Castle in north Italy and dated to about 1380–1390.

The armorer also continued to improve the armor for the limbs. From about 1340 cuisses were shown made from plates, rather like the brigandine (see the sections that follow) and poleyns were made smaller to just cover the front and sides of the knee. After 1370 the cuisses were made from a single iron plate and the greaves usually consisted of two plates, at the front and back of the leg, fastened together with straps and buckles. The defenses for the arms developed in much the same way as those for the legs, although there were many variations in shape and form across Europe. Tubular or gutter-shaped plates for the upper and lower arm, *canons*, with or without a couter at the elbow, secured to the hauberk were the most common form. Until about 1375 gauntlets were made from small plates, but from about 1380 the hourglass form in which a single plate covered the back and sides of the hand and the wrist appeared. The fingers were protected by small overlapping plates, and these were sometimes decorated with *gadlings,* small decorative figures attached to the knuckle plate, as on the gauntlets of the Black Prince in Canterbury Cathedral.

The bascinet remained a popular helmet throughout the period, and by about 1330 it extended down to the base of the neck and forward to cover the rear of the cheeks. After about 1330 it was usually fitted with an aventail, a mail extension covering the neck and shoulders, which was secured to the helmet by *vervelles,* iron pegs with a transverse hole. The bascinet was fitted with a visor, called a *Klapp-visier,* which, at first, was rounded and pivoted at the sides of the skull, although later was attached to the top center of the face opening. The tall form of the bascinet with a point at the rear and a visor pivoted at the sides became very common throughout Europe from about 1380. It is sometimes called a "pig-faced bascinet" by modern scholars although the term visored bascinet was more common at the time. A variation of the bascinet, fitted with plates resembling the aventail, and called a great bascinet was used primarily for jousting. The kettle hat was still popular, and the great helm changed very little throughout the fourteenth century, although after about 1350 it was relegated to the tournament.

By the second decade of the fifteenth century complete full-plate armor had developed and two very distinct areas of armor making had emerged—northern Italy, mainly in Milan and Brescia, and southern Germany, especially Augsburg, Nuremberg, Landshut, and Innsbruck. Each area produced armor of a distinctive style and both were dominated by a small number of great armorers: the Missaglia family of Milan and the Helmschmied dynasty of Augsburg were possibly the greatest of these. Of course armor was made in other parts of Europe, such as England, France, Spain, and the Low Countries, but very little is known about these workshops and armorers. All produced not only high-quality armor, tailor-made to fit an individual who could afford it, but also cheaper armor. Indeed, the workshops in Italy practiced an early form of mass production—specialists in the different parts of armor supplied a central arms merchant who made up complete armors to fulfill orders from all over Europe. The richest patrons, such as the dukes of Burgundy, were able to bring armorers to work at their courts, while others, such as the dukes of Milan, often made an annual payment, a retainer, to an armorer to ensure better service. Men of lesser wealth like Sir John Paston, a well-to-do English knight, had to rely on "mail order." He wrote to an armorer in Bruges, Martin Rondelle, to purchase a "complete harness," but Rondelle was not prepared to commit himself to a price until he knew exactly what Sir John wanted! High-quality armor was shaped and fitted to every part of the body and closely followed the fashion of the dress of the day—for example, the high waistlines and closely fitted clothes of the later fifteenth century were closely copied by armorers.

Italian full-plate armor is characterized by its rounded form, while that made in Germany or in the German fashion had a more angular shape. For much of the fifteenth century, the Italian breastplate was formed of an upper breastplate, which was rounded and cut off at the waist, and a lower breastplate, the plackart, fastened together with leather straps and buckles. The plackart was usually fitted with a skirt, or fauld, of two or three plates. The backplate was similar and attached to the breastplate at the shoulder and waist. The vambraces consisted of a short tubular upper cannon, a couter with a disc-shaped plate covering the elbow joint, and a lower cannon extending to the wrist. The rectangular-shaped pauldrons were usually asymmetrical, that on the wearer's left larger than that on the right, allowing greater freedom for the right arm for fighting. The armor for the legs was very similar to those used earlier and consisted of plate cuisses and greaves attached to poleyns at the knees. The feet were usually covered with mail rather than plate sabatons.

From about 1430 the bottom plate of the fauld was cut in half to form two rectangular plates, called tassets, which were hung from the breastplate on straps and buckles. Sometimes additional tassets were added to the sides and backplate. The arm defenses changed little over the following decades although the asymmetrical pauldrons were made larger at the back, sometimes even overlapping one other, and the upper cannon was extended to cover the upper arm. Earlier fingered gauntlets developed into mittens, the right consisting of a wrist plate with two plates covering the fingers, and the left of a single plate over the hand. The leg harness changed very little except that the side wings on the poleyns were made larger.

The typical helmets of the Italian workshops were the sallet, the armet, and the kettle hat. The sallet, a helmet closely fitting to the front of the head and formed into a long "tail" at the rear covering the neck, developed early in the fifteenth century, with the first reference in Italian sources in 1407, and became popular after about 1430. The front was cut out around the face and closed with a visor, fastened to the sides of the helmet skull, which could be lifted to provide extra ventilation. A slit between the top of the visor and the helmet bowl provided vision when the visor was down. The armet consisted of a shallow bowl covering the top of the head with a narrow extension down the back. Two large plates, hinged to the lower edge of the bowl, covered the sides of the face. The opening over the face was fitted with a pointed visor, pivoted at the sides. The kettle hat continued to be worn, although it was not as popular.

The German breastplate of the 1420s and 1430s was more angular; the upper part flared out and the lower back angled into the waist, giving it a very characteristic "box" shape. However, from the 1460s it developed into a more slender, elongated form, often with ripple-like fluting and applied brass borders, sometimes known as the "High-Gothic style," as shown by two armors made for the archdukes Maximilian and Sigmund of Tyrol in about 1480 by Lorenz Helmschmied.

In the 1420s a small arm defense covering the shoulder, the spaudler, came into use, and by the 1450s this was attached to the upper cannon, a feature that continued into the sixteenth century. The leg harness was very similar to that of the Italian style, although with smaller side wings on the poleyns and sabatons made of horizontal plates in the shape of contemporary footwear. In Germany the kettle hat, often with a wide brim, was popular until about 1450, and the bascinet continued to be worn. However, the armet was not as popular as in Italy until the sixteenth century. The sallet is first mentioned in the 1420s but was rare until the 1460s when a combination of the kettle hat and the sallet developed to form the characteristic German sallet—a helmet with a long tail over the neck, sometimes formed of several plates, and a deep skull fitted to the shape of the head. The German sallet had either a visor pivoted at the sides, the eye slot formed between the lower edge of the skull and the upper edge of the visor, or was in one piece with eye slots cut in the front.

From about 1500, the separate styles that had evolved in Italy and Germany merged, resulting in a single line of development. Still the two main armor centers continued much as before, supplying both the fine armors for those who could pay as well as the more mundane, plain armor for the common soldier. During the first decades of the sixteenth century a popular style of armor was introduced where the surface was decorated with parallel lines of ridges, the so-called "Maximilian" style, probably a fusion of the earlier German ripple-fluting and Italian rounded styles. The ridges were not only decorative but also helped strengthen the armor by providing additional rigidity. At much the same time, the applied brass borders of the earlier period were replaced by turned edges, usually decorated with roping.

The breastplate was now usually globular in shape with attached tassets. The arm defenses were almost always in one piece, the lower and upper cannons joined permanently to the couter with internal leathers and rivets, and the whole frequently also joined permanently to the pauldron. The collar, gorget, became a standard feature, worn underneath the cuirass, to which the arms were attached. The almain collar also became popular, in which the spaudlers were attached to the collar, covered the shoulders, and were worn with mail sleeves. For the first decades of the century, mitten gauntlets were very common, though they were replaced from about 1530 by fingered gauntlets. The leg harness changed very little; the cuisses, poleyns, and greaves were either made separately and joined together with fastenings or made all of a piece and secured together with leathers and rivets. Sabatons, often attached to the greaves, were usually of plate, although in Italy there was still a tendency to wear mail sabatons.

The armet continued to be popular and was joined, shortly after 1500, by a new helmet type, today called the close helmet. The quintessential knight's head protection of the sixteenth century, the close helmet was somewhat similar in form to the armet. It consisted of a bowl covering the top of the head and extending down round the back of the head and neck. The visor, usually formed of three separate plates, was hinged at the sides and could be lifted when needed. Slots for sighting and breathing were provided.

The skull of the burgonet was similar to that of the close helmet, but instead of a visor covering the face, the front was left open. Above the eyes a small peak jutted forward, and hinged cheek-pieces, which were tied together with a cord beneath the chin, protected the sides of the face. The burgonet allowed for much greater vision and was less uncomfortable to wear than other helmets as it left the mouth and nose open, although in some examples an additional piece, the buffe, was fitted to the front to protect the face when necessary. Used especially by the infantry and the light cavalry, it was popular throughout the sixteenth century. The kettle hat was still popular, but was now called the morion; it had a tall skull and a narrow brim and was usually fitted with cheek-pieces that were tied together under the chin.

The infantry, poorer and less well paid than the knights on horseback, were usually more simply armed. For those who could afford it, especially those recruited from towns, urban militias, and mercenaries, mail shirts and helmets were common and could be augmented by other pieces of armor, for example a breastplate. For those less well off, protection might be nothing more than a quilted jacket perhaps with a simple helmet. Increasingly though, the armor that was adopted by the infantry was the brigandine and the jack. The brigandine was made of small rectangular plates of iron riveted to a sleeveless fabric jacket that fastened up the front or on one side, providing a continuous but flexible protection, very similar to modern flak jackets. The plates overlapped one another to provide good protection for the chest and back, especially against sword thrusts. Extant examples show just how well the problems of armor were understood. The iron plates, very prone to rusting, especially from the sweat produced in the extremes of battle, were coated with a protective layer, applied by dipping the plates in a molten bath of a lead and tin mixture very similar to modern solder. Though mostly used by the poorer soldiers, deluxe versions for knights and princes were also produced and were made using costly silks and brocades.

The jack was made from small square plates of iron, each with a hole through its center, laced between two layers of fabric with cord, giving them a characteristic quilted appearance. Jackets and hats were made in the same way but, unlike brigandines, jacks seem to have been only made from cheap, coarse materials for common soldiers. Both the jack and the brigandine were especially popular in the fifteenth century, but they were in use before then and were still being used by the light infantry, with mail sleeves and a pike, in the late sixteenth and early seventeenth centuries.

After about 1500, it became more usual for the infantry, and the light cavalry, to wear a corselet, consisting of a collar, breastplate, backplate, tassets, vambraces, and gauntlets with an open helmet.

Surface decoration, quite rare in the fifteenth century, became more common in the sixteenth century, and armors were often "etched and gilded." Patterns were drawn on the surface, usually in narrow bands, and these were treated with acid, which etched them into the surface of the metal. The patterns were then gilded, giving the armor a glittering and rich appearance, though in extant armors this surface decoration, especially the gold, has been worn away by centuries of cleaning. Fine armor was always a status symbol, proclaiming one's wealth and position in society, and this reached a climax in the sixteenth century when highly elaborate and decorated "parade" armors were produced. Often copying ancient Roman originals, or more fanciful in nature, for example imitating fashionable contemporary dress, these were usually not suitable for actual use in battle. Frequently through the later fifteenth and sixteenth centuries, very fine armors were given by one ruler to another as a form of diplomatic gift, or from a wife to her husband for special occasions such as weddings, or as Christmas presents.

Although armor might appear to be heavy, and there is a popular myth that the armored knight needed to be winched into his saddle, this was never the case. A full suit of battle armor weighed in the region of 50–90 pounds (20–40 kilograms) distributed over the entire body. The way that each of the joints of the body was mimicked by the armor, at the elbow and knee for example, meant that the knight was able to move very much as in normal life, although with some curtailment of the extremes of movement.

The exception to this was armor for tournaments, which could be very heavy and very restrictive to safeguard the life of the contestant. From at least the middle of the fifteenth century, there was an increasing demand for armors designed and made for specific uses, especially for the growing fashion and proliferation of the tournament. From ancient times knights trained to fight and to develop their combat skills in the melee, a mock battle where groups of mounted knights fought one another in a "friendly" fashion. However, melees could get out of hand and result in serious injury or even death. By the 1200s the tournament had changed so that, instead of many knights fighting together, individual knights fought one another. This could take many forms, from jousting on horseback with blunt lances to fighting on foot with *pollaxes* or halberds. The idea in all cases was much the same: the knight gained valuable experience in fighting; the contestants competed against one another, scoring points and winning prizes and hearts, and the audience was entertained—much as in any sport today.

At first the armor for tournaments was similar to that worn for war, but gradually specialized harnesses were developed. For jousting on horseback, the knight used a special saddle and was protected with extra plates of iron or thick wooden shields. Sometimes for foot combat, the knight wore armor with a wide skirt of iron to protect his legs. Unlike armor for war, armor for jousting could be very heavy and often did not allow very much movement—just enough to be able to hit the opponent in fact.

Tournaments were frequently very elaborate affairs lasting days, or even weeks, complete with all sorts of entertainments, fighting of every kind, score sheets, and winners and losers. At the other extreme, individual knights sometimes challenged other knights in single combat. As tournaments became ever more elaborate and special armor was needed for each type of fighting, the garniture was developed—a basic suit of armor supplied with additional plates, more than 60 in very elaborate garnitures, which could be added or exchanged with pieces for each type of fighting. These extra pieces were often secured with nuts and bolts, and special tools were needed to put them together, thus adding to the myth of the armored knight bolted into his armor.

Horse Armor

The mail trapper or trappers made rather like the coat of plates continued in use into the fourteenth century. Unfortunately, the caparison, the large textile covering for the whole horse that had first appeared in the late twelfth century and often bore heraldic colors or the rider's coat of arms, hides what was worn underneath, making it difficult to be sure of the early developments of horse armor. Popular throughout the thirteenth and fourteenth centuries, caparisons disappear by about 1450, except for use in tournaments. However, plate defenses, including the shaffron, the head defense, began to appear, at much the same time as did plate armor for the rider, in about 1250. The shaffron is commonly depicted from about 1275 protecting the upper portions of the horse's head. These earliest references to plate defenses, made from either *cuir boulli* or metal, also mention flanchards, for the sides, and cruppers, for the rear, of the horse. It is likely that trappers of plate, similar to the coat of plates for the rider, were also used, though the evidence is scarce. During the fourteenth century, the shaffron, increasingly made of metal, was extended to cover the front and sides of the horse's head from behind the ears to the muzzle and had both eye and ear guards. Examples are rare before 1450 except for two, one of metal, the Warwick shaffron, of the first quarter of the fifteenth century and a second dating to the first half of the century made from hardened leather. The top of the head and the neck were protected by the poll plate and the crinet, respectively. From the 1320s plates were worn over the mail trapper at the front, sides, and rear, and illustrations show many different combinations of plates. The mail trapper continued in use until the 1420s, after which there are increasing references to horse armor made from metal and some also made the same way as brigandines.

By the middle of the fifteenth century, the full bard, or horse armor, consisted of a shaffron, crinet, peytral, covering the front of the horse, and flanchards and crupper, covering the rear. Over the course of the later fifteenth century, the shaffron become narrower and was more open, while the peytral, which earlier had been very deep and fitted close to the front legs, was shortened and flared away from the body, presumably to allow greater freedom of movement.

From late in the century, horse armor was increasingly decorated with fluting, embossed ridges, or other patterns and was often made to match the armor of the rider. In the sixteenth century, the shaffron was reduced still further in size until it covered just the upper half of the head and the crinet covered just the top of the neck, rather than fully enclosing it. The full bard was common until the 1550s, after which it increasingly went out of fashion except for use in tournaments. Horse armor was used in tournaments from about 1450 and was often specially designed for it. For example, shaffrons were made with no eye holes and had a prominent medial ridge. In some forms of tournament, the armor was replaced by a large semi-circular padded cushion, the *buffet,* which fitted across the front of the horse and was worn with a shaffron and full caparison.

Shields and Pavises

Shields continued to be used through the fourteenth century, but by the early decades of the fifteenth century were becoming less and less common until mid-century, after which they were used rarely in battle. They were, however, used for some types of joust where small wooden shields were secured to the left side of the armor to protect the shoulder.

From the later thirteenth century a type of shield called the pavise was developed, which went on to be extensively used throughout the fourteenth and fifteenth centuries, most notably by crossbowmen archers and handgunners. Pavises were large roughly rectangular shields of varying sizes. The largest measured about 5 feet (1.8 meters) high by 2–3 feet (60–90 centimeters) wide. Weighing more than 20 pounds (8.5 kilograms), these were propped up by a wooden or metal brace that, when not in use, was stored in a groove made in the back of the shield. Shorter pavises, measuring 2–2 1/2 feet (60–75 centimeters) high by 1–1 1/2 feet (30–45 centimeters) wide and weighing less than 10 pounds (4 kilograms), could be held in the hands of assistants, called *pavesarii.* When set on the ground, often in long rows, archers could either shoot from behind them or use them as protection between shots. Surviving examples are frequently painted with heraldic or symbolic devices, especially of Germanic towns, though they seem to have been used throughout Europe.

As the name suggests, the earliest pavises—thought to have originated sometime in the early to mid-thirteenth century—were associated with the northern Italian town of Pavia. However, the first solid evidence for their use in warfare are Florentine regulations issued shortly before the Battle of Montaperti in 1260 that demanded the service of all of the town's soldiers, including archers, crossbowmen, and their *pavesarii*. The latter were required to carry their pavises near to the crossbowmen and to be ready to use these shields to protect them. When the army was not involved in fighting, the pavises were to be carried in the baggage, but the *pavesarii* were also to remain close to them so that they could be retrieved quickly if needed. However, they do not appear elsewhere in Europe until the fourteenth century. During this century and the next one, pavises became very popular throughout Europe, as shown by their frequent references in written documents, illustrations in artistic sources, and extant examples. Yet by the early sixteenth century they had largely disappeared.

CAVALRY WEAPONS

Mounted on his horse, the fully armored knight was a formidable opponent and a fighting force to be reckoned with. His primary task was to break up the enemy's frontline troops, killing and causing panic and disorder to the extent that they would take fright and flee. Most had, by this time, discarded the shields of the earlier centuries, and they fought with the couched lance for the initial charge. Once the lance had done its task, it was discarded and the knight fought at close quarters with sword, war hammer, and axe.

Lances

As throughout the Middle Ages, the late medieval lance was usually made from ash, although other woods were used where and when necessary, and fitted with a slender, pointed iron head. A disc of iron, the vamplate, was attached to the rear as a hand-guard, and it was gripped between the arm and the body, couched.

Swords

The sword began to change in the later thirteenth century from a cutting and slashing weapon with a relatively wide blade to a thrusting and piercing weapon where the point was used more than the edges. It was a change that no doubt is related to the development of plate armor. During the first half of the fourteenth century, sword blades were made narrower with longer points and were diamond or hexagonal in cross-section. Over the same period, the grip was lengthened and extended so that it could be used in one or two hands. The simple straight cross guard of the earlier sword also changed, and by around the middle of the fifteenth century was curved toward the blade, and the simple wheel-shaped pommel was replaced by pommels of triangular, conical, or oval shape. National characteristics also emerged during this period, and swords of different designs developed in various areas of Europe.

An extra ring at the base of the blade was sometimes added through which the forefinger was inserted, and from the early fifteenth century an iron ring was also added to one quillon as extra protection. From about 1450, a second ring was added to the other quillon, and by the end of the century pieces of iron, called guards, were added from the quillons to the pommel to provide added protection for the hand. Over time there was a tendency for the hilt to become more elaborate and additional guards were added, which in some cases almost enclosed the hand in a cage of iron bars. However, this development was neither straightforward nor regular, and many early features, such as straight quillons, continued to be used on some types of swords. During the fifteenth century, there was a tendency for swords to be made lighter, and at the end of the century, they had become an essential part of everyday dress. As a result, swords became more highly decorated and ornate, leading eventually to the development of the rapier in the sixteenth century, the civilian sword par excellence.

Training in the use of swords was of course very important, and swordsmanship was taught in a master/pupil relationship. From the early fourteenth century, the techniques of fighting with the sword started to be written down and illustrated, and there are manuscripts showing the various starting positions, called wards, and sequences of movements that were to be learned. Although few examples from the fifteenth century survive, such as the *Fectbuch* of Hans Talhoffer, written in 1467, fencing books proliferated after the 1530s when fencing became part of every gentleman's education. During the early sixteenth century, a number of schools also began to be established throughout the capitals of Europe and a number of different techniques developed.

Daggers

Together with the sword worn on the left hip, most soldiers would also carry a dagger, either suspended from his right side, hanging down vertically at the front, or carried almost horizontally across the back. When worn at the front, it would normally be drawn with the blade below the hand in the stabbing grip, and if worn at the back it could be grasped so that the blade was either above or below the hand.

Beginning in 1300 a number of different types of daggers appeared across Europe. The quillon dagger probably first developed around the middle of the thirteenth century. The earlier versions of these daggers have quillons and pommels that curve away from the grip, known as antennae-pommels, or pommels in a crescent or ring form. Later quillon daggers are characterized by guards that resemble quillons of swords, and indeed most often look like smaller versions of contemporary swords. Pommels could be of almost any form—discs, wheels, octagonal, or spherical pommels among others. The grip could be of one or two pieces and was usually wrapped in leather and wire. The quillons often curve forward toward the blade, which is usually short and could be double edged, of flattened diamond section, or single edged and triangular in shape. In both, the blade tapers from the hilt to the point. Surviving scabbards are rare, especially early ones, but were probably of leather with a metal throat and chape. Usually a knightly weapon, they were worn on the right side hanging from the sword belt on a cord or thong.

The rondel dagger was introduced around 1300 and was in widespread use all over Western Europe from the middle of the fourteenth century. Most often slender and elegant in form, like the quillon dagger, it too was a knightly weapon. It gained its name from the discs of wood or metal at either end of the grip. The blade was relatively short, double edged, and of flattened diamond section, and tapered from the hilt to the point. Later on, the blades became longer, up to about 15 or 16 inches (38–40 centimeters), and single-edged blades became more common. Scabbards were usually just simple leather sheaths, often with decorative tooling.

Perhaps the most common and widely used form of dagger was the baselard, which probably originated in Basel, Switzerland, in the late thirteenth or early fourteenth century, and quickly spread all over Europe. Baselards were very common from 1350 until the late fifteenth century. An anonymous English writer of the early fifteenth century declared that:

There is no man worth a leke,
Be he sturdy, be he meke,
But he bear a basilard

(G. F. Laking, *A Record of European Armour*
and Arms Through Seven Centuries, 5 vols.
[London, 1920–1922], III:8).

Although during the fourteenth century baselards were particularly a knightly weapon, especially in southern Germany and Italy, in the fifteenth century they became more of a civilian weapon. They were commonly worn on the right hip, suspended at the front or from a hanger attached to the sword belt. The hilts have a very characteristic form with cross pieces at both the guard and pommel ends giving it the shape of an "H" on its side or a capital "I." The cross pieces can be of equal length and both can be quite small, but the typical baselard has a cross piece at the guard slightly longer than that at the pommel. The grip is usually made of two pieces of wood, ivory, horn, or bone, riveted through the tang, often with many rivets. Although early examples have single-edged blades, they are most commonly of double-edged or flattened diamond form. Scabbards, again rare survivals, were made from leather with metal mounts at the throat, middle, and chape. Luxury versions of baselards were also made, and a few have survived in which the scabbard is made from carved ivory or bone. Some baselards have elaborately carved hilts of boxwood, bone, or ivory and another type has curved cross pieces shod with metal.

An intriguing type of dagger was developed about 1300 in which the hilt was made from wood with no metal and shaped with two prominences at the guard and a bulbous knob at the top. The contemporary name was ballock dagger, obviously derived from the shape of the guard, but more prudish historians in the nineteenth century called them kidney daggers, even though some are remarkably phalliform in shape. The grips of ballock daggers that survive are made in one piece and, although most are made from plain wood, ivory, or horn, later metal examples are known. Early examples have a single-edged blade of triangular cross-section tapering evenly from the hilt to the point, but from about 1400, double-edged versions appear. Scabbards were usually made of leather with no metal mounts. The ballock dagger was worn on the left hip, hanging vertically at the front or sometimes horizontally at the back.

The eared dagger, characterized by two discs at the pommel rather like ears, developed in Spain at the end of the fourteenth century and spread to Italy, France, Germany, and England in the fifteenth. In general, eared daggers are elegant and usually highly decorated with enamel, incised, or colored decoration to a grip of bone or ivory, together with etching, damascening in gold or silver, niello work, and, in the sixteenth century, cast medallions. The guard is usually of disc form, larger early on, and reducing in size until it almost disappears. The blade is broad and double edged, often with a broad ricasso.

The final distinct type of dagger, the so-called cinquedea (literally "five fingers"), was a specialty of Italy. The very broad flat blade, which tapers evenly from the hilt to the point, has either a strong medial ridge or is fluted. The flutes are almost always arranged in three layers running with the axis of the blade, two at the tip, three immediately behind those, and four near the hilt. The hilt can be of two forms, either with a wheel pommel, a grip like a sword, and quillons curved toward the blade or, more commonly, it had an arched pommel with strongly down-curving quillons of rectangular cross-section. Cinquedeas can be very long and indistinguishable from a sword, or short and dagger-like. Scabbards were usually made from *cuir boulli*, shaped to fit the blade, and often covered in tooled decoration.

Of course, throughout the late Middle Ages a wide range of knives and peasant daggers of many different forms were also in use.

Maces, War Hammers, and Pollaxes

While swords were primarily used for slashing and thrusting, mounted cavalry also used a number of other close-range weapons, although none as common as the sword. The mace, which had been used since the twelfth century, was now often made entirely of iron, as opposed to earlier versions that consisted of a copper alloy or iron head mounted on a wooden shaft. It was therefore heavier and more capable of inflicting greater damage, and was especially effective against more heavily armored foes. The mace still interested many who described warfare in the late Middle Ages, as seen, for example, in the following statement of Geoffrey Chaucer: "With mighty maces the bones they to-brest." Short war hammers consisting of a rectangular head, often with a backward protruding spike, were very effective from horseback and were common from the mid-thirteenth century, when one is shown in the hand of an anonymous English knight's effigy in Malvern Priory Church. A surviving war hammer, dating from around 1450, in the Wallace Collection in London, has a hammer head that is square in shape, although turned at a 45 degree angle to present a diamond-shaped front; the pick is short, slightly curved, and equal in length to the head.

The axe, which earlier had, for the most part, been used primarily by the infantry and had fallen into disuse, again became popular and was used for fighting on foot, as well as by cavalry and in foot tournaments. Fitted with a long two-handed shaft, they were also usually furnished with a backward-facing short spike—a weapon called a pollaxe. Injuries, causing death, from the spikes of both war hammers and pollaxes have been identified in the skulls recovered from the graves of soldiers killed at the battles of Visby in 1361 and Towton in 1461.

INFANTRY WEAPONS

Late medieval infantry were armed with a variety of weapons. For personal protection, it was common to carry a sword or a dagger and usually both. However, the infantry soldier's main weapon in this period was the staff weapon.

Swords and Daggers

Swords and daggers used by infantry were similar to those used by the cavalry, but they were usually simpler and therefore cheaper to own.

Staff Weapons

Staff weapons, used both by foot and equestrian soldiers, are of great antiquity, but the period from 1300 was when they especially came into their own as an infantry weapon. In 1302, at the Battle of Courtrai, the Flemish townsmen from Bruges, Ypres, and Courtrai, armed, in the main, with staff weapons routed a superior and supposedly better-armed French army. The reaction to this victory, essentially by the lower and middle classes, and the large numbers of French cavalry dead, were noted throughout Europe and caused uproar among the nobles, knights, and the upper classes of society. The weapon, called a *goedendag* (literally "good morning" or "good day"), which caused such a devastating and unexpected victory, far from being sophisticated or innovative, was basically a heavy-headed club to which iron spikes were attached. Their use at Courtrai and, equally important, the discipline of the Flemish forces, mark the rise of the infantry armed with staff weapons as a potent force on the battlefields of Europe. This victory was followed by that of the Swiss using staff weapons at the battle of Morgarten against the Austrians in 1315. From this time on staff weapons played an increasingly important part on the battlefield—blocks of disciplined, well-trained, and well-drilled infantry, all armed with similar weapons, were common down to the seventeenth century.

The traditional infantry weapon, the spear or long spear as it became known in the fourteenth century, was around 15 to 18 feet long (5 to 6 meters) and was essentially a defensive weapon. It was used to extend the reach of the foot soldier in a thrusting motion that, when well directed, was effective against other infantry and mounted troops, especially when used in closely ordered formations. By the beginning of the fourteenth century, the spear had been joined, as already described, by other forms of staff weapons, in particular the *goedendag*. However, the increase in the use of armor, especially the development of the full-plate harness, led to the need for an infantry weapon that was capable of both thrusting and cutting actions. Essentially, the ability of plate armor to resist penetration, coupled with its smooth, rounded surfaces, which tended to deflect blows, meant that the thrusting spear was less effective. From the very end of the thirteenth century, there developed a new type of staff weapon, the halberd, which combined the spear with the long, two-handed axe. At first it consisted of a fairly broad blade with a spike projecting from the top secured to the end of a long pole— around 6 feet (2 meters) in length. It was used in a similar way to the spear as a thrusting weapon, but it could also be swung over the head and brought down with considerable force. During the fifteenth century, an extra spike was added to the axe portion of the head making it an even more formidable weapon.

The halberd is most closely associated with the Swiss armies of the later thirteenth and, especially, the fourteenth and fifteenth centuries. The Swiss had been granted rights of freedom, which carried with them the right to bear arms, and this resulted in a population that carried weapons as a norm of everyday life. This familiarity with arms, especially staff weapons, resulted in the creation of a voluntary, part-time army that was both well disciplined and skilled. And, in fact, Swiss mercenaries gained a considerable reputation all over Europe during the fifteenth and early sixteenth centuries and were much sought after by military leaders and commanders. By the end of the fifteenth century, a very characteristic Swiss halberd had developed, although it is important to note that it was not just the weapon that made the Swiss such a formidable force but discipline and the ability to fight as a unit.

The halberd and the *goedendag* were joined by a variety of other staff weapons over this period, some very characteristic of particular areas and some more widely distributed around Europe. The glaive, a large cutting and thrusting weapon, had a long blade with a convex front edge and a straight back. Although it was never very common, it probably first appeared in Europe during the thirteenth century and was used throughout the end of the Middle Ages. Later, in the sixteenth century, it came to be used very much as a ceremonial weapon carried by official guards and in processions. The bill was far more commonly used throughout Europe in the later medieval period. Although there were considerable variations in its form, it generally consisted of a forward-facing hook with one or more spikes projecting from the rear and/or front. Simpler bills were very similar to halberds and were probably used in much the same way. Other, more complex types were developed. For example, the Welsh bill had a long slender curved blade and a right-angle spike, and the *roncone*, developed in Italy, had a long straight blade with a smaller curved hook and both top and backward-facing spikes. Finally, the partisan, a later type of staff weapon used throughout Europe from about 1500, was basically a long, flat blade tapering to a point, rather like an elongated spear.

MISSILE WEAPONS

Slings

Slings were still being used on the battlefield during the late Middle Ages, although they were not common nor numerous. Although stones remained the main ammunition, they were also used to throw firepots and other incendiaries. These were fitted with a fuse that could be lit before throwing and, on shattering, the contents ignited, spreading fire and confusion.

Crossbows

The crossbow, although basically the same weapon as in the preceding centuries, became increasingly powerful with the introduction of the steel bow. This needed more force to draw the string back to the firing position and therefore it was a more potent weapon than its composite bow counterpart—imparting a greater velocity to the bolt or quarrel, and thus a greater range, and making it capable of shooting a heavier missile. Estimates as to the range vary between 400 and 550 yards (370 and 500 meters). To draw the string back, special devices were required. The *cranequin* worked on the rack-and-pinion principle, and the windlass used a system of pulleys to increase the power of the shooter and enable him to pull the string back to the firing position. Although both slowed the rate of fire of the crossbow, the crossbow was still used extensively on the battlefield and at sieges.

The crossbow became very much a specialty of soldiers from certain areas, notably from Genoa—although it is unclear whether "Genoese crossbowmen" mentioned in late medieval sources referred to soldiers from Genoa alone or was just a convenient way to refer to mercenary crossbowmen. Genoese crossbowmen were especially valued and frequently employed as mercenaries by leaders from all over Europe. Crossbows continued to be used as a weapon throughout the fifteenth century, although declining in popularity. By the early decades of the sixteenth century, they had became almost exclusively a hunting weapon.

Longbows

Before becoming famous as the English weapon that significantly influenced the events of the Hundred Years War, the longbow was a specialty of the Welsh and those who lived on the Marches of England. Fully the height of an average man, these formidable weapons took great skill and strength to draw and shoot. Evidence from the skeletons of archers of the fifteenth and sixteenth centuries show distinct changes to the bone structure that long-term practice and shooting of bows brought about. Just how powerful these bows were is impossible to ascertain, but evidence from the longbows found on the wreck of the English ship *Mary Rose,* which sank in 1545, indicates that their draw weight, that is, the force needed to pull the string back to the firing position, was in the order of 110 pounds (50 kilograms). Whether all longbows were of similar weight cannot be known, however, and it is likely that longbow draw weights might have varied based on the ability and experience of the respective archer. It is also estimated that a fully trained longbowman could probably shoot as many as 10–12 arrows per minute. However, whether this rate of fire was ever achieved, or, more importantly, ever required, is open to question. Firing as and when the archer had a suitable and achievable target was probably more normal.

No doubt because of its increased use by the middle of the four-teenth century there were occasional shortages of weapons and pro-jectiles. In 1356 the Black Prince ordered the arrest and forced labor of all fletchers in Cheshire until his supply of arrows could be re-plenished. And between 1360 and 1381 the supply of bows and ar-rows in England had declined from a total of 11,000 bows and 23,600 sheaves of arrows—each sheaf holding 24 arrows—to no bows and only 1,000 sheaves of arrows. By the middle of the fif-teenth century, it was not a shortage of arms but a shortage of skilled archers that became the problem. In 1450 Edward IV requested 20,000 archers to be raised, but had to settle for fewer than 13,000, and in 1456 he decreed that playing football or other sports and amusements by all men between the ages of 12 and 60 be proscribed and archery practice substituted in its stead. But nothing could halt the decline of longbow archery in England and by the early sixteenth century the weapon had largely been replaced by gunpowder weapons.

Unlike composite bows, the longbow was made of a single piece of wood, usually yew, although other species, ash especially, were sometimes used. During the reign of Edward II (1307–1327), the longbow was to be made of yew, either imported from Spain or grown in England, be an average 2 ells in length, 4 thumbs thick in the middle, and fire an arrow a yard long. By a skillful combination of the sapwood, which is strong in tension, and heartwood, which is capable of withstanding compression without losing flexibility or strength, the bow maker was able to make a bow that was both pow-erful and strong. Bowstrings were made from strands of linen and obviously easily broken, as inventories frequently list extra supplies per bow. The bows recovered from the wreck of the *Mary Rose* also show that the ends of the bow, the nocks, were sometimes reinforced with bone or horn.

Arrows were usually made from ash, but a variety of other woods could also be used as available. The arrowhead was made from iron in a large variety of shapes—presumably suiting their use, although exactly what purpose each shape was used for is not always clear and has been closely discussed and debated in recent years. Larger winged arrowheads were probably used for hunting. The bodkin head, a long thin head, has often been thought to be armor piercing, but recent experimental work has shown that it cannot pierce armor but instead curls up on impact. The more likely candidate for the armor-piercing arrowhead is a small winged head that has been shown by analysis often to have steel edges and tip. This small, highly sophisticated design would certainly be fully capable of piercing armor. It is also worth noting that these arrowheads could be made in the hundreds of thousands in a relatively short time.

Feathers, the fletching, or flight, were attached with glue to the rear of the arrow to stabilize it in flight. There is some evidence to show that these were sometimes put on at an angle so that the arrow would rotate about its long axis in flight, giving the arrow greater accuracy. The archer usually wore a leather bracer to protect the inside of the left arm from the string as the arrow was loosed and also had a quiver in which to keep his supply of arrows. When in position in the battle line, archers usually placed their fresh arrows either point down in the ground in front of them or else stuck through their belt—both easy ways to quickly grasp the next arrow.

The English made a lot of use of longbowmen, especially against France in the wars that made up the Hundred Years War. Of note was the way the English developed the use of archers in their battle tactics over that period and particularly at the battles of Crécy (1346), Poitiers (1356), and Agincourt (1415). In each the use of the archers was critical to the English success, and their tactical use has been the subject of many long and detailed studies and debates. Essentially, the English used a combination of archers on the wings of a solid central formation of non-archer infantry, the men-at-arms. Traditionally, the arrow "storm" unleashed by the English archers is seen as the primary cause of the defeat of the French forces in these and other battles. But this may be far too simplistic an interpretation. It is difficult to see how arrows fired at long range could have impeded the advancing enemy—protected by armor and charged up with adrenalin for the attack. What really counted was a combination of the terrain over which the battle was fought and the fact that the English forces were able to stand in a reasonably coherent formation without fleeing. The terrain over which the battles were fought was such that, as the French advanced, they were funneled into an ever-smaller front, causing severe crushing within their ranks. Harangued by the archers, their charge finally came to a halt at the English lines where, their charge broken up and dissipated, they were no match for the English men-at-arms.

In these particular battles, perhaps more so at Crécy than anywhere else, credit must also be given to the steadfastness of the English who did not turn and fly when confronted by the advancing enemy. It was this more than anything else that led to success in medieval battles. Disrupting the enemy lines, whether attacker or defender, and causing panic, alarm, and confusion, which resulted in rout, led almost inevitably to triumph.

SIEGE WEAPONS

Non-gunpowder Weapons

During the later Middle Ages, the gain and loss of territory remained of considerable importance, and in this the siege was the most frequently followed strategy. Indeed, despite the fame of Crécy, Poitiers, and Agincourt, the Hundred Years War can be seen as a war of sieges rather than battles. Defending or attacking castles, towns, and fortresses was the primary focus of most of the warfare that took place. Ideally, a siege would consist of a complete encirclement of the enemy stronghold, the prevention of any chance of resupply, the battering down of the walls in a strategic place, followed by its overrun. Of course, in reality, attackers rarely had enough troops to complete an encircling position, walls could resist the heaviest battering, and defenders put up a spirited and stout defense.

The usual method of breaking down the walls of towns, castles, and fortifications continued to be traditional artillery, primarily the counterweight trebuchet, or mining and often, of course, both together. Even the rise of gunpowder artillery, especially in the fifteenth century, when large guns were being made in some numbers, did not completely oust the trebuchet from sieges until the later decades of the fifteenth century.

Gunpowder Weapons

The major development in arms and armor of the period was the discovery and use of gunpowder and gunpowder artillery. Although gunpowder itself is now known to have been a Chinese invention, it is clear that the use of fire has always been a major weapon to be deployed wherever and whenever possible, and in whatever possible guise. Unfortunately, the materials that make up all incendiary devices, including gunpowder, quickly vanish upon detonation and deteriorate in long-term storage, meaning that we have little or no evidence of its historical use.

The vital ingredient in gunpowder is saltpeter (potassium nitrate), now known to have been first discovered in China around the year 500 by alchemists searching for the elixir of life. Its first warlike use, in the tenth century, was as part of an inflammable mixture that, once alight, was difficult, though not impossible as many contemporary sources claim, to extinguish. By the 1040s, it had been discovered that mixing saltpeter with sulfur and charcoal produced an explosive material. Over the next two to three centuries the Chinese developed a bewildering array of handheld fire devices, fire lances, and bombs, and by the twelfth century had developed the first guns, though exactly when is still disputed. Certainly by the middle of the thirteenth century gunpowder was being used to fire projectiles at their enemies.

Just how the secrets of gunpowder traveled westward to Europe will probably never be fully known, although it seems likely that there was not just one route but several—via the ancient trading route known as the Silk Road, by travelers from the West, by the Mongols, or by peoples of the Russian lands. By whatever means, the secret of gunpowder was known in Europe by the mid-thirteenth century when writers like Roger Bacon and Albertus Magnus described its effects. However, it was not until the early decades of the fourteenth century that it is certain that guns had finally arrived. In 1326–1327 there is not only the first documentary evidence, but the first illustrations of guns. The former refers to guns made in Florence, while the latter is contained within two manuscripts made in England and illuminated by the same artist.

For the next fifty years, references to guns and their ammunition are frequent throughout most of Western Europe, from England to Italy and from Spain to northern Germany, but it is clear that their use was at a very low level—the guns themselves were small and supplies of saltpeter were limited and expensive. The two were inextricably linked, of course. Just where Western Europe obtained its saltpeter at this period is not known, although its contemporary name, "Chinese snow," would suggest that it was being imported from the East—the cost of transport making it a high-cost luxury product that only kings and princes could afford. From the late fourteenth century, references to larger cannon and saltpeter "plantations" in Western Europe appear, the two probably going hand in hand—the increasing availability of saltpeter and its lower cost stimulating the production of larger and larger cannon.

Saltpeter, or potassium nitrate, is produced by the action of bacteria on animal waste products, primarily feces, although urine must also be added, which convert ammonia salts to nitrates. The earth removed from stables and dovecotes was a rich source of raw material for the salpeterman. It is a slow process, taking from one to two years to obtain good yields. Piles of the raw material, called saltpeter beds, together with a source of chalk, were made and left to "ferment." The saltpeter was extracted and purified from the bed by a process of leaching out with water, followed by evaporation and crystallization. Adding wood ashes to convert the calcium nitrate to potassium nitrate was a crucial part of the process. Although well understood today, the making of saltpeter in this way was difficult and time-consuming, making it relatively expensive. The product was also liable to be very impure, and possibly fraudulently adulterated. The *Feuerwerkbuchs*, treatises on gunpowder and guns produced from the early fifteenth century, are full of ways, based on taste, feel, and the way that it burns, to check that saltpeter is good.

Gunpowder, or black powder as it was also called, was made by mixing finely powdered saltpeter, sulfur, and charcoal. The mixture was then pounded together for several hours in a stamp mill to ensure that the ingredients were thoroughly combined. The rate, that is how fast, at which gunpowder burns and the force it produces on ignition depend on a number of interrelated factors including the composition of the powder, how much of each of the ingredients is present, the manufacturing process, and the physical size of the grains of powder itself.

The amount of each of the components—saltpeter, sulfur, and charcoal—is critical, and the amount of saltpeter is most important. The late medieval gunner quickly realized that the best composition was when saltpeter made up about 75 percent of the total. The quantity of sulfur and charcoal was less important and a composition of 75 percent saltpeter, 15 percent charcoal, and 10 percent sulfur, often abbreviated today as 75:15:10, was discovered to be about the best proportions. However, using less saltpeter in the mixture and increasing the amounts of sulfur and charcoal, though it resulted in a powder which was not as strong, was sometimes used as it was safer and meant that guns were less likely to be damaged when fired.

The actual manufacturing process was also important, and it was soon discovered that grinding the ingredients together for a long time, up to several hours, made a better powder. At some stage, though just when is still disputed, it was discovered that if the mixture was wetted with vinegar or alcohol as it was being ground, the resultant powder proved to be more powerful and more reliable than a mixture that was dry mixed.

In addition the size of the grains of powder, called corns, is also important. Small grains are very good for small caliber weapons such as handguns, while larger corns, from about 1/4–1/2 inch (6–13 millimeters), were best in larger guns. All these factors affect the way gunpowder mixtures explode and they were, largely though not completely, understood by the late medieval gunner.

The study of early cannon and firearms is made difficult as there is no way to understand just what a contemporary scribe meant when he used a particular name for a gun. Although from the sixteenth century on the names of cannon were fairly well fixed and were dictated by the size of the bore of the piece, in the fourteenth and fifteenth centuries names of guns do not appear to follow any easily identifiable system. Guns of widely differing size, bore, length, and weight frequently have the same name in original sources. This has meant that it is difficult, if not impossible, to be sure of what is being referred to and has hindered an understanding of the development of guns in this period. Before about 1420 there are few names for artillery. In the Burgundian sources, for example, which are particularly rich and have been well studied, only two names for artillery are used, bombard and *canon*. During the fifteenth century other names occur, including *couloverine*, *veuglaire*, and *crapaudeaux*, leading to the assumption that different types of guns were developed, probably for different purposes.

The bombard developed as a type of gun in the fourteenth century, and during the first half of the fifteenth century it became a major feature of most siege trains. Although large and heavy, weighing up to 15 or even 20 tons, they were not, as most modern historians state, difficult to the point of impossible to move around. Late medieval armies of 10,000–20,000 men were not that mobile themselves, and had a rate of movement normally in the region of 8–12 miles (12–20 kilometers) a day, and much the same as has been calculated for some of the largest bombards in the fifteenth century. These large guns were moved around on specially reinforced carts capable of taking their enormous weight and on campaign were escorted by pioneers who ensured that the road was suitable and that bridges would take the weight—though accidents occasionally happened. Once at the siege they were taken off their carts by means of cranes, called in the French sources, *gins*, and were then mounted within large reinforced frames of wood for firing.

Ranges were, on the whole, very short, perhaps in the region of less than 200 yards (180 meters). To protect the artillerymen working the piece from attack, wooden hoardings and walls, prefabricated and transported to the siege or made up on the spot, were set up in front and around the gun position.

Whether bombards made a difference to the outcome of sieges is hard to ascertain, although their continual use and transport to siege operations certainly strongly suggests that they were seen as important, even vital, weapons. The larger guns always fired stone shot, which, in modern tests, has been shown to be very effective against almost all defenses. However, evidence for their use and effectiveness on the battlefield is, for the early period at least, circumstantial. They were stockpiled by rulers and kings and taken on campaigns, but written sources neither state what they were capable of nor whether they made a difference to the outcomes.

From the 1420s, other types of gunpowder weapons are noted in accounts and inventories. In the Burgundian sources, for example, *veuglaires* seem to have been a shorter weapon with a large bore, while *crapaudeaux* were long and thin. This mirrors the development at the end of the fifteenth century and the beginning of the sixteenth century of the two classes of guns that went on to dominate artillery in the subsequent three centuries, the cannon and culverin. The former was a shorter large-caliber weapon used for battering walls and fortifications, while the latter was used for longer-range fire. Both fired iron shot and were, from the beginning of the sixteenth century, cast from a copper alloy.

From the 1420s, handguns were being ordered in large quantities and must have been used extensively on the battlefield, although again there are few written sources, and only rare glimpses of them in the chronicles of the period. Presumably they augmented the archers and crossbowmen and were probably used in much the same way. Whether they were more effective than these two traditional weapons is not an easy question to answer. While the longbow needed long years of practice and considerable skill to shoot, the crossbow was a relatively easy weapon to master, and both could be shot considerably more quickly and were more accurate than the early handgun. The fact that it was loaded by the muzzle was not the only reason for the speed of fire—it also had to be loaded with propellant and projectile, while the bows had to be loaded with only projectile. Some recent experimental work has, however, indicated that the velocity of a bullet was considerably greater than either the crossbow's bolt or the longbow's arrow—

handguns offered a greater range and firepower, which offset their inaccuracy and low rate of fire.

Although it is clear that round shot was used from the introduction of gunpowder weapons, a common form of ammunition throughout the fourteenth century were large arrows, called *garros*. Though this might, at first, seem strange, it should be seen as a logical extension of the traditional projectile weapons of the period, the crossbow and the longbow. Firing at a low trajectory, too, *garros* can be seen as highly dangerous weapons, especially against soldiers standing shoulder to shoulder in dense formations. During the Middle Ages, however, the main ammunition for almost all guns was a stone ball cut by masons using hammer and chisels. They were made from whatever stone was commonly available; thus, many Burgundian references mention marble cannonballs while in sixteenth-century England, Kentish ragstone was used. Contemporary accounts of artillery mention the great frequency that the mason's chisels needed to be sharpened and the use of moulds, wooden boards with a hole of the correct size cut in them, to check that they were the correct size and completely spherical. For smaller guns, primarily handguns, lead was also used for ammunition cast into suitable moulds.

Although there are occasional references to cast-iron ammunition in the early decades of the fifteenth century, these did not become common until the last quarter of the fifteenth century. Cast-iron shot, almost three times heavier size-for-size than stone, is noted from the early decades of the fifteenth century, but quantities seem to have been small at first. It was perhaps not until the 1470s that cast-iron shot was produced and supplied in large quantities. The technology of casting iron into moulds was developed in the fifteenth century for domestic implements and for shot, but it was not until 1543 that it was perfected enough to allow for the commonplace manufacture of gunpowder weapons.

The impact that gunpowder weapons made on the battlefield and at sieges in the fourteenth century has been questioned by modern historians, who have suggested that they were just a means of creating noise and confusion and were not necessarily effective weapons in their own right. However, their very use would suggest that they were seen as a useful addition to the military arsenal and argue strongly that they were effective in whatever role they played. By the final decades of the fourteenth century larger guns were being produced, and in the early decades of the fifteenth century, the manufacture of gunpowder had progressed to the extent that a differentiation was made between powders for smaller handguns and for larger pieces. From about 1420, there is also a growing differentiation between types of guns, which points to their increasing sophistication and the development of cannon for specialized uses. The handgun, for example, is first noted around 1380. The dukes of Burgundy, in particular, ordered considerable quantities of handguns in the middle decades of the fifteenth century, and it is clear that they were extensively used by their soldiers.

By the later fifteenth century, some rulers had considerable artillery trains, most notably the kings of France, the dukes of Burgundy, and the kings of Aragon, but it is questionable how effective these were. Two particular examples show just how difficult it is to evaluate these new gunpowder weapons. After the death of his father, Philip the Good, Charles, Duke of Burgundy, embarked on a campaign of conquest and vengeance against the Duchy of Lorraine. In response to the declaration of the people there to free themselves from Burgundian control, Charles marched with his army to bring them to heel. He quickly recaptured the town of Nancy and restored his rule over the duchy. His next move was to march against the Swiss who had helped the Lorrainers in their rebellion. Although possessing one of the most up-to-date and numerous artillery trains in Europe, as well as having the necessary funds, Charles was resoundingly defeated outside the small town of Grandson in the Vaud, losing virtually everything except the clothes he was wearing at the time. The resounding success of the Swiss was as much the result of surprise and resolution on their part, but it does make the point that having some of the best equipment in Europe does not guarantee success. And this was not an isolated case. Less than three months later, Charles was once more soundly defeated outside the walls of Murten, again by the Swiss. In the early days of 1477, Charles had rearmed and returned to try to retake Nancy, lost to him over the preceding months. In a daring move by the city's defenders, Charles's forces were outflanked and he himself was cut down and slain.

In 1494, King Charles VIII of France invaded Italy, taking with him a significant artillery train. He swept all before him on his dramatic and sudden march through the entire length of the country, only pausing on reaching Naples. Our knowledge of this spectacular event has been much influenced by the words of Francesco Guicciardini who claimed that his success was due completely to the use of a new type of artillery mounted on mobile carriages that enabled him to subdue town after town and fortification after fortification. A detailed modern analysis has shown, however, that perhaps this was not quite the whole truth. What Charles did was to use terror tactics to get his own way. Arriving at the town of Monte San Giovanni to which he laid siege and managed to take by force, he then proceeded to massacre the entire population—ostensibly for resisting his approach. As he then marched south, each town or fortification threw open its doors to him—thus sparing themselves the fate of Monte San Giovanni. When he reached Naples, where the local forces put up a spirited defense, he had to mount a prolonged siege and was eventually forced to retreat, losing considerable numbers of troops to disease.

Guicciardini's comments have influenced almost every subsequent writer so that these events are still used to prove that a new form of artillery, together with mobile carriages, was invented by the French in the late fifteenth century. What he appears to have been doing, however, was putting the best spin on events that did not reflect well on the fighting qualities of his Italian compatriots. Far from having new forms of artillery and carriages, Charles used a superb grasp of tactics and psychological terror to get all his own way—until someone stood up to him.

THE ENEMY: THE OTTOMAN TURKS

The Ottomans Turks burst onto the scene at the very beginning of the fourteenth century when the founder of the central Asia Minor dynasty, Ghazi 'Osmān, using mainly familial forces, defeated a much larger Byzantine army at the Battle of Baphaeum in 1301. Byzantine leaders had thought little of putting down what they saw as a simple rebellion by a religiously motivated minority. Over the next 150 years they and, by extension, Europe were to pay deeply for their presumption.

In 1304, 'Osmān captured Nicaea and almost took Philadelphia, their siege of the latter raised only when the Latin Grand Company in Greece came to the aid of the defenders. In 1329, 'Osmān's successor, Orkhān beat a Byzantine army led by Emperor Andronicus III Palaeologus at the Battle of Pelekanon, and in 1337 he conquered Nicomedia. It was on these victories that he established the first Ottoman state in western Anatolia and Thrace. But it was his son, Murād I, and grandson, Bāyezīd I, who are credited with adding the largest amount of land and making the Ottoman Turks a military power to rival any in the Western world at that time. They added Seres and Demotika in 1361, Macedonia in 1371, Armenia in 1375,

Sofia in 1385, Nis in 1386, the rest of Bulgaria in 1393, Salonika and Rum in 1394, and Dobrudja in 1395. In two major battles, at Kosovo in 1389 and Nicopolis in 1396, Ottoman armies crushed Western opponents. At Kosovo, they defeated a Serbian army, killing Prince Lazar of Serbia, while at Nicopolis, they destroyed a crusading force drawn from England, Burgundy, France, Germany, Hungary, Wallachia, Transylvania, and the Teutonic Knights, massacring almost all those captured without regard for class or rank. Only twice did the Ottoman Turks lose significant military engagements during this period, at Rovine in 1395 when a Hungarian and Wallachian army defeated them in battle, but were unable to turn back their Balkan campaign, and at Ankara in 1402 when Tamerlane (Timur the Lame) and his Mongols trounced the until-then indefatigable force in battle and then captured their former capital of Bursa.

A succession crisis between Bāyezīd I's sons, Süleyman and Musa, halted Ottoman expansion for several years, but Murād II, who ruled from 1421 to 1451, continued his predecessors' military policies. Although starting out badly, having to break off his siege of Constantinople in 1422 because of a rebellion by his brother, Mustafa, he annihilated Hexamilion and desolated the Morea the following year. He took Smyrna in 1424 and in 1428 defeated the Hungarians on the Upper Danube. In 1430 he recaptured Salonika and took Albania in 1432. So effective were these campaigns that in 1440 Pope Eugenius IV called for a crusade against the Ottoman Turks. The response from the West was less than overwhelming, but the call to crusade inspired a response in those who were defending their lands against the Turks. In 1441 Vladislav of Poland and Hungary raised the siege of Belgrade; the next year the Hungarian hero, János Hunyadi, defeated the Ottomans invading Transylvania; in 1443 the Albanians revolted and regained their independence; and in 1444 Hunyadi won the Battle on Mount Kunovica. After this defeat a truce was arranged, but when it failed three months later, the tide turned. Late in 1444 Murād II demolished a crusading army at the battle of Varna, and in 1448 he defeated Hunyadi at the Second Battle of Kosovo, recovering control of the Balkans, except for Albania, and ravaged the Morea.

On 3 February 1451, Murād died and was replaced by his son, Mehmed II. Perhaps the West breathed a sigh of relief, but if so it was premature. For Mehmed diligently followed his father's example. Indeed, his greatest achievement came early in his reign when he conquered the city of Constantinople in 1453, making it the new capital of his empire. In 1456 Hunyadi had some revenge when he raised the siege of Belgrade, but this was but a momentary break in the Ottoman successes. Southeastern Europe fell quickly: Athens fell in 1456, Serbia in 1459, the Morea in 1460, Trebizond in 1461, Herzegovina in 1467, Kaffa in 1475, and Albania in 1478. Hunyadi's son, Matthias Corvinus, did have some successes—in 1463 at Jaysca, and in 1475 at Savacz—and the Knights Hospitaller skillfully defended their headquarters at Rhodes in 1480. But the Ottomans could not be halted. In the early sixteenth century, Süleyman the Magnificent added Rhodes, Belgrade, Egypt, Buda, and Hungary. Only in 1529 was he stopped, when the Holy Roman Emperor Charles V raised the Turkish siege of Vienna.

Contemporary writers frequently remark on the originality and uniqueness of Ottoman Turkish military administration, strategy, tactics, and equipment, at the same time emphasizing the differences between the Ottomans and their enemies. Of course, almost all of these characteristics had predecessors. But one should not fault late medieval commentators for ignoring those, especially when they could see little more than constant victories from this new Eastern power, victories won indiscriminately against Byzantine, European, or other Middle Eastern Islamic armies.

The earliest Ottoman soldiers were almost exclusively horse archers. Not very numerous, such troops were ideal for the raiding tactics used by 'Osmān and his immediate successors. They were armed with bows known by this time as Turkish bows—despite being little different than those carried by previous non-Turkish horse archers—composite bows with recurved arms that were bent forward and, in stringing, were pulled back against that natural position, thereby giving the bow its ballistic power. A very skilled archer, which these early Ottomans are said to have been, could accurately fire several arrows a minute while moving around its targets. Contemporaries do not record how effective these arrows were when fired at a well-armored enemy, although against unarmored opponents they must have been quite lethal. But the power of their bows may not have been very important to the Turks, success being determined more from the panicked flight of an adversary than sustained fighting that, even if ending favorably, would decrease the numbers of an already depleted military force. Mounted archers remained a central part of the Ottoman Turkish force until 1400.

No doubt the direct descendants of Ottoman mounted archers were the *akinjis* or raiders. Also light cavalry, in both arms and armor, which they provided themselves, the raiders had already appeared in Ottoman ranks by the turn of the fifteenth century. Traditionally these troops were said to have come from the Rumelia region of the Balkan peninsula, with late medieval chroniclers suggesting a unity that existed beyond the battlefield. Descriptions from Constantine Mihailovic, written between 1453 and 1463, and Spandounes, whose work appeared initially in 1509, indicate a pastoral people specializing in cultivating crops and raising cattle and particularly quick horses, the latter providing mounts for the troops raised from among them. They supplemented their pastoral income with booty and slaves gained from warfare and raiding, and they were especially feared along the borders of Ottoman Turkish lands, where their ruthlessness was legendary. Mihailovic depicts these raids with hyperbolic metaphor:

> [They came] like torrential rains that fall from clouds. From these storms come great floods, until the streams leave their banks and overflow, and everything this water strikes, it takes, carries away and moreover destroys . . . Thus also the Turkish Raiders do not linger long, but wherever they strike, they burn, plunder, kill and destroy everything, so that for many years the cock will not crow there (Colin Imber, *The Ottoman Empire, 1300–1650* [Houndmills: Palgrave Macmillan, 2002], p. 261).

By these attacks the raiders weakened potential border defenses, thus preparing targeted lands for Ottoman conquest.

Elite Ottoman Turkish cavalry units were provided for by *timar*-holding landowners. *Timars* were small amounts of lands, similar to fiefs in Western Europe. They, too, generally contained a village or groups of villages, from which a mounted soldier gained an income to allow his full-time military service. It could also be withdrawn from the soldier should he fail to appear for military service, or if he failed to have male heirs who would continue the *timar's* military role after his death. *Timar*-holding cavalry seem to have used several different weapons, but were renowned for their skill in using short swords. Their standard armor was a mail shirt and helmet. The mail armor was not as heavy as similar Western armors, nor was it as long, covering only the torso. There was also never a move to use full-plate armor in its stead, although sometimes small plates of metal, both iron and copper alloy, were added to the mail. Ottoman helmets were very distinctive, shaped like a turban and fitting low around the head and sometimes cut around the eyes. Often they were quite ornate, damascened or inlaid with silver and gold. These arms and armor were to be provided by the *timar*-holding cavalrymen themselves, with threats of decapitation or amputation if they were not up to standard. They were also to provide mail horse-armor.

It was not until the reigns of Orkhān and Murād I (1362–1389) that Ottoman armies reorganized to take better advantage of infantry, and there is little doubt that this was the reason for the increased military success in capturing more lands and facing new enemies. In particular, Murād I used a mixed array of ordinary and elite infantry troops and mounted archers and more traditional cavalry to defeat opposing Serbians at the Battle of Maritsa in 1371 and crusaders at the Battle of Nicopolis in 1396. In both, Turkish infantry—the first ranks composed of ordinary soldiers and the rear of elite ones—were used to lure opposing heavy cavalry into a trap between two flanks of their own lighter, more maneuverable cavalry forces where the now halted and exhausted attackers were immobilized and defeated.

The most irregular infantry soldiers were the *yaya*, who served primarily as armed laborers. They could also be and often were put into battle as fighting troops, but their skills were, of course, limited. Above them were the *azabs*, literally the "bachelors," who had been recruited from the peasantry. Their service was most often determined by conscription, and almost all families in the Empire were required to provide a recruit. Both *yaya* and the *azabs* carried traditional infantry weapons—spears and swords—although some were also outfitted with small axes. Those who were experienced hunters carried bows and could provide nonmounted archery support when needed. After 1380 some *azabs* were trained in the use of crossbows. All irregular troops carried shields and some were armored in light mail and helmeted.

The most famous Ottoman Turkish infantry were the *yeni ceri*, or janissaries. Janissaries seem not to have existed before the middle of the fourteenth century, and the early units numbered only a few hundred soldiers. But these proved extremely effective in warfare, and success added quickly to their numbers. Their bravery was renowned throughout Europe, Byzantium, and the Islamic world. At the Battle of Ankara in 1402 they stood their ground, even though the rest of the Ottoman Turks had fled, though this did not bring victory. However, at the Battle of Varna in 1444, during the flight of fellow soldiers, they protected their sultan, Murād II, and then turned the battle in their favor. They eventually captured and killed the Hungarian king Vladislav. By the reign of Mehmed II the janissaries numbered nearly 5,000 and, by the reign of his successor, Bāyezīd II, more than 10,000.

The janissaries were the elite infantry troops of the Ottoman Turkish army and they also provided a bodyguard for the sultans. At times this could work against the ruler, however, as Mehmed II experienced in 1446 when a janissary rebellion returned his father, Murād, to the throne for a brief time and in 1512 when they forced the abdication of Bāyezīd II.

Perhaps the most famous characteristic of the janissaries was their recruitment. The legend of captive male children, especially the sons of Christians, being required to serve with the janissaries may have been stretched by frightened contemporaries who exaggerated the ruthlessness of the Turks. But the core of the legend seems accurate. Raised with arms and armor, and trained in the art of warfare, they proved to be superb warriors, whose conversion to Islam strengthened their resolve and no doubt added to their military effectiveness.

The janissaries were well armed and armored. Their armor and helmets were similar to those carried by the *timar*-holding cavalry. Early janissaries were armed traditionally with spears and swords, mostly sabers, the latter being their principal weapon. However, as guns began to be made small enough to be handheld, the janissaries quickly adopted them, and soon the two became linked in every commentator's writings. However, unlike the other units of the Ottoman army, all of these weapons and armor were provided by a central store, thus guaranteeing quality and tactical unity.

Before the first quarter of the fourteenth century, fortifications and walled towns in Byzantium and elsewhere had been safe from Ottoman attack. However, with greater numbers of combatants, 'Osmān and his successors turned to siege as another means of conquest. Of course, the large number of walled towns in the region necessitated this. Initially, Ottoman soldiers attacked fortifications without siege artillery. As there was usually no army to provide relief from these actions, time was not an issue. Yet only rarely were the Ottomans patient enough to await surrender from starvation. Instead, Turkish leaders resorted to assaults against fortified sites: scaling walls and gates using ladders, battering them down using rams, or mining under them.

Compared with Europeans, Byzantines, and other Islamic realms, the Ottoman Turks were late in acquiring and using gunpowder weapons. Sultan Bāyezīd I seems not to have had them at his siege of Constantinople in 1396–1397, at least they are not mentioned by contemporary chroniclers among the artillery pieces present. In fact, Ottoman gunpowder artillery is not mentioned until 1422, at Murād

II's siege of Constantinople, when they are recorded to be large, of "excessive" weight and caliber, constructed on site, and operated by German cannoneers. Where these originated and whether this was their first actual use by Ottoman military leaders is a mystery. But it is certainly clear that they quickly impressed the Turks, for from then on, in almost all sieges and many battles, they used large numbers of gunpowder weapons: for example, at the siege of Novo Brdo in 1427, at the battle of Kosovo in 1436, at the siege and battle of Varna in 1444, and, most notably, at the siege of Constantinople in 1453.

By the middle of the fifteenth century the Ottomans were building gunpowder artillery of all sizes, including handheld guns, but they are especially famous for their continuous use of the largest of these, bombards. The story of Mehmed II's employment of a Hungarian named Urban or Orban to build cannon of very large size for the siege of Constantinople is quite famous and bears repeating:

> Mehmed asked him if he was able to cast a cannon large enough to fire a shot which would make an impression on the walls of the city, in spite of their strength and thickness. He replied, "If you wish, I can cast cannon as large as the shot which is being shown to me now. I know what the walls of the city are like. The shot of my cannon could reduce them, and even the walls of Babylon itself" " . . . Build me the cannon," the Sultan replied . . . So they started to collect bronze, and the craftsman began to make the moulds for this work. The operation of casting was completed within three months, and the result was a monstrosity of the most fearful and extraordinary kind. (Michael Ducas, *Byzantine History,* in *The Siege of Constantinople: Seven Contemporary Accounts,* trans. J. R. M. Jones [Amsterdam: Adolf M Hakkert, 1972], 70–72).

The first of these bombards was tested in the presence of the sultan and the public, although pregnant women were asked to stay away so that they would not miscarry. This test proved to be extremely impressive:

> In the morning the gunpowder was lit, there was a great rush of hot air, and the shot was driven forth, leaving the cannon with a loud explosion which filled the air with clouds of smoke. The sound was heard a hundred *stadia* away, and the shot traveled a thousand paces from the point of firing, making a hole six feet deep at the point where it landed (Michael Ducas, *Byzantine History,* in *The Siege of*

Constantinople: Seven Contemporary Accounts, trans. J. R. M. Jones [Amsterdam: Adolf M Hakkert, 1972], 70–72).

This and other gunpowder weapons of similar size were used well into the sixteenth century.

The capture of Constantinople in 1453 was one of the most decisive military victories. Some modern historians even see in its fall the end of the Middle Ages. With its defeat, the Byzantine Empire, which dated its founding to Constantine's relocation of the Roman Empire's capital to Constantinople, the city he named after himself, also effectively ended. Mehmed II chose it also to be the capital of the already vast Ottoman Empire. It would remain such for 470 years.

Conclusions

THE MIDDLE AGES, as defined by modern historians, lasted for about 1,200 years—from the fall of the Roman Empire in the fourth century to around 1500. Over this vast period of time there were some obvious changes in the economics, politics, and society of Western Europe. Chieftains became nobles and some became kings. Field rotation and the plow drove agricultural advances and increased production of cereals and foodstuffs. Increasing specialization resulted in the growth of towns and urban centers and the development of an urban class. Industrial activity and trade brought about further urbanization and increased "middle class" wealth. But while these momentous changes were slowly laying the foundations of the modern world, the art of war remained much the same.

At least until the end of the Middle Ages and the advent of gunpowder weapons, the process of winning battles and sieges, and the arms and armor used to do so, did not change significantly. Throughout most of this period warfare was, and largely remained, a conflict fought man to man, warrior to warrior. Every soldier faced an individual opponent, smelling his breath and seeing the fear—or confidence—in his eyes. And largely, the arms each fought with were the same throughout the period—the sword, dagger, axe, spear, and polearm. They did not change significantly throughout the Middle Ages, nor had they changed much since the earliest conflicts. Essentially, by the beginning of the Middle Ages these traditional weapons were already well developed. Any further improvements—in shape or material—could only be minor and secondary to their use and effectiveness. And while it is true that javelins and arrows were effective at greater distance these, too, were almost completely developed by the early Middle Ages.

The *spatha*, the long sword of the Romans, was in essence similar to the swords used throughout the Middle Ages. Of course there were changes but these were relatively minor—changes in length, for example, or whether the blade had a single or double edge.

In a similar way, the Roman *gladius* can be seen as the precursor of the medieval dagger. A weapon frequently neglected by most medieval military historians, the dagger was a useful secondary weapon. Although its form was very much influenced by fashion, it was, and remained, basically a stabbing weapon for use at close quarters.

The axe, too, changed little throughout this period. Essentially a weapon that developed from the common woodcutting axe, it, like the sword and dagger, was little altered throughout the Middle Ages.

Much the same can be said of spears and polearms. The spear, essentially a simple weapon—a long shaft with an iron head—underwent few, if any changes during the Middle Ages. And while polearms—again, a wooden shaft with an iron head or blade—certainly changed in detail and form, it can be argued that they changed little, if at all, over this period.

The bow saw perhaps the greatest change, although this was more quantitative than qualitative—its range and power both increased, especially during the later Middle Ages. Even the crossbow, which has almost always been seen as a specifically "medieval" weapon, had its ancient antecedents with the Greek *gastraphetes* or "belly-bow." While it changed little at first, the introduction of the steel bow greatly increased its ballistic power later in the Middle Ages.

The same can be said of armor. Throughout most of the Middle Ages, from the beginning of the third century to the beginning of the fifteenth century, armor always consisted of a mail shirt or coat, which was a direct descendant of the Roman lorica hamata, as well as a shield and a helmet. After 1400, mail was quickly replaced by plate armor, so that by 1450 almost all armor worn by Western European nobles and elite soldiers was plate. At the same time, the shield became smaller and then disappeared altogether. Helmets, too, changed to match the efficiency of the new plate armor. Intriguingly though, from the late fifteenth century, plate armor increasingly became a fashion statement, and a very costly one, prized for its ability to show the wealth and status of the wearer even more than his military prowess.

But did medieval arms and armor determine medieval tactics, or did medieval tactics determine the arms and armor? Why were there no really significant changes in either until the end of the Middle Ages? The answer is not easy to formulate, but it is clear that change in almost every area of life was slow and the reasons for change are not often clear to us today.

Both the Visigothic and Eastern Roman troops who met at Adrianople in AD 378 consisted of three basic forces: infantry, cavalry, and missile troops. The battle was not decided by the superior use of these individual troops separately by the Visigoths, but by the tactics of the army as a whole. At Hastings in 1066, those same three military forces were also present on both the Norman and the Anglo-Saxon sides. Interestingly though, it is commonly perceived—even contemporarily—that this was a victory of cavalry over infantry. In fact, King Harold Godwinson had dismounted his cavalry to join with his infantry and missile troops, while Duke William used his infantry—which was as numerous as his cavalry—to initiate the attack of the Anglo-Saxon shield wall. And his archers shot arrows throughout the conflict, with one particular arrow ultimately deciding the outcome of the battle when it ended the life of Harold. Finally, at Agincourt, in 1415, where English longbow archers were so decisive that they were immortalized in one of Shakespeare's greatest plays—*Henry V*, Act III, Scenes 3–4—it might easily be forgotten that the English infantry and cavalry were also present. But they were, although in small numbers because many had been disabled by dysentery. The cavalry had dismounted and joined the infantry, and they held the center ground where most of the hand-to-hand fighting took place. Nor did the French only have cavalry, so effectively defeated by the longbowmen, but infantry and archers too, and all were defeated on that field.

So the three types of soldiers persisted throughout the Middle Ages. At times, changes in tactics were effected and there were improvements in leadership, training, and the availability of arms and armor, but their purpose on the battlefield did not alter significantly. Early medieval cavalry, even before the advent of the stirrup, were used to charge against other cavalry, to break an infantry line, and to chase away missile troops. The stirrup, of course, facilitated this and added the ability to use couched lances, but the cavalry's purpose remained the same—to charge other cavalry, to break an infantry line, and to chase away missile troops.

Medieval infantry could be classed as either heavy—meaning they were wearing heavy armor—or light—meaning they were more lightly armored or were unarmored. These divisions remained valid from the fall of Rome to the Hundred Years War. Heavy infantry were usually experienced and professional, paid to fight in whatever might become the "hottest" part of the battle. Light infantry were recruited from the populace at large—initially by conscription, later by obligation (what has often been called feudalism), and finally by indenture and the payment of wages. Once more, though, the purpose of medieval infantry, both heavy and light, did not change.

At the beginning of the Middle Ages missile troops largely used bows and arrows, although some slingshots, javelins, and throwing axes provided supplementary firepower. While the number of slingers and javelin throwers declined markedly and axe throwers disappeared, archers remained the most prominent missile troops for all medieval armies. The technology of their weapons changed slightly—as mentioned above—but it was only when the numbers of archers themselves increased that their tactics changed. When Genoese crossbowmen became available for hire in large numbers, their influence on the battlefield—for good or bad—also increased. And when large numbers of skilled English longbowmen began to be recruited into the English armies of the Hundred Years War, their impact on tactics became legendary. Still, no matter how numerous, these troops never removed themselves from their military purpose: they were there to supplement the infantry and cavalry, to provoke a disordered enemy cavalry or infantry charge, to focus that charge onto the infantry lines, and to cause a rout of enemy light infantry or missile troops.

As with all premodern warfare, most medieval conflicts took place not on the battlefield but at sieges. Battles were risky and often did not accomplish much, whereas sieges resulted in the capture of cities and fortifications. But sieges were also time-consuming and costly endeavors, and a successful outcome for the besiegers generally meant that they had to starve the inhabitants into submission, find someone inside the besieged location who was willing to betray his neighbors, or lose a large number of soldiers in an attempt to conquer the site by force. Trying to starve out the inhabitants or cause one of them to turn traitor greatly lengthened the time it took to bring about a successful siege, so it was not unusual for a medieval siege to last for more than a year or longer. Thus, generals often tried to decrease the time by attempting to go over, under, or through the fortifications. Such ancient besieging techniques as using ladders or siege towers to climb over the walls, mines to weaken the earth under the walls, or battering rams and catapults to blast through the walls proved to be the same techniques that proved effective in the Middle Ages. The technology of ladders, siege towers, and battering rams changed only very slightly, if at all; although trebuchets, both traction and counterweight, were markedly different than their catapult precursors, the idea of using machine-driven ballistic force to throw projectiles into and over fortifications was not.

While developments in medieval arms and armor were relatively minor, there were of course changes, although it is perhaps surprising just how slow these were in coming and the length of time they took to have a widespread effect. Yet it is worth noting that change was not a simple matter and should never be seen in a simple, deterministic way—improvements were not always adopted and innate conservatism and resistance to change were always very potent forces. During the later Middle Ages, however, it is clear that there were two areas in which changes did have a significant and widespread effect. The first was the rise in importance of infantry forces. The victories of the Flemings at Courtrai (1302), the Scots at Bannockburn (1314), and the Swiss Confederate forces at Morgarten (1315), where massed foot soldiers fighting together proved they could be a decisive force on the battlefield, shook the whole of Europe and initiated widespread, although slow to us, changes in tactics. The second area was the changes that affected arms and armor. Of these, the development of gunpowder and gunpowder weapons, especially from around 1400, and the developments in the iron industry at about the same time were certainly the most important. The latter led to greater production capacity and greater control of quality, especially in the production of steel, and therefore in the production of plate armor. These developments were to provide the basis for warfare from then into the early modern period.

ILLUSTRATIONS

LATE ROMAN TETRARCHY
Allan T. Kohl/Art Images for College Teaching

The tetrarchy (literally "rule of four") led the Roman Empire from 293 to 313. Established by Emperor Diocletian to share the responsibilities of government for the Empire and to prepare the next leaders for rule, it could not survive the bellicose jealousies of its second generation, with Constantine the surviving emperor. This statue, carved around the time, depicts the unity of the then peaceful four leaders. As they were also military leaders, they are dressed in lorica segmentata armor, a bronze breastplate from which bronze strips descend in a skirt of two connected layers to the knees. The shoulders and upper arms are covered with three layers of bronze strips. (Layering aids in the movement of the arms and lower torso.) An undergarment to which this armor may be connected can be seen on the arms and slightly below the skirt. Their scabbarded weapons are spathas, long swords especially popular among Roman cavalry, although the long hilts may also indicate that they could be grasped by two hands and used for fighting when the soldier had dismounted. Currently, the statue is outside the Basilica of San Marco, brought there from Constantinople by the Venetian Fourth Crusaders after their sack of that city in 1204.

LATE ROMAN GENERAL STILICHO

Alinari, Basilica di San Giovanni Battista, Monza, Italy/The Bridgeman Art Library

Stilicho (ca. 359–409), the son of a Vandal father and a Roman mother, rose through the Roman military ranks to lead the Eastern Roman army at the Battle of Frigidus in 394, which placed Theodosius I on the throne of the last united Roman Empire. After his death a year later, Stilicho led the armies of Theodosius's son, Honorius, as Western Roman Emperor, a position he held until he fell out of favor and was executed in 409. In this superb contemporary ivory Stilicho appears with his wife, Serena, and son, Eucherius. He is armed with a long spear (perhaps 7 feet or 2.2 meters, depending on his height) with a long, sharp head. A scabbarded sword with a well-formed hilt is hung from two belts around his waist. He is unarmored but carries a large, oblong shield covered with scales, perhaps metal plates. The shield has a sharp, conical, fluted boss, the only other decoration being two unidentified busts.

LATE ROMAN EMPEROR THEODOSIUS I OR JUSTINIAN
Louvre Museum, Paris/Giraudon/The Bridgeman Art Library

The Barberini Ivory, generally dated to the sixth century, is half of a Byzantine diptych, the centerpiece of which portrays an emperor—indicated by his crown—thought to be either Theodosius I or Justinian. The emperor is mounted on a strong horse, and he wears a lorica segmentata, with a solid bronze torso plate and a skirt and shoulder armor of two layers of bronze strips. He wears no other armor and carries no weapons. Of equal interest to the study of arms and armor is the soldier depicted on the right side of the emperor. He wears the same armor as the emperor, although his shoulder armor appears to be a solid plate—the emperor's is hidden. He also wears a long sword in a scabbard attached to his left side.

EMPEROR JUSTINIAN AND HIS COURT
Archivo Iconografico, S.A./Corbis

This justifiably famous mosaic of the Eastern Roman (or Byzantine) Emperor Justinian (482–565) was placed on the wall of the Basilica of San Vitale in Ravenna shortly after his capture of what had been the capital of Ostrogothic Italy in 540. In it Justinian is flanked by clergy—including Maximian, Bishop of Ravenna—government officials, and soldiers. Four of the soldiers carry spears with large iron heads, although they seem not to be too long as none are shown reaching the ground. Only one of the soldiers is clearly seen to be wearing armor, a mail shirt covering the torso and shoulders. But it is his shield that dominates the mosaic: a large oblong shield colorfully decorated with the Greek letters chi and rho, symbolizing "Christ the shepherd," placed first on the shields and banners of Roman soldiers by Constantine at the Battle of Milvian Bridge in 312. However, a second shield, only partially visible, is colored differently and may not contain the same symbol.

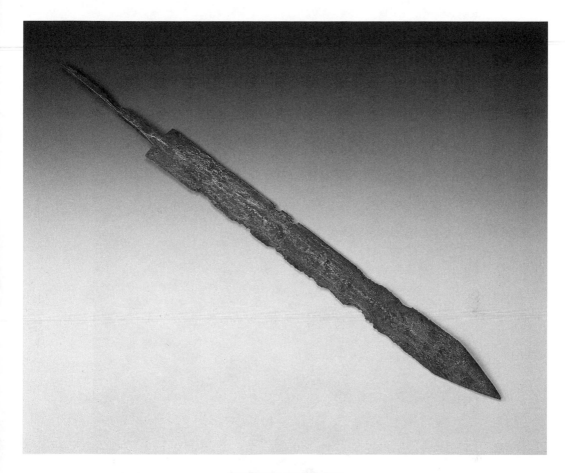

ROMAN GLADIUS
National Museums of Scotland/The Bridgeman Art Library

From the first century BC to the fifth century AD all Roman infantry soldiers carried a gladius. Closing for hand-to-hand combat, once he had thrown his pila, the soldier drew his gladius from its scabbard. This fine example of a gladius is from the end of the first century AD and was excavated at Newstead near Melrose, Scotland. It shows a sharp-tipped short sword with two edges, indicating a weapon that could be used either for slashing or thrusting at an enemy. A long tang is the only surviving part of a hilt that would have been comfortable but probably not decorated. It is currently held in the National Museums of Scotland, Edinburgh.

ROMAN BALLISTA
Alinari/Art Resource

Although the Greeks may have invented the torsion catapult, or ballista, it is perhaps the Romans who used it most successfully in warfare. Power was supplied to the projectile of the ballista by two bow arms anchored in springs made of rope and sinew and wound tightly together. These were then locked into place by metal washers and covered with a metal casing to protect it from inclement weather. A sinew bowstring was spanned between the two bow arms. This apparatus was mounted on a bed to which were attached a slider to facilitate firing, a winch to withdraw the string, a ratchet to hold the string in place while loading the projectile, and a trigger to discharge the projectile. Larger ballistae were most often used in siege warfare, but smaller cheiroballistaes, like the one portrayed here on Trajan's Column in Rome, were more mobile and could be used on the battlefield as well as at siege. This column, celebrating the victories of Emperor Trajan against the Dacians, was erected in AD 113, but there were few changes between the ballista depicted on the lower right of this image and the Roman catapult of the fourth and fifth centuries.

BARBARIAN FIGHTING A ROMAN LEGIONARY
Lauros/Giraudon, Louvre, Paris, France/The Bridgeman Art Library

The Romans and Germanic barbarians had fought frontier engagements for many centuries before the Goths crossed the Danube River and invaded the Empire. Before this the Romans fought the barbarians in their lands. In this beautifully carved relief from the second century AD—currently in the Louvre Museum—a Roman legionary fights a barbarian soldier in the latter's village, as represented by the house in the background. The barbarian wears no armor and wields a thick sword with a large pommel and a thick but small cross guard. The Roman soldier wears the lorica squamata, armor made of a large number of metallic scales attached to each other by leather laces and to an undergarment by linen thread. His helmet is made from a bronze bowl that covers the head and lower neck but is cut out for the ears, a thick decorated brow rising to a point above his nose, and hinged cheek-pieces that would have been tied together with leather laces under his chin. A horsehair crest may have shown rank or unit. Because the relief is broken, the weapon of the legionary cannot be determined.

BARBARIAN HORSEMAN
Foto Marburg/Art Resource

Contemporary depictions of barbarian soldiers are rare. This grave stele was found in Hornhausen, Germany, and has been dated from the fourth to the seventh century. The stele shows a barbarian cavalry soldier, probably a Frank—as he is portrayed wearing long hair, a symbol of nobility among that barbarian tribe. He wears a helmet with large cheek-pieces and a distinct nasal. Most likely it is a spangenhelm, although this cannot be determined from the weathered sculpture. A decorated shield is also clearly portrayed, large, round, and with a distinct boss and rim—probably iron. Body armor is not depicted, although the decorated garment on the thigh may indicate that he is wearing armor similar to the lorica segmentata. Two weapons are visible. The soldier holds a spear with a long, wide, and thick head in his right hand. A sword is attached to the soldier's left side; the scabbard has a clear rim and chape. The grave stele is currently in the Landesmuseum, Halle, Germany.

MEROVINGIAN HELMET

Musée Dauphinois, Grenoble, France/Lauros/Giraudon/The Bridgeman Art Library

Despite their obvious expense, most barbarian soldiers wore helmets, many differing in construction from those worn by Romans. This marvelous Merovingian helmet is thought to be from the seventh century and is currently in the Musée Dauphinois in Grenoble, France. It is a spangenhelm, consisting of an iron cap made of a decorated, gilded metal band encircling the head attached by rivets to six metal bands flayed at the bottom and rising to a circular metal piece at its peak. Covering the spaces between these bands are iron plates that are also attached by rivets. Two hinged metal pieces descend from the lower band to protect the cheeks; there are holes in these and in the back of the helmet for attaching mail protection for the neck and lower face. The decoration indicates that this was likely the helmet of an elite or noble soldier.

NYDAM WEAPONS CACHE

Landesmuseum fur Vor- und Fruhgeschichte, Kiel, Germany/The Bridgeman Art Library

This cache of barbarian weapons was excavated from the Nydam bog outside Schleswig, Germany, by Conrad Engelhardt between 1859 and 1863 near two intact clinker-built boats, one made of oak and one of pine. However, they may not have been directly connected. The bog served as a ritual burial spot for "spoils of war," trophies of arms, armor, and other items taken from defeated foes. They date from as early as the late third century, although how late they go cannot be determined. It is thought that they were pre-Christian. The cache contains a large number of swords, spearheads, axes, and arrowheads, all well preserved by the bog. All weapons are iron, but the bog also preserved some wooden arrow and spear shafts, as well as the wood of some shields.

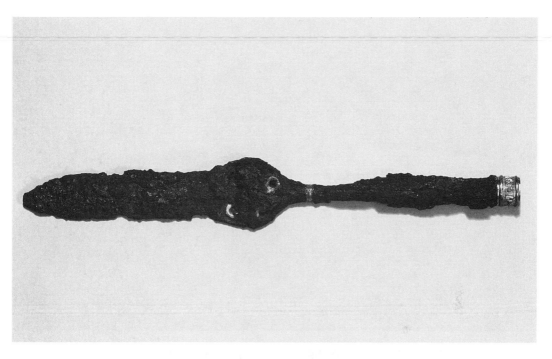

BARBARIAN SPEAR
Trustees of The British Museum, M & ME 1964, 7-2.491

According to contemporary sources, the barbarian spear was used from horseback as a lance, for close combat as a thrusting weapon, and, when thrown, as a javelin. Consequently, many different types of early medieval spearheads have been found, of varying sizes and weights. This artifact, currently held in the British Library, was found in Great Chesterford, Essex, buried with an early Anglo-Saxon warrior whose grave has been dated to the sixth century. It is unusual in that it contains an inlaid ornament, probably indicating that the warrior with whom it was buried was of the nobility or the elite.

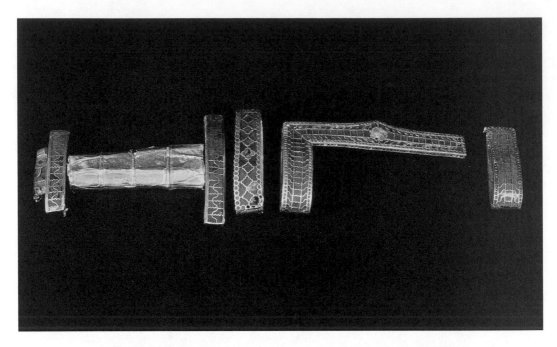

SWORD ORNAMENTS FROM THE TREASURE OF CHILDERIC I
Bibliothèque Nationale, Paris, France/The Bridgeman Art Library

Childeric I was the Merovingian king of the Salian Franks from 457 until ca. 481. A strong military leader, during his reign he added much territory to his kingdom. When he died he was buried at his capital, Tournai, in a rich grave that was opened in 1653. Found among the heaps of treasure—which included a golden bracelet, jewels of gold and cloisonné enamel with garnets, gold coins, a gold bull's head, more than 300 golden bees, and a ring with the inscription "Childerici regis" (of Childeric the King)—were two richly decorated swords, a spatha and a seax. (Unfortunately, much of this was destroyed in the early nineteenth century.) The hilts and scabbards of both swords were decorated with gold inlay and cloisonné. Pictured here are the hilt and scabbard metal of the spatha, currently held in the Bibliothèque Nationale in Paris.

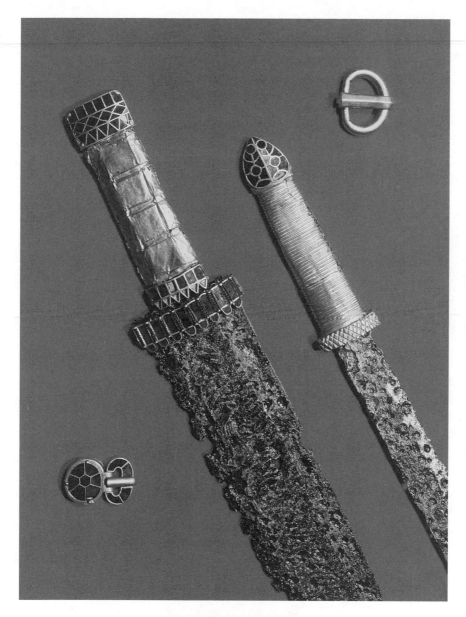

BARBARIAN SWORDS

Musée des Beaux-Arts et d'Archéologie, Troyes, France/Giraudon/
The Bridgeman Art Library

The sword was the close-combat weapon of choice for almost all barbarian soldiers, both cavalry and infantry. While the Romans preferred the short gladius, which was used primarily for thrusting, the barbarians chose the longer spatha, which was both a slashing and a thrusting weapon. As can be seen in these Merovingian Frankish swords, currently found in the Musée des Beaux-Arts et d'Archéologie, in Troyes, France, they were well-made iron weapons, which often had decorated grips of wood and leather, and sometimes, as in these examples, of bronze.

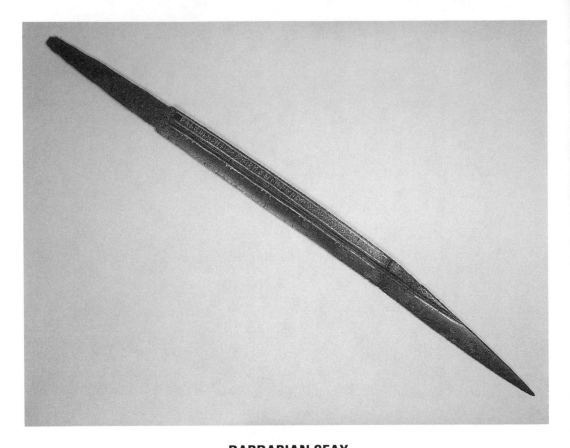

BARBARIAN SEAX
HIP/Art Resource/British Museum, London

A seax or scramasax, a single-edged sword with a sharp point, was popular among barbarian soldiers of all tribes during the early Middle Ages. Shorter than a two-edged sword of the period, they were used for close combat between infantry soldiers. This sword, from ninth- or tenth-century England, is not only famous as an exquisite example of a seax, but also because it is the only artifact bearing the complete Anglo-Saxon runic alphabet. Another inscription bears the word "Beagnoth," which may indicate the name of the owner or maker.

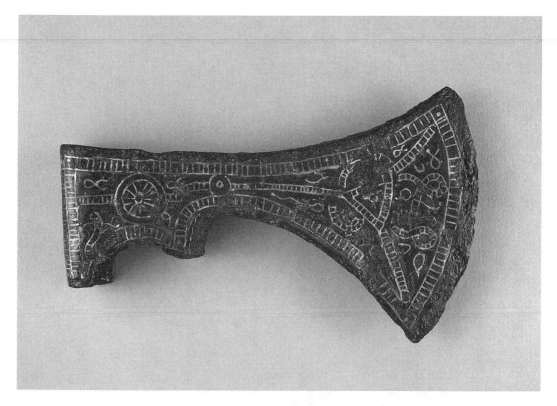

MEROVINGIAN FRANCISCA
Trustees of The British Museum

The francisca was a widely used barbarian throwing axe; such artifacts have been found throughout Europe. With a heavy head and short handle, the francisca was usually thrown by the warrior before closing in for hand-to-hand combat with sword, spear, or another francisca. This particular head of a francisca, Merovingian Frankish and dated to the seventh century, is exceptional in that it is inlaid with silver, which may denote ownership by an elite or noble soldier. It was found in the area of Neuwied, Rhineland-Palatinate, Germany, and is currently in the British Museum (M & ME 1961, 5-5, 1).

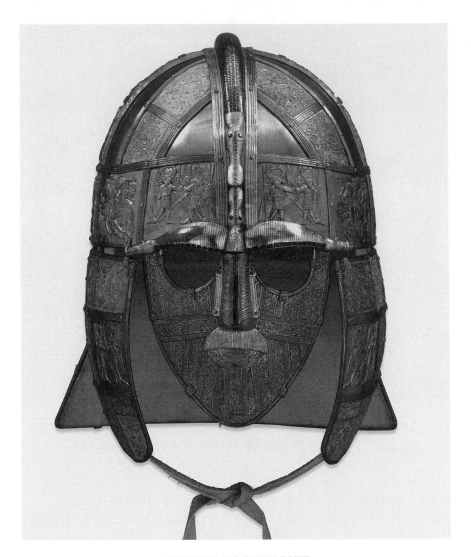

SUTTON HOO HELMET
British Museum/Art Resource

This is a modern reconstruction of the extraordinary helmet found in the Sutton Hoo ship burial. Dating from the early seventh century it is one of only four helmets from the Anglo-Saxon period. The decoration includes interlacing, animal ornaments, and heroic scenes, motifs that were common in the Germanic world at this time. One scene shows two warriors, wearing horned helmets and holding short swords and downturned spears. Another shows a mounted warrior trampling a fallen enemy, a theme handed down from the Roman Empire. The face mask is the most remarkable feature of the helmet: it has eye sockets, eyebrows, and a nose, which has two small holes cut in it to allow the wearer to breathe freely. The nose, eyebrows, and dragon make up a great bird with outstretched wings that flies on the helmet rather like the bird of prey on the shield. Although it belonged to a king of East Anglia, it came originally from Sweden and was probably about 100 years old when it was buried.

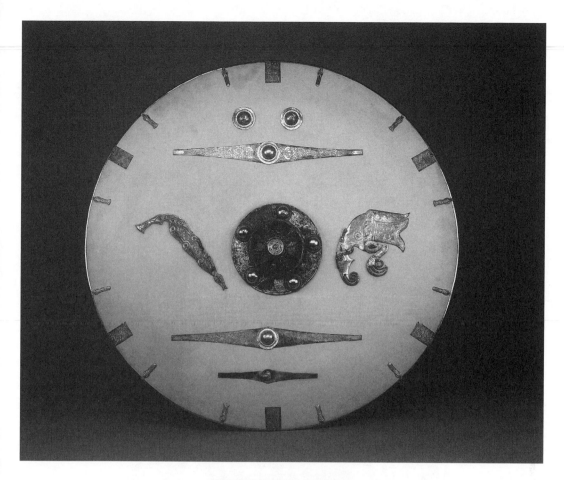

SUTTON HOO SHIELD
Trustees of The British Museum

All barbarian soldiers carried a shield. Shields could be easily constructed from hard wood slats held together by glue, a metal rim, and probably a leather cover. As evidenced in this replica of the shield found in the Sutton Hoo burial, an Anglo-Saxon shield was round with a metal rim, reinforced frequently by two sizes of metal pieces clamped around the rim—six wide and twelve narrow. A large, round, and thick metal boss placed in the center of the shield anchored a leather grip that has now disappeared, as has the wood of the shield, thought to be limewood. That this was the shield of an elite warrior is suggested by the well-carved jeweled decorations of an eagle and a dragon.

THE TRIUMPH OF VIRTUE OVER EVIL

Museo Nazionale del Bargello, Florence, Italy/The Bridgeman Art Library

Charlemagne's empire contained artisans who were especially adept at ivory carvings. These, although small, show great detail. This, the lower half of an ivory carving of the Triumph of Virtue over Evil, is from Ambronay Abbey and was made in the ninth century. It depicts Virtue as a Carolingian soldier. He is dressed in the mail byrnie required to be worn by all Carolingian soldiers to protect his torso, upper arms, and groin. He wears no helmet but carries the required circular and concave shield, with a large, heavy boss and decoration as seen in several other contemporary illustrations. His weapon is a wooden spear, its long tapering iron spearhead resting on the neck of his captive, Evil. This ivory is currently housed in the Museo Nazionale del Bargello of Florence, Italy.

THE COURT OF CHARLES THE BALD

Bibliothèque Nationale, Paris, France/The Bridgeman Art Library

Charlemagne's empire stayed intact through the reign of his son, Louis the Pious (814–840), after which it was divided among his three grandsons, Lothair, Louis "the German," and Charles "the Bald." Each ruled a part of the empire as its king. Charles the Bald's realm in West Francia encompassed much of modern France. In this depiction of Charles's court—painted ca. 843–851—he receives a Bible from Abbot Vivian and the monks of Saint-Martin de Tours. Two soldiers attend him. Their helmets consist of a shallow skull cap fitting closely to the head and flaring out above the level of ears in a wide brim, which covered the neck and was turned up in the front. It is difficult to know the purpose of this brim, unless it was purely for fashion. Unfortunately, no artifact exists to test this theory or to determine how a Carolingian helmet was constructed. The soldiers also carry spears characteristic of their time. However, their armor, although protecting the same parts of the body as the traditional Carolingian byrnie, does not appear to be mail but plate, likely bronze, and imitative of the style of Roman armor.

EARLY NINTH-CENTURY CAROLINGIAN SOLDIERS
Bibliothèque Nationale, Paris, France/The Bridgeman Art Library

One of the most important Carolingian manuscripts is the Utrecht Psalter made at Reims between 816 and 835 and currently held at the University of Utrecht Library—hence its name. Its particular value is that it contains numerous pictures of everyday life, although drawn with what some have called an unrefined hand. The soldiers depicted in this later copy are from the Carolingian period, although they are meant to illustrate a Biblical psalm. There is no fighting, although the infantry in the center left of the illustration are taunting their indeterminate enemy by raising their weapons, suggesting that they are anxious for combat. Instead, both infantry and cavalry are pictured on the march or at rest. Almost all carry long spears and lances, with a single, possibly re-curved bow held by a soldier at the front of the taunting infantry. Many troops can be seen wearing Carolingian-style helmets, distinguishable by the large peaked brims. Some infantry and cavalry soldiers also carry shields, two of which are depicted from the inside where their carriers have their left forearm looped through a thong while holding a grip anchored to the boss on the outside of the shield. Two or three distinctively shaped unit banners are also portrayed.

SIEGE OF A FORTIFIED TOWN

Bibliothèque Nationale, Paris, France/The Bridgeman Art Library

This depiction of a besieged Biblical site is copied from the Utrecht Psalter. Although the size of the illustration makes it difficult to determine details of arms and armor, it nicely shows how these were used in military conflict. Spears are carried at rest by soldiers inside the city, but cavalry use the spears overhand when attacking. The spears lying on the ground may indicate that some were thrown, although at least one horseman uses the weapon to thrust down at the infantry soldier below him. Swords are also used, as slashing weapons by the cavalry and thrusting weapons by the infantry. The only distinctive protection shown is the shield, round and convex in shape, with a large boss that rises out of the shield to a point. Shields are used by both infantry and cavalry.

CAROLINGIAN CAVALRY
Time & Life Pictures/Getty Images

Charlemagne's army has been characterized throughout history by its cavalry. Although always smaller in number than the infantry, the Carolingian cavalry dominated the battlefield. This contemporary illustration, from the late ninth-century Golden Psalter held in the library of the Saint-Gall Monastery (Saint-Gallen-Stiftsbibliothek, MS 22), Switzerland, is the best depiction of these soldiers and their arms and armor. The men in the lower half of the illumination all wear the mail byrnie to protect their torso, upper arms, and thighs. Their heads are protected by traditional Carolingian helmets, with their distinctive wide brim, unique in shape and style. And they carry a long lance, its head shaped like the "Holy Lance," except for the lead horseman who carries a banner in the shape of a fish or dragon, which may be the unit's symbol. The cavalry pictured in the top half of the illumination wear helmets and carry lances similar to those of the lower warriors, but they are not wearing byrnies, which may indicate that they are a light cavalry unit while their counterparts are heavy cavalry. However, what is perhaps most important is the depiction of stirrups on all the saddles, a relatively new invention that cannot be seen more clearly than here.

CAROLINGIAN SIEGE
Topham/The Image Works

This late ninth-century illumination of a Biblical siege by Joab found in the Golden Psalter (now held in the library of the Saint-Gall Monastery in Switzerland [Saint-Gallen-Stiftsbibliothek, MS 22]) beautifully depicts all the arms and armor used by Carolingian soldiers. Both infantry and cavalry are portrayed, although there is little distinction in their arms or armor. All wear the Carolingian mail byrnie, made of several thousand interlinked metal circles. This armor, so highly valued by Charlemagne that he forbade its sale outside his empire, on pain of death, protected the soldiers' torso, upper arms, groin, and thighs. All wear the Carolingian helmet, its very distinctive wide brim rising to a peak in the front. Also depicted are several large, round shields, their convex shape, large and pronounced boss, and traditional decoration are clearly seen on the one held by a soldier in the besieged town at the top of the illustration. A number of weapons are also shown: lances used by cavalry; spears used by infantry—who thrust them with two hands; long swords wielded by both cavalry and infantry, but also worn by the infantry using lances; and a bow surprisingly fired only by a mounted archer and not by any of the besieged soldiers as is common in many medieval siege scenes. A banner different from those seen in other Carolingian illustrations is carried by a cavalry soldier in the upper siege. Finally, stirrups can be clearly seen descending from the horses' saddles.

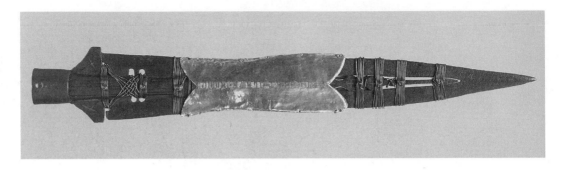

THE "HOLY LANCE"
Vienna, Kunsthistorisches Museum, 8028/435

Called the "Spear of Destiny," this spear-head was once thought to be the Holy Lance that Longinus used to pierce the side of Jesus Christ while he hung on the cross, thus making it one of the greatest relics of all Christendom. It is not. It is, in fact, the sole surviving Carolingian spearhead, dating from at least the reign of Otto I (936–973). It has the characteristic thin tapered form with two cross-wing projections at the base. These projections may have been added to prevent the blade from penetrating a body too deeply. This spearhead is iron but sheathed in a gold cover with the inscription "Lance and Nail of the Lord." This was added by Charles IV, Holy Roman Emperor, in 1350 on top of a silver sheath, which had been placed there in 1083 by Emperor Henry IV. When both sheaths were removed in 2003 it was discovered that the spearhead was broken in two and contained a further relic bound in the center.

ELEVENTH-CENTURY INFANTRY
Bibliothèque Nationale, Paris, France/The Bridgeman Art Library

Dating from the eleventh century, this illumination fragment from the Life of St. Aubin of Angers (Vie de Saint Aubin d'Angers) is one of the best illustrations of a contemporary infantry unit. The unit consists of twenty-four infantry soldiers and one officer. The armor of the common soldiers is difficult to distinguish, although they seem to be clothed in some torso armor with sleeves that end at the wrist in bands. They also seem to be wearing armor to cover the knees. Two kite-shaped shields are visible, although the tops of others can be seen further back in the unit, indicating that at least some, if not all, of these soldiers had shields.

All the infantry soldiers are armed with spears, roughly six feet (two meters) in height, with the spearheads similar to the extant Carolingian "Holy Lance." Two also wear swords. The better-equipped officer wears a Carolingian mail byrnie to cover his torso, groin, and upper arms, but he does not appear to be wearing armor on his knees. His nasal helmet is attached to a mail coif that hangs to his shoulders, protecting his neck. A kite-shaped shield is slung around his back by a leather cord, and he is armed with a spear and sword like those carried by his soldiers.

SIEGE AND COMBAT OF ANGLO-SAXON SOLDIERS
British Library

In this illumination from the early eleventh-century Harley Psalter (British Museum, Harley MS 603, f. 57v), produced at Christ Church in Canterbury, England, soldiers fight both in a battle and at siege. Although meant to illustrate a Biblical scene, those fighting carry contemporary Anglo-Saxon arms and shields. The shields are both round—used by the besiegers—and kite-shaped—used by the besieged. The shield held by the warrior on the far left nicely shows its round and deep concave shape. The large iron boss and thick rim are also clear, as are the shield's designs, which may in fact represent reinforcing ribs. The metal rims and bosses of the kite-shaped shields are also visible, although the shields themselves seem to be smaller than those depicted in the *Bayeux Tapestry* later in the century. Both spears and swords are wielded. The spears are long, with long and thin heads—almost indistinguishable in size from the shafts—and are used solely as thrusting weapons. The swords are long and quite thick, tapering from the cross guards to a rounded point; large pommels are also clearly visible. One of the swordbearers wears a scabbard attached to his waist by a belt. The soldiers do not wear armor or helmets.

COPPERGATE HELMET
Topham /The Image Works

This helmet, which was found in York, England, dates from the eighth century. It is Anglo-Saxon in origin and may have been hidden deliberately. On the brass band across the crest of the iron helmet is an inscription in Latin that identifies the owner as Oshere and includes a short prayer invoking God's protection. It has two deep curving cheek-pieces and a curtain of mail to protect the neck. It is owned by the Yorkshire Archaeological Trust and is currently on display in the York Castle Museum.

A SEVENTH-CENTURY SPANISH VERSION OF
THE TAKING OF JERUSALEM BY NEBUCHADREZZAR

Museu Diocesa d'Urgell, La Seu d'Urgell, Spain/Lauros/
Giraudon/The Bridgeman Art Library

In this tenth-century Spanish manuscript illumination portraying the Biblical capture of Jerusalem by Nebuchadrezzar, several soldiers on both sides of the conflict are displayed. All are armed in the same way. This is different from most medieval depictions of similar Biblical accounts, which usually show the Israelites as Christians and the Babylonians as Muslims. There is no visible body armor on the soldiers, although it may be hidden under their clothes. All but the archers carry small, round shields, known as bucklers. The soldiers carry three weapons: a long spear, with a distinct spearhead, only wielded by the infantry; swords, used by infantry, cavalry, and as an executioner's weapon, that are longer than other contemporary swords; and bows, fired by the besiegers from horseback and by the besieged from the walls of the distinctly Muslim fortification—probably an attempt by the artist to display a fortified Middle Eastern town. The very odd style of horse archery should not be taken as literal, however; instead, it probably shows the inadequacy of an artist attempting to paint a three-dimensional action before the use of perspective. While wielding a sword one cavalry soldier also carries a banner, holding it with the same hand he uses to hold the reins of his horse. Unfortunately, the size of the illumination prohibits one to determine any details of the weapons.

PROCESSION TO VALHALLA BY DEAD VIKING WARRIORS
Werner Forman/TopFoto/The Image Works

Death in battle ensured an eternity in Valhalla for a pre-Christian Viking warrior, where he would continue to fight daily mock battles on the plains of Asgard in anticipation of assisting Odin in his final conflict with the giants. At night, he would feast on boar and drink mead with other celebrated soldiers, drunkenly telling their war stories. This was heaven for a soldier in the militaristic culture of the Vikings, and a soldier's greatest fear was that he would otherwise end up in the much more boring Hel. On this funerary picture stone found on the island of Gotland, off the coast of Sweden, and dated to early Viking age, a procession of dead soldiers makes its way to Valhalla. Although much of the detail has been lost to centuries of weathering, the helmets of these soldiers can be distinguished, with their nasal guards and peaked caps. Some seem also to be carrying shields. Swords are scabbarded at their waists. A mounted warrior—perhaps their valkyrie guide—rides before them. He (or she if it is a valkyrie) wears a helmet similar to those worn by the other soldiers and carries a much more clearly visible decorated round shield.

VIKING SWORDS, STIRRUP, AND SPEARHEAD
Nationalmuseet, Copenhagen, Denmark/The Bridgeman Art Library

The spearhead, stirrup, and swords pictured here are currently found in the Nationalmuseet of Copenhagen, Denmark. They date from the Viking period and were excavated from different locations. The two swords are similar in type and construction, although one has a more decorated cross guard and pommel. The blades are pattern-welded iron, made by building them up from many smaller pieces of iron welded together, twisted, and worked in such a way that the resultant surface of the blade exhibited a visible pattern of waves, ripples, or herringbone designs. The spearhead is long, flat, and thick at the rounded end near the socket, tapering to a sharp point. A reinforcing ridge runs down the center of the blade from the point to the socket. The single stirrup is heavy, large, and well crafted, much better made than elsewhere in Europe at the same time, showing—with the weapons—the metal-working skills for which the Vikings were so well known.

VIKING SWORDS
Library of Congress

Viking warriors took justifiable pride in their swords. They were expensive and well made, some crafted by smiths who signed their work down the middle of the blade. They were made from iron welded together and then twisted and remade, and then twisted and remade again, over and over until the strongest blade was achieved. The resulting designs gave the process its name: "pattern-welding." Also distinctive were the grips of these swords; the pommels and cross guards were often decorated and sometimes inlaid with silver, as can be seen in these three examples from the Universitetets Oldskamling in Oslo, Norway.

VIKING WEAPONS
Museum of London/The Bridgeman Art Library

Scandinavian ships brought warriors to England for close to three centuries, from 787 to 1085, but many also brought colonists who were attracted by England's rich agricultural and fishing potential. Most of these settled in the north and east, but London also seems to have been a site for tourism, as well as raids. This is confirmed by these weapons, found under London Bridge in the Thames River and now located at the Museum of London. The iron spearheads are long, narrow, and diamond-shaped rather than flat. They also contain wing projections at the base similar to early Carolingian spearheads. The iron axe-heads, from "Danish axes" or "broad axes," are triangular in shape and quite heavy with a sharp cutting edge. The numbers of spear- and axe-heads in this and other collections indicate the popularity of these weapons for Vikings.

VIKING SHIELD
Topham/The Image Works

As can be seen in this artifact recovered from a ship burial, the Viking shield was round and made of wooden slats, held together by an iron rim and probably a hard leather covering. The grip on the inside of the shield was anchored by a thick and heavy iron boss. Viking shields were often decorated with animals and fauna, although any such decorations on this shield have disappeared. The round shape of the Viking shield allowed for easy attachment to the sides of their ships, increasing the height of the gunwales and therefore adding protection to the rowers.

THE BATTLE OF HASTINGS IN THE *BAYEUX TAPESTRY*
Art Archive/Corbis

The *Bayeux Tapestry* (ca. 1080) is undoubtedly the best pictorial source of information about arms and armor in the eleventh century. The infantry in this part of the tapestry, Anglo-Saxons, are shown standing shoulder to shoulder and using their long kite-shaped shields to form a shield wall for added protection. Both they and the Norman cavalry charging them are armed with spears. Some of the spears are thrown while others appear to be thrust overarm. The soldiers all wear mail shirts descending to the knees and elbows, mail coifs, and simple conical helmets with nasals.

BAYEAUX TAPESTRY CAVALRY, INFANTRY, AND ARCHERS

Erich Lessing/Art Resource

King Harold's Anglo-Saxon army is fiercely attacked at the Battle of Hastings (1066) in a detail from the *Bayeux Tapestry*. Harold's opponents, the Norman cavalry, are shown wearing long mail shirts and conical helmets. They are armed with spears, although some are also shown wielding a sword or a club of some sort. The kite-shaped shields are held by an internal leather strap. The saddle has a high front (the pommel) and back (the cantle), and the riders' stirrups are long. The horses do not wear any armor or other protection. The Anglo-Saxon infantry are outfitted with armor, helmets, and shields that are similar to those of the Normans and are fighting with swords, axes, spears, and javelins. The lower margin of this part of the tapestry shows unarmored archers with long bows and arrows with large barbed heads. It is not known whether these represent Anglo-Saxon or Norman archers.

TRANSPORTING ARMS AND ARMOR IN THE *BAYEUX TAPESTRY*
Erich Lessing/Art Resource

William of Normandy had to transport to England not only the army but also all of its equipment. The *Bayeux Tapestry* portrays mail armor, helmets, swords, and spears, together with food and drink, all en route to England. The square neck opening of the armor shows that it was lined with what appears to be textile.

NORMAN KNIGHT
Snark/Art Resource

This mounted knight depicted on a tapestry that once hung in Baldishol Church, Norway, wears the characteristic long mail shirt and nasal helmet of the eleventh and twelfth centuries. He carries a kite-shaped shield and is armed with a spear. He rides with long leather stirrups in the typical straight-legged fashion of the medieval horseman. The tapestry, representing the month of May, is currently in the Kunstindustrimuseet, Oslo, Norway.

NASAL HELM
Kunst Historisches Museum

The common helmet of the eleventh and twelfth centuries was a simple conical shape with a long projection, the nasal, to protect the nose. Although illustrations appear to show that these helmets were made from several pieces, like the earlier Anglo-Saxon and Viking helmets, this very rare survival is made from a single piece of iron. It is now held in the Wapen und Rustkammer, Kunsthistorische Museum, Vienna, A 41.

REGIN REMAKES SIGURD'S SWORD
The Art Archive/Oldsaksammlung Oslo/Dagli Orti

The Sigurd/Siegfried legend relates how Regin forges a sword for Sigurd, which he then uses to slay the dragon, Fafnir, and capture the dragon's treasure. While cooking the heart of Fafnir, Sigurd tastes the dragon's blood and gains the power to understand the birds, which tell him that Regin plans to kill him and take the treasure. Sigurd slays Regin instead. On this twelfth-century wooden panel from the Setesdale Church in Norway, Regin forges Sigurd's sword in his smithy. After heating the sword in his forge, while an assistant pumps the bellows to increase the heat, Regin hammers out the sword on an anvil.

SAINT MAURICE ON HORSEBACK
Erich Lessing/Art Resource

This silver casket from the Treasury of the Abbey of Saint-Maurice in Switzerland shows Saint Maurice as a medieval knight in mail armor of about 1150. He is wearing a nasal helmet and carrying a long kite-shaped shield. A pennon is attached to his lance. Both pennon and shield are decorated with a cross identifying Maurice as a crusader.

KNEELING CRUSADER KNIGHT
HIP/Art Resource

This justly famous image from the Westminster Psalter depicts a knight of about 1175–1200 (British Library, Royal 2 A, XXII, f. 220). He wears a surcoat over his mail coat with long sleeves that extend to protect the backs of his hands. His legs are protected with mail; the mail on his lower legs is tied at the back and extends to cover his feet. He also wears simple prick spurs. His head is protected with a mail coif fastened by a flap secured to his left. To the upper right is his great helm, held for him by his lady. His sword is double edged, tapers to a sharp point, and has a simple disc pommel and cross guards. It is encased in a scabbard hanging from his belt. A pennon is attached to his lance below the spearhead. The pennon and his surcoat indicate that he is a crusader.

WAR ELEPHANT FROM A MEDIEVAL BESTIARY

British Library, Harley MS 4751, f. 8, London/The Bridgeman Art Library

This fantastic image of an armed elephant, from about 1230–1240, shows many of the weapons of the thirteenth century. At the far right a man is shown with a sling loaded with stone shot, while other soldiers are armed with axes, longbows, and crossbows. There are a variety of different helmets, including the great helm, although most are of the simple, open kettle hat type. All are armed in mail armor, and the driver carries a triangular shield that covers his head and most of his torso. This illumination comes from a bestiary made in England, possibly Salisbury.

MAIL-CLAD KNIGHTS AND MOUNTED ARCHER
FROM THE CHANSON D'ASPREMONT

British Library, Lansdowne MS 782, f. 10

This illustration from the Chanson d'Aspremont (1225–1250) shows a mounted archer with his bow and quiver at his side into which he is reaching with his right hand. All the soldiers are clad in mail from head to toe and are wearing surcoats. They are fighting with couched lances and swords and are using the smaller heater shield.

KNIGHTS WITH COUCHED LANCES
ON A TWELFTH-CENTURY CHESS PIECE
Erich Lessing/Art Resource

These two knights are shown on an ivory chess piece of about 1140. They are probably wearing long mail coats, although the carving suggests that their armor is made of scales. The skulls of their nasal helmets are made from four plates joined together, instead of a single piece. Their long, kite-shaped shields are curved to fit around the body for extra protection and are supported by a strap that goes over the shoulder. They are fighting with couched lances and are outfitted with long stirrups and simple prick spurs. Currently in the Louvre Museum, Paris.

SWORD, CA. 1250–1330

Trustees of The British Museum

Found in the River Witham in Lincolnshire, England, this sword has the characteristic tapering double-edged blade, simple cross guard, and disc pommel of the period. The hilt, which would have covered the tang, the extension of the blade between the cross guard and the pommel, is missing.

DAVID DEFEATING THE PHILISTINES FROM THE MORGAN PICTURE BIBLE

The Pierpont Morgan Library/Art Resource

This miniature, made in France in about 1250, shows David defeating the Philistines. The mounted knights wear mail armor and great helms or kettle hats; most are also wearing long surcoats. The knights are shown charging with their lances couched or wielding a long, tapered, double-edged sword. Shields are now shorter than the long kite-shaped shield popular in the previous two centuries. This beautifully illustrated manuscript, once known as the Maciejowski Bible, is now in the Pierpont Morgan Library in New York City (MS M.638, f. 39).

DAVID DEFEATS THE SYRIANS FROM THE MORGAN PICTURE BIBLE
New York City, The Pierpont Morgan Library, MS M.638, f. 40/Art Resource

This miniature, from the former Maciejowski Bible—now called the Morgan Picture Bible—was produced in France in about 1250, and depicts King David defeating the Syrians. The mounted knights are in full charge with couched lance and sword, but the infantry soldiers to the right are scaling the walls of a town using ladders while another soldier is attacking the gate with a pickaxe. All soldiers are wearing mail that covers the entire torso, arms, and legs, including the hands and feet. Several different helmets are shown, including great helms on the cavalry and kettle hat helmets on the infantry.

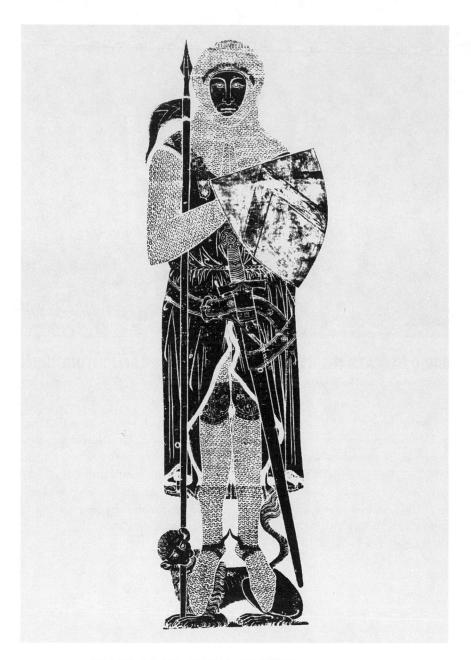

BRASS OF SIR JOHN D'ABERNON THE ELDER
Stoke d'Abernon Church, Surrey, England

The armor of Sir John d'Abernon, from his monumental brass of 1277, is predominantly mail from his head—the coif—to his feet. However, his knees are protected with plate armor—possibly made from *cuir boulli* and not from iron. His shield is now the much shorter type rather than the long kite shape of earlier. His sword is long and tapers down its length.

THE SIEGE OF ACRE, 1191
Library of Congress

This miniature of an attack on a castle shows the characteristic siege tactics of the crusading period. On the lower left is a simple counterweight trebuchet loaded with a round stone ball. The soldiers to the right are digging a mine under the castle walls using pickaxes. Defenders are shown shooting longbows. All soldiers on both sides wear mail armor covered by surcoats of single color without heraldry. The illumination is said to depict the siege of Acre and is currently housed in the Bibliothèque Royale de Bruxelles.

ASSYRIANS AT THE SIEGE OF JERUSALEM

Erich Lessing/Art Resource

This illumination from the Silos Apocalypse (British Library, Add. MS 11695, f. 102v) depicts the Four Horsemen of the Apocalypse—Famine, Plague, War, and Death—represented by four cavalry soldiers (likely Spanish Muslims) riding colorful horses. While one rider is holding a set of scales, two are brandishing long tapering swords and one has a recurved bow armed with an arrow. All are wearing long mail coats that appear to be edged with decorative borders. The Silos Apocalypse is a commentary on the Book of Revelation by Beatus of Liébana and was written in 1109 in Silos, Spain.

MEDIEVAL MUSLIM HORSEMEN
British Library Add. MS 18866, f. 140a

This fourteenth-century manuscript illumination shows four Muslim horsemen carrying swords and small circular shields. Their swords are slightly curved and have simple cross hilts. The horsemen have also looped the reins around their right arms leaving them free to wield their swords.

KNIGHTS AND INFANTRY AT THE BATTLE OF BANNOCKBURN

British Library MS Add. 47682, f. 40/The Art Archive

This early fourteenth-century manuscript illumination shows a wide range of both soldiers and arms and armor. At the top, cavalry, wearing mail armor and plate helmets, fight on horseback. Their weapons include swords, axes of various shapes, daggers, and lances. At the top center one cavalry soldier wields a sword called a falchion. The horses are unarmored and are just wearing cloth trappers. In the lower scene the infantry fight with swords, axes, polearms, and bows and arrows. While some of these soldiers wear mail, most are unarmored except for a helmet. The two soldiers to the left of center fight with a small round shield called a buckler. This illustration is from the Holkham Bible Picture Book.

THE CAPTURE OF DAMIETTA
Archivo Iconografico, S.A.,/Corbis

This miniature, from a manuscript held in the Bibliotheque de l'Arsenal in Paris, dates to the end of the fourteenth century and shows how armor had developed. The soldiers are wearing plate armor on their arms and legs and, although it is unclear what they are wearing on their torsos, one man on the left appears to be wearing a breastplate. Each also wears a helmet, mainly a bascinet or a kettle hat, with a mail coif or collar. Weapons include the tapered stabbing sword with disc pommel and simple cross guard, the rondel dagger, an axe, and a variety of polearms.

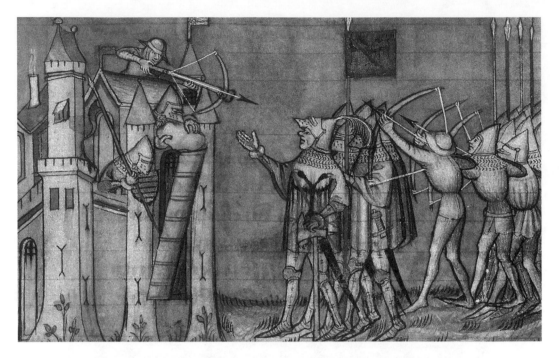

BERTRAND DU GUESCLIN'S CAPTURE OF PESTIEN CASTLE
British Library, Yates Thompson 35, f. 51 /HIP/The Image Works

Dating to about 1400, this illustration shows soldiers wearing mail and plate armor. The figures in the middle are wearing leg harnesses and visored bascinets. The defenders are wearing similar armor and are armed with crossbows and spears. It is not clear if they are wearing breastplates as the torsos are obscured by fabric coverings. The attackers are using longbows and are armed with spears and swords. While most are wearing bascinets, with or without visors, some are wearing kettle hats. The scene celebrates Bertrand Du Guesclin's capture of Pestien Castle in 1364 and is found in Cuvelier's "Life of Bertrand Du Guesclin."

BATTLE OF AGINCOURT
Stapleton Collection/Corbis

This fine fifteenth-century manuscript illustration of the Battle of Agincourt shows a wide range of armor and weapons. Most of the foot soldiers are wearing brigandines, as shown by the pattern of rivets on the fabric, and poleyns on their knees. They are armed with the longbow and the sword. The mounted knights also wear brigandines but with armor on their arms and legs. All are shown wearing simple helmets, sallets or kettle hats.

BATTLE OF SAN ROMANO
Erich Lessing/Art Resource

This famous picture by Paolo Ucello (1397–1475) shows the condottiere Niccolo da Tolentino leading the Florentine forces against Siena at the Battle of San Romano in 1432. The knights are wearing complete plate armor of the very latest fashion. Most are armed with lances, although on the right a knight is fighting with a war hammer. Note that the horses are completely unprotected. National Gallery, London.

BRASS OF SIR JOHN D'ABERNON THE YOUNGER

Stoke d'Abernon Church, Surrey, England

This monumental brass of the knight Sir John d'Abernon the Younger (ca. 1327) shows the armor of that time. It consists of a combination of both mail and plate armor. Under Sir John's surcoat he is wearing a coat of plates and a mail haubergeon—both can be seen at the front. His arms and legs are covered in mail and further protected at the front by the addition of simple "gutter-shaped" defenses. His bascinet is very rounded, and his neck and shoulders are protected by mail. His long sword has an almost parallel-sided blade and is secured to his waist belt. Compare this to the brass of John d'Abernon the Elder, of 50 years earlier, who is predominantly wearing mail with only very small plate defenses.

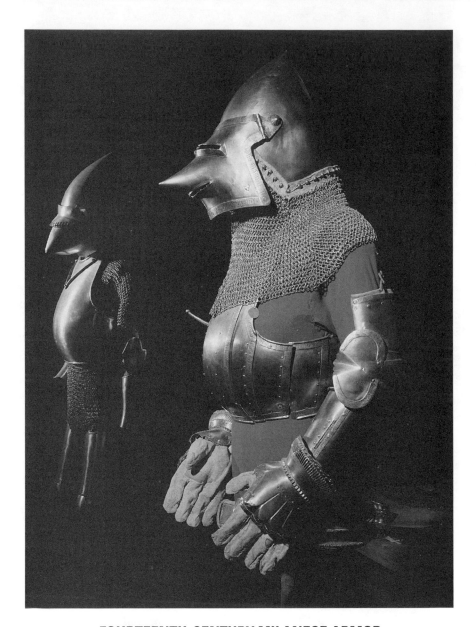

FOURTEENTH-CENTURY MILANESE ARMOR
Erich Lessing/Art Resource

This very rare early armor was made for a member of the Matsch family and dates from around 1390. The breastplate is, unusually, made from small plates and is very rounded, while the armor for the arms is of simple shape. All the pieces of armor are edged with a copper alloy border. The helmet, a bascinet, is complete with its visor and aventail, which is attached to the helmet by means of *vervelles*.

ARMOR FOR MAN AND HORSE, CA. 1480
Royal Armouries II.3 and VI.379 — Trustees of the Royal Armouries

This complete armor for man and horse is composed of pieces made by different armorers working in south Germany in the late fifteenth century. It shows just what the fully armored knight was wearing at the time armor had reached the very peak of its development. He is wearing a sallet and is completely encased in plate from head to foot—a veritable "knight in shining armor." His horse is also armored in a plate shaffron and barding.

GREAT HELM CA. 1350–1375

Royal Armouries IV.600 — Trustees of the Royal Armouries

This extremely rare great helm—only two others are known to survive—was possibly made in England. This type of helmet was very popular on the battlefield until the end of the fourteenth century but was then often used for jousting after that. The cross-shaped holes at the lower edge of the helmet were for the attachment of a toggle-ended chain by which the helmet was secured to the breastplate. The edges of the sight, formed between the edges of two of the plates, are turned out to present a glancing surface to turn blows away from the eyes.

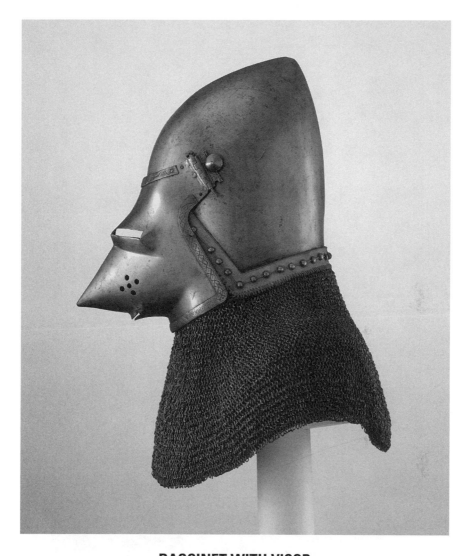

BASCINET WITH VISOR
Royal Armouries IV.470 — Trustees of the Royal Armouries

This very fine bascinet with visor and mail aventail was made in north Italy between 1380 and 1400 and is very characteristic of the period. The visor is nicely hinged and could be open during conflict to aid breathing or communication. The engraved copper-alloy border around the visor is a rare survival. The aventail is secured to the lower edge of the helmet by means of a leather strip that fits over pegs, *vervelles*, through which a cord is threaded.

THE ALTARPIECE OF ST. VINCENT OF SARAGOSSA
Giraudon/Art Resource

The two figures on either side of St. Vincent of Saragossa are wearing brigandines, as shown by the pattern of rivets covering the rich fabric. The brigandines open at the front and are secured together by laces and points. The figure to the left is also wearing mail at the lower waist and shoulders as well as plate armor on his thighs, knees, and elbows. The altarpiece of which this is a detail was painted by Nuno Goncalves or Gonzalvez ca. 1495 and is now in the National Museum of Ancient Art, Lisbon, Portugal.

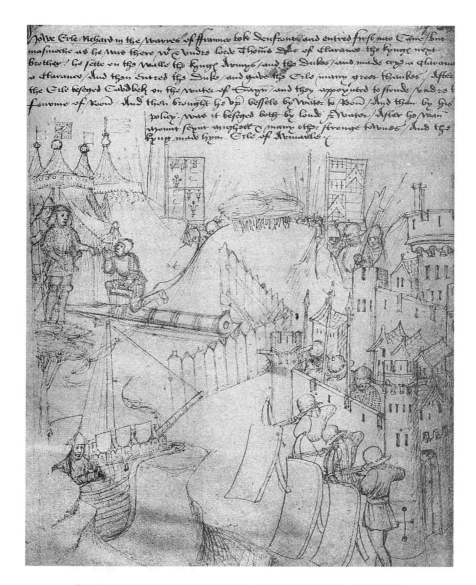

SIEGE OF ROUEN FROM THE BEAUCHAMP PSALTER
British Library, Cotton MS Julius E IV, f. 19/The Art Archive

This scene from the pageant of the life of Richard Beauchamp, Earl of Warwick (1389–1439), produced in about 1485, shows the siege of Caen in 1418. At the bottom right three crossbowmen, only wearing sallets and no other armor, are shooting from behind the protection of large shields, pavises, propped up on a single leg. The ship at the bottom left is armed with artillery, and the walls of the city are being bombarded by a large breech-loading cannon. The soldier behind the cannon is holding the powder chamber in his left hand.

FEDERIGO DA MONTEFELTRO
The Bridgeman Art Library

This 1472 portrait of Federigo da Montefel-tro, Duke of Urbino, shows him wearing a superb up-to-the-minute Italian armor that covers him from head to foot. His helmet and gauntlets are on the floor in front of him. A fringe of mail with a brass border can be seen below his armor. His sword is hung from his waist by an elaborate set of straps, which ensured that it was held in such a way that it could be easily drawn with his right hand. This famous painting, by Piero della Francesca, is a detail from the Brera Altarpiece and is now in the Pina-coteca di Brera, Milan, Italy.

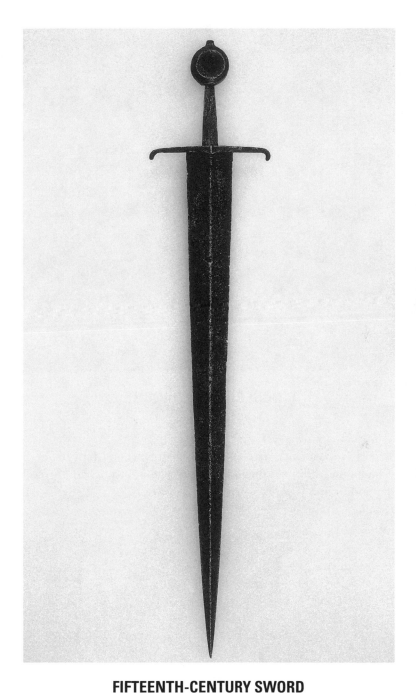

FIFTEENTH-CENTURY SWORD

Trustees of the Armouries/Heritage-Images/The Image Works

This is a very characteristic "knightly" sword of about 1400. The double-edged blade is wide at the hilt and tapers sharply to the point, making it a good weapon for both stabbing and slashing. The hilt is very simple, consisting of a simple disc pommel and cross guard. Royal Armouries, IX.3683.

CINQUEDEA AND BARBUT
Scala/Art Resource

On the right is a cinquedea with its characteristic wide blade and hilt. The helmet is a type called a barbut and is very characteristic of the Italian armorers. Both date from the second half of the fifteenth century and are from the Museo Poldi Pezzoli, Milan, Italy.

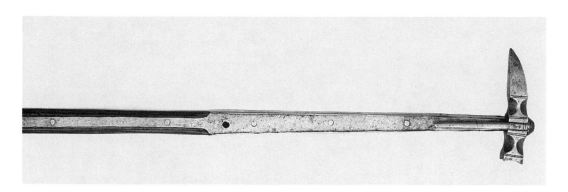

WAR HAMMER
Trustees of the Royal Armouries

A war hammer of the late fifteenth century of a type used extensively by mounted knights as a secondary weapon. Shaped rather like a hammer, one side is a simple "hammer head" while the other is longer and pointed for greater effectiveness as a piercing weapon. War hammers were often attached to the wrist by a leather strap fastened to the end of the handle, leaving the hand free until the hammer was needed.

FIFTEENTH-CENTURY LONGBOWS
British Library, Royal 16 G. VIII, f. 189 /HIP/The Image Works

Two armies face each other in battle from a Flemish manuscript of Caesar's Histories (ca. 1473). The front lines consist of archers armed with longbows. All are wearing complete plate armor with visored sallets and cloth-covered upper breastplates. Just behind the archers are the cavalry, mounted on unarmored horses, with couched lances. They are wearing armor similar to that of the archers, but they are also wearing great bascinets and wooden shields are protecting their left shoulders. Behind the cavalry, to the left, the massed infantry are wearing armor and are armed with polearms. To the far left one soldier has a handgun to his shoulder.

THE EARLY CANNON OF THE SECRETIS SECRETORUM
British Library Add. MS 47680, f. 44v

This is one of the earliest depictions of cannon, from 1326–1327, and it shows a large vaselike barrel lying on a table. The cannon is loaded with an arrow projectile, which was common throughout the fourteenth century. One of the four soldiers at the left is firing the gun, while all appear to be shielding their faces from the blast.

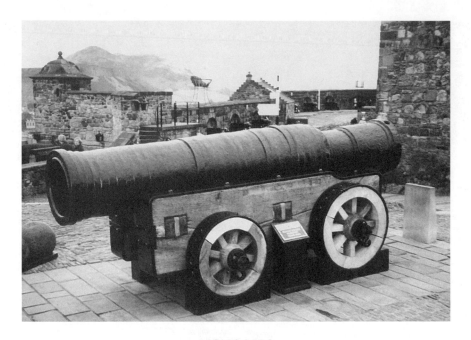

MONS MEG
Courtesy Robert D. Smith

This justifiably famous cannon, known as Mons Meg, was made in 1449 for Philip the Good, Duke of Burgundy, in the workshop of Jehan Cambier, a well-known arms maker and dealer in Mons, now in present-day Belgium. It is made from long staves of iron bound with iron rings in much the same way wooden barrels are still made. Of a type called a bombard, it fired a stone ball of about 285 pounds (130 kg) and was used in sieges to break down and shatter walls. These huge guns were used from the first decades of the fifteenth century but from about 1475 were replaced by smaller cast bronze cannon firing iron cannon balls.

KUMLA FRESCO DEPICTING LATE MEDIEVAL WEAPONRY
Courtesy Robert D. Smith

Handguns were used from the very early days of gunpowder in the fourteenth century. This fresco, dating from the end of the fifteenth century, in the Kumla Church in Sweden, shows that handguns were used alongside all the other projectile weapons, especially the longbow. The handgunner on the left is, unlike the other soldiers, not wearing any armor. His weapon is a simple iron tube with a long extension at the rear which serves as the "handle."

OTTOMAN JANISSARY
Alinari Archives/The Image Works

This very fine pen drawing was produced in about 1479–1481 by the Venetian artist Gentile Bellini, who worked at the Ottoman court in Istanbul. The figure wears the characteristic tall hat of the janissaries, the crack troops of the Ottoman army. His sword has the characteristic curved hilt with a simple cross guard. At his left waist is his recurved bow, and his quiver of arrows hangs to his right.

GLOSSARY

Ailettes: Rectangular plates, probably made from *cuir boulli*, attached to the shoulders of a knight and projecting upwards, bearing his arms or other identifying features.

Aketon: Padded undergarment worn beneath the hauberk.

Almain Collar: Plate armor for the top of the shoulders and neck which when joined together added protection to that area of the body.

Angon: An early medieval light spear or javelin generally thrown at an opponent before closing in for an attack.

Antenna-Pommel: A dagger pommel which curved away from the grip.

Armet: Type of helmet with large cheek-pieces attached by hinges to the lower edge of the bowl of the helmet that met under the chin.

Arrow: Wooden shaft with an iron head on one end and a flight (feathers) on the other to be shot from a bow.

Aventail: Mail defense attached to the lower edge of a helmet, usually a bascinet, draping over the shoulders.

Axe: A weapon with a thick iron head—one edge of which was sharpened—attached to a wooden shaft. It could have a long shaft with a large triangular-shaped head or it could be small with a short head. Some types of smaller-shafted axes were meant to be thrown while others, both long and short, were used in one or two hands as a close combat weapon.

Backplate: Armor defense for the back. Almost always used with a breastplate.

Ballista: An ancient torsion catapult used by both Greeks and Romans which used tightly wound springs made of sinew and rope to anchor bow staves. They fired either large bolts or stone balls from a thick string stretched between the two staves and drawn back by a winched tiller.

Ballock Dagger: Type of short dagger, usually with a blade of triangular section. At the lower part of the handle were two lobes from which the dagger derives its phallic name.

Bard: Complete horse armor.

Bascinet: Type of helmet introduced around 1300 consisting of a conical bowl often raised to a peak on the top of the head. During the following three centuries several types of bascinet developed, differing slightly in shape but all open faced, although usually fitted with a movable and removable visor.

Baselard: Type of dagger very common from 1350 until the late fifteenth century. Their hilts have a very characteristic form with cross pieces at both the guard and pommel ends, giving it the shape of an "H" or a capital "I" on its side. These cross pieces can be of equal length and quite small, but the typical baselard has a cross piece at the guard slightly longer than that at the pommel.

Besagew: Small circular plate of iron attached to the front of armor which hung down and protected the armpit.

Bevor: Part of a helmet which protected the lower face. It could be attached to the helmet bowl or separated from the helmet itself and attached to it with a leather strap and buckle.

Bill: Type of polearm commonly used throughout Europe during the later medieval period. Although there were considerable variations in its form, it generally consisted of a forward-facing hook with one or more spikes projecting from the rear and/or front. However, other, more complex types were developed, for example, the *Welsh bill* and the *roncone*.

Bodkin: Type of arrowhead which was long and very small in cross section similar to a bodkin needle.

Bolt: Short, thick arrow fired by a crossbow or ballista.

Bombard: Type of cannon which, although somewhat undefined in the early period, came to denote a cannon of very large size that fired a stone ball.

Boss: Circular, bulbous element fixed to the front of a shield which was often attached through the shield to the grip. They were usually made of iron.

Bow: Used to fire arrows—consisting of a springy, elastic shaft to the ends of which a string was attached. The commonest types were the longbow and the composite bow.

Bracer: A defense to protect the inner arm from the string when shooting a bow. Bracers could be made of a variety of material including leather, bone, or *cuir boulli*.

Brazil Nut Pommel: The pommel of a sword which in shape resembled the outer shape of a brazil nut.

Breastplate: Armor to protect the front of the chest. Usually, though not always, worn with a backplate, the two together called the cuirass.

Brigandine: Armor for the upper body consisting of overlapping small iron plates—usually with a protective coating of tin—riveted to the inside of a fabric jacket.

Buckler: A type of small round shield held in the left hand and used especially when fighting with the sword.

Buffe: A separate defense for the face usually worn with a burgonet.

Buffet: Large semicircular padded cushion fitted across the front of the horse and worn with a shaffron and full caparison.

Burgonet: Type of open-faced helmet similar to the close helmet, but, instead of a visor covering the face, left the front open. A small peak above the eyes jutted forward adding protection for them, and hinged cheekpieces, tied together with a cord beneath the chin, protected the sides of the face. A burgonet could also be worn with a buffe for extra protection for the face.

Butted Rings: Rings to form mail armor where the ends of the rings were not connected one to another but were simply butted up close and not joined.

Byrnie: Mail armor worn by Carolingian soldiers that extended from the neck to the thighs or knees. It was worn fairly loose with short sleeves reaching to the mid-arm or elbow.

Cannon (*canon* in French): Gunpowder weapons larger than those which could be held in the hands. Cannons ranged from small pieces firing shot of 8 ounces to extremely large artillery pieces firing stones weighing 300 or more pounds.

Caparison: A large flowing cloth covering the horse which, especially later in the Middle Ages, was emblazoned with the rider's colors or arms.

Carolingian Helmet: Helmet open on the face and cheeks worn by continental European soldiers between the eighth and tenth centuries. It had a fairly shallow skull fitted closely to the head and flared out just above the level of ears to form a brim, narrow at the sides but more pronounced over the back of the head to protect the neck, and turned slightly upward at the front.

Catapult: Generic name for projectile-firing siege machines, which included ballistae, *onagers*, and trebuchets.

Cervelliére: A simple conical helmet of more rounded form than the earlier nasal helmet. The *cervelliére* became common by about 1300.

Chape: A protective covering, usually made from metal, for the tip of a scabbard to keep the point of a sword or dagger from piercing it.

Chausses: Mail defenses for the legs.

Cheiroballistra: smaller, more portable version of the ancient Greek or Roman ballista.

Cinquedea: A type of dagger (literally "five fingers") with a very broad flat blade, tapering evenly from the hilt to the point, with either a strong medial ridge or fluting to add strength to the blade.

Close Helmet: The quintessential knight's head protection of the sixteenth century. It consists of a bowl covering the top of the head, but extended down round the back of the head and neck. The visor, usually formed of three separate plates, was hinged at the sides and could be lifted when needed. Slots for sighting and breathing were provided.

Club: Any form of hafted weapon with a heavy head which can be used to hit an opponent; usually a weapon of the poorer class of soldier.

Coat of Plates: A textile or leather coat developed by the late thirteenth century to the inside of which small iron plates were attached. Its exact form and construction is not always clear in artistic representations as it is often hidden by the surcoat which was worn over it.

Coif: Mail armor worn over the head.

Composite Bow: A type of bow made from horn, bone, and sinew which utilized the different properties of each to produce a very springy and strong bow stave.

Corselet: A term used, mainly after 1500, for armor worn by the infantry and the light cavalry consisting of a collar, breastplate, backplate, tassets, vambraces, and gauntlets with an open helmet, usually a burgonet.

Couched Lance: The method of holding the lance on horseback in which the lance was held in the hand and the rear was tucked underneath the arm. It was used by the cavalry to add the impetus of both the horse and its rider to deliver a shock blow to the enemy.

Coulverine (*Culverin*)**:** During the fifteenth century a type of handgun. Later, from the early sixteenth century, the English translation of the name, *culverin*, identified a cannon firing an 18-pound shot.

Counterweight Trebuchet: A catapult similar in design to the traction trebuchet but with a substitution for the pulling ropes of a fixed counterweight, usually a box filled with stones, sand, or some other heavy body, which provided the power to discharge the projectile.

Couter: Armor defense for the elbow.

Cranequin: A loading device working on the rack and pinion principle used for drawing the string back on a very powerful steel crossbow.

Crapadeaux: A small cannon popular in fifteenth-century France and Burgundy.

Crest: A family emblem often molded in three dimensions and worn atop the helmet as a means of identification.

Crinet: Armor for the horses' heads.

Cross Guard: The bar crossing the lower end of the hilt of a sword which prevents an opponent's sword sliding up one's blade onto the hand.

Crossbow: The crossbow was a mechanical bow basically constructed as a small bow attached to a stock which provided a groove for the bolt and handle. The bowstring was held in place on the handle ready for release by a trigger mechanism. Probably descended from the ancient Greek *gastraphretes* (or "belly-bow"), the crossbow was popular in western Europe from the eleventh century until the end of the Middle Ages.

Crupper: Plate defense for the rear of a horse.

Cudgel: See *Club*.

Cuir Boulli: Leather which has been softened and molded into shape.

Cuirass: The breastplate and backplate together.

Dagger: A bladed weapon shorter than a sword and usually wielded in the left hand meant for stabbing in very close fighting.

Damascus or Damascene Blade: A sword blade made from pieces of iron expertly welded together so that the final product appears to have a watered effect. It is not known whether the word "damascene" derived from the location "Damascus" or vice versa.

Disc Pommel: A form of sword or dagger pommel in the shape of a disc or wheel.

Eared Dagger: A highly decorated dagger characterized by a disc-shaped guard and two discs at the pommel like ears.

Etching: A form of decoration usually in iron or steel. The surface was first covered in a resistant layer with the required pattern scratched into the surface. The piece was then put into an acid or etchant bath with the unprotected areas eaten away revealing the pattern on the surface.

Falchion: A short sword with a very broad, curved, single-edged blade, shaped similar to a modern machete.

Fauld: A separate plate, or sometimes two or three plates, riveted to the lower edge of the breastplate or plackart, sometimes called a skirt.

Flanchard: Armor for the side of a horse.

Flanged Head: Mace head with sharpened or dulled flanges wrapped around it.

Framea: Early Germanic spear with a short and narrow blade that could be thrown or wielded in close combat.

Francisca: Early medieval axe especially favored by the Franks that was primarily used as a missile weapon.

Gadling: A small decoration attached to the knuckle plate of a gauntlet, the most famous being the leopards on the gauntlets belonging to Edward the Black Prince.

Gambeson: Trying to pin down just what a gambeson was is confusing as both it and the term *aketon* seem to have been used indiscriminately for garments worn both over and under the hauberk. However, it is likely that it refers to a garment worn over the mail shirt, rather like the surcoat.

Gamboised Cuisses: Padded thigh defenses, which start to appear in the later thirteenth century.

Garniture: A suit of armor supplied with additional plates, over 60 in very elaborate garnitures, which could be added or exchanged with other pieces of armor for different types of warfare and martial games, i.e., various forms of tournament, foot combat, fighting on horseback.

Garros: See *Bolt.*

Gastraphretes: Ancient Greek "belly-bow" that probably inspired the medieval crossbow.

Gauntlet: Plate armor to protect the hand that became popular after the end of the thirteenth century.

Gilding: Decorating the surface of a weapon or armor with gold.

Gladius: Roman short sword with a blade made of iron and a grip of bronze-covered wood, bone, or ivory.

Glaive: A type of polearm, the long blade of which had a convex front edge and a straight back.

Goats-Foot Lever: A simple mechanical device for spanning (drawing back the string) of a crossbow, consisting of two interlocking frames pivoted about their ends.

Goedendag: A simple polearm favored by the urban militias of the southern Low Countries during the fourteenth century which was basically a heavy-headed club to which iron spikes were attached.

Gorget: Plate armor to protect the neck and chin.

Great Bascinet: A form of bascinet, fitted with plates resembling the aventail, and used primarily for jousting.

Great Crossbow: A large mounted crossbow used as a siege engine or as a defense against sieges.

Great Helm: A type of helmet of fairly simple cylindrical shape with a flat top and sight and breathing holes cut into the front. It was worn over the mail coif and an arming cap, although it had its own padded lining and a chin strap.

Greave: Plate armor to protect the lower legs.

Greek Fire: An enigmatic material, the discovery of which in the early eighth century has always been attributed to a Greek named Kalinikos. The Byzantine Greek fire is now suggested to have been a low-boiling-point distillate of a natural deposit similar to modern gasoline, although its exact composition is obscure. The early users of the weapon forced the fluid under pressure out of a simple pump device over an open flame igniting it—rather like a modern flamethrower. Later on, in the twelfth century, another material named Greek fire began to be used by Muslim forces in the crusades. This was not the liquid of the Byzantines but a mixture of flammable materials such as tar-like substances, gums, and resins mixed with sulfur and other chemicals. It was packed in ceramic pots or small wooden containers and either thrown by hand or from a trebuchet.

Grip: The part of the sword or dagger which is actually "gripped" by the hand.

Guard: The bars that make up the grip of a sword. It can consist of as little as a single curved bar round the hand to a complex of many bars, almost forming a cage, as on many later rapiers.

Guisarme: A type of polearm with an extremely long, axe-shaped head.

Gunpowder: A mixture of sulfur, charcoal, and saltpeter which, when confined in a barrel, explodes. It is a complex material which was used in many ways, for rockets and fireworks, as an incendiary, as well as in cannon and firearms, to propel projectiles.

Halberd: A type of staff weapon combining the spear with the long, two-handed axe. At first it consisted of a fairly broad blade with a spike projecting from the top secured to the end of a long pole—around 6 feet (2 meters) in length. During the fifteenth century, an extra spike was added to the axe portion of the head making it an even more formidable weapon.

Hammer: A weapon consisting of a short handle, made of wood or steel, with a head like a hammer.

Handgun: A gunpowder weapon which could be carried and used in the hands, usually consisting of a barrel set into a wooden stock. In the medieval period the arquebus was the common type, fired by means of a handheld match, but later locks were developed as the trigger mechanism: snaplock, snaphaunce, flintlock, etc.

Haubergeon: A hauberk shortened at the sides that became popular after 1250.

Hauberk: A mail shirt which covered the torso and arms extending to just above the elbow.

Heater Shield: A smaller triangular-shaped shield that replaced the kite shield in the thirteenth century.

Helmets: The armor to cover and protect the head. Helmets came in many forms: the kettle hat, bascinet, burgonet, close helmet, great helm, etc.

Heraldry: Essentially used as an identifier for groups of medieval soldiers, it eventually came to indicate the family of the nobles leading these forces. Heraldry appeared on shields, surcoats, gambesons, and banners.

Hilt: The part of the sword which is grasped in the hand.

Inlay: The filling of etchings in blades, hilts, and scabbards with precious metals—gold, silver, and bronze—as a means of decoration.

Jack: A type of body armor consisting of small rectangular iron plates, slightly larger than an inch square with a hole in their center, which were laced between two layers of fabric with string, giving them a characteristic quilted appearance.

Javelin: A type of spear, around 6–9 feet (2–3 meters) long with a small leaf-shaped head, intended to be thrown at an opponent.

Kettle Hat: A type of helmet formed by a close-fitting bowl with a wide, flat brim.

Kite Shield or **Kite-Shaped Shield:** A long shield, extending from the waist to the knees and shaped like a triangular kite. It was usually curved across its width to fit the body and was held by a leather strap at the back.

Klappvisier: A type of visor for the bascinet, which, at first, was rounded and pivoted at the sides of the skull although, later, was attached to the center of the face opening.

Lamellar Armor: See *Scale Armor.*

Lance: A long spear used by the cavalry. It was usually couched, held under the arm to carry the impetus of both man and horse into a target, and as such struck enemy forces as a shock weapon.

Lance Rest: A short projection on the right side of a breastplate from which the knight could more easily manipulate his lance.

Leaf-shaped Blade: A blade shaped like a leaf—wide in the center and tapering both back and front.

Longbow: A type of bow made from a single piece of wood carefully selected to be springy and resilient. Usually about 2 meters long and used especially by English and Welsh archers, becoming one of the most important weapons of the Hundred Years War.

Longsword: A sword especially favored by early medieval barbarian soldiers usually of simple broad shape. These swords could be single or double edged with a rounded point made for slashing and cutting rather than thrusting.

Lorica Hamata: Roman armor constructed of metal rings, as many as 35,000 to 40,000, which had been either punched out of sheet metal or made of wire.

Lorica Segmentata: The most popular Roman armor, it was a cuirass made of six or seven thick horizontal bronze strips attached by hooks and buckles onto a leather undergarment to cover the lower chest and stomach area to below the waist. The shoulders were covered with several curved strips of bronze secured to a pair of front and back metal plates attached to two sets of horizontal strips protecting the lower part of the body.

Lorica Squamata: Roman scale armor made of a large number of metallic pieces, measuring about 0.6 inches (1.5 centimeters) long and 0.5 inches (1.3 centimeters) wide, attached to each other by leather laces and affixed to a linen undergarment by linen thread.

Mail Armor: Armor made from small rings of iron joined together in a way so that each ring is linked through four others. The rings were made either by forming wire into rings and riveting their ends together or by punching out rings from solid metal. To make a piece of armor many thousands of rings were needed, and shaping was achieved by increasing or decreasing the numbers of rows, rather like in knitting.

Mail and Plate Armor: A type of armor, used exclusively in the East, produced by joining small iron or steel plates together using rows of rings.

Mangonel or Manganum: A rotating beam siege engine used by the Merovingian Franks to defend Paris by throwing huge stones against the Vikings, similar to the later medieval trebuchet.

Morion: A late form of kettle hat with a tall skull and a narrow brim usually fitted with cheek-pieces which were tied together under the chin.

Muffler: The extension of the sleeves of the mail shirt to cover the backs of the hands, forming so-called mufflers, a fashion which lasted until the early years of the fourteenth century.

Nasal: An extension from the front center of a helmet to cover the nose which was especially common in the eleventh and twelfth centuries.

Onager: A Roman catapult which used a single horizontal spring and one arm swinging upward. At the end of the single arm was a sling in which a missile, usually a stone ball, was placed for launching. The trigger was a piece of rope used to anchor the arm ready for loading which was mounted on two large and heavy horizontal beams.

Partisan: A later type of staff weapon, used throughout Europe from about 1500, with a long, flat blade tapering to a point, rather like an elongated spear.

Pattern-Welding: A means of making swords by building up the blade of a weapon from many smaller pieces of iron which were then welded together, twisted and worked in such a way that the resultant surface of the blade exhibited a discernible and visible pattern akin to waves or ripples or somewhat like woven patterns, especially herringbone work.

Pauldron: Plate armor to cover the shoulders.

Pavise: Large roughly rectangular shields of varying sizes developed in the thirteenth century and used mainly to protect crossbowmen, archers, and handgunners. When set on the ground, often in long rows, archers could either shoot from behind them or use them as a protection between shots.

Perrière: See *Traction Trebuchet.*

Petrobole: An Avero-Slavic catapult, literally meaning "rock thrower," possibly indicating that it was a traction trebuchet.

Peytral: Armor covering the front of the horse.

Pig-Faced Bascinet: A tall form of the bascinet with a point at the rear and a visor pivoted at the sides which became very popular throughout Europe from about 1380. Although called a pig-faced bascinet by modern scholars, the term *visored bascinet* was common at the time.

Pike: A type of very long spear, around 16 feet (5 meters) long with a small iron head used by the infantry, typically in large organized formations.

Pilum: A heavy spear used both for thrusting and for throwing. *Pila* had a leaf-shaped iron head, 2–3 feet (60–90 centimeters) long, embedded in or socketed onto a wooden shaft with a short iron spike at the rear.

Plackart: A breastplate for the lower torso used especially by the Italian armorers of the fifteenth century, who specialized in making it from two plates, placed one on top of the other. It was often fitted with a skirt, or fauld.

Plate Armor: A term to differentiate mail armor from that made from large plates of iron or steel.

Polearm: A general name for a weapon in which an iron or steel head was attached to the end of a long wooden pole or shaft. Used by the infantry, polearms took many forms over the medieval period.

Poleyns: Plate armor to protect the knees.

Poll Plate: Plate armor to protect the top of a horse's head and usually attached to the crinet or neck defense.

Pollaxe: A type of staff weapon, usually about 5 feet long, consisting of a wooden shaft, often reinforced with iron bands, to the end of which is attached an iron or steel head in the shape of a hammerhead often with one side rectangular while the other is pointed. Used for fighting on foot, especially in the tournament called the "foot combat."

Pommel. The button at the top of the sword which secures the hilt to the blade and which also prevents the hand from sliding off the grip. It can take many forms, for example the brazil nut and disc.

Pourpoint: A type of quilted textile defense which began to be worn in the second half of the twelfth century, although its exact purpose and use are somewhat difficult to ascertain.

Quarrel: The "arrow" fired by a crossbow. It was shorter and thicker than the arrow shot by a bow.

Quillon: Another term for the cross guard, the transverse bar at the top of a sword or dagger blade.

Quillon Dagger: A type of dagger with quillons which first developed around the middle of the thirteenth century. Later versions had guards resembling the quillons of swords, and indeed most often look like smaller versions of contemporary swords.

Recurved Bow: See *Composite Bow*.

Riveted Rings: See *Mail Armor*.

Roncone: A type of bill, developed in Italy, which had a long straight blade ending in a smaller curved hook with both top and backward-facing spikes.

Rondel Dagger: A type of dagger, introduced around 1300 and in widespread use all over western Europe from the middle of the fourteenth century which was most often slender and elegant in form. Its name was derived from the discs of either wood or metal at either end of the grip.

Sabaton: Plate armor for the foot.

Saddle: The seat, secured to the back of a horse, on which the rider sits.

Sallet: A type of helmet developed early in the fifteenth century that closely fitted to the front of the head and formed into a long "tail" at the rear which covered the neck. The front was cut out around the face and closed with a visor fastened to the sides of the helmet skull which could be lifted to provide extra ventilation. A slit between the top of the visor and the helmet bowl provided vision when the visor was down.

Scabbard: A protective sheath for the sword usually made from leather, or wood, or wood covered in leather. Its tip was protected by the chape.

Scale Armor: Armor made of a large number of metallic scales attached to each other by laces and affixed to an undergarment.

Scutum: A large oblong shield, favored by the Romans, that was constructed from layers of wood, usually three, glued together. Each layer was made of strips, with the outer pieces laid horizontally and the inner piece laid vertically, and the whole covered in canvas and calf hide. A long wooden boss ran the entire length of the shield and anchored the hold on the inside.

Seax or **Scramasax:** A light, short, single-edged sword favored by barbarian soldiers in the early Middle Ages.

Shaffron: Armor covering the front of the horse's head which could be used on its own or attached to a poll plate and a crinet.

Shield: A defense held in the left hand to protect the body when fighting. It was usually made from wood, covered in leather, and sometimes reinforced with iron bands. Shields ranged from the small buckler used in sword fighting to the large kite-shaped shields of the eleventh and twelfth centuries to the very large pavises of the thirteenth to fifteenth centuries.

Skull-plate or **Skull Cap:** A simple helmet covering just the top of the head.

Sling: A missile weapon consisting of a length of string with a wide pouch in the center. The two ends were held in one hand and the sling, with a shot in the pouch, was twirled around the head and released. Although stones were the main ammunition, slings also threw firepots and other incendiaries.

Solid Rings: See *Mail Armor*.

Spangenhelm: A type of helmet consisting of a wide band encircling the head to which two narrow bands were attached—one from front to back, the other from side to side. The resulting triangular-shaped spaces were then filled with metal or horn. A nasal extended down from the front of the encircling band to cover the nose.

Spatha: A long and thick Roman sword that was primarily used by cavalry.

Spaudler: Plate armor to cover just the tops of the shoulders which was much simpler and smaller than a pauldron.

Spear: Perhaps the most widely used weapon in the pre-modern world, the spear was a rod of wood with a sharpened head, made of metal during the Middle Ages. It could be shorter and lighter—a javelin—or longer and heavier—a lance or pike—all of which could be thrust or thrown.

Springald: Although it is uncertain what type of catapult this was before the thirteenth century, in the later Middle Ages it became a type of great crossbow where the bow was made in two halves attached to either side of a wooden frame by means of a twisted and tensioned skein of horse hair, a string attached to the outer ends of the two bows.

Staff Weapon: See *Polearm*.

Stirrup: A device attached to a leather strap and hanging down on each side of a horse's saddle where a rider can place his feet. The stirrup made a couched lance and mounted shock combat possible.

Stop-Rib: A bar of iron riveted to the breastplate just below the neck which acted as a stop if the wearer was hit by a weapon. These were common on armor until about 1450.

Subarmalis: A Roman garment worn under armor.

Surcoat: A long textile garment worn over armor from the middle of the twelfth century and often carrying the heraldry of the wearer's leader.

Sword: A weapon consisting of an iron or steel blade with either one or both sides sharpened. The hilt was fitted over an extension of the blade, the tang, and the whole fastened together with the pommel.

Tang: See *Sword*.

Tasset: Plate armor to protect the tops of the legs and usually attached to the lower edge of the breastplate.

Thoracomachus: A Roman garment worn under armor.

Torsion Catapult: See *Ballista*.

Traction Trebuchet: A medieval catapult consisting of an arm set unequally on two upright supports, to the shorter end of which was secured many lengths of rope with the other end containing a sling for the projectile. When the ropes were pulled down, the arm swung about its pivot, launching the projectile.

Trapper: Armor to protect the horse, covering it from the head down to the knees, and made either from mail or from plates.

Turkish Bow: See *Composite Bow*.

Vambrace: Plate armor protecting the arm.

Vamplate: A disc of iron attached to the rear of the lance which protected the hand.

Vervelles: Small iron pegs with transverse holes attached to the lower edge of a bascinet and over which the aventail was secured to the helmet.

Veuglaire: A name for a medium-sized type of cannon, used especially in France, Burgundy, and the Holy Roman Empire.

Visor: The part of a helmet covering the face which was usually movable, so that when not needed it could be pushed up out of the way, allowing the wearer to breathe and communicate more easily.

Visored Bascinet: A type of bascinet with a visor.

Welsh Bill: A type of bill with a long slender curved blade and a right-angle spike.

Windlass: A device for pulling back the string of a crossbow using a system of pulleys to enable the shooter to pull the string of a more powerful bow back to the firing position.

BIBLIOGRAPHY

GENERAL

Military History

Bachrach, David S. *Religion and the Conduct of War, c.300-c.1215*. Woodbridge, UK: The Boydell Press, 2003.

Barber, Richard. *The Knight and Chivalry*. 2nd ed. Woodbridge, UK: The Boydell Press, 1975.

Bennett, Matthew, Jim Bradbury, Kelly DeVries, Iain Dickie, and Phyllis Jestice. *Fighting Techniques of the Medieval World: Equipment, Combat Skills, and Tactics*. New York: Thomas Dunne Books, 2005.

Bradbury, Jim. *The Medieval Siege*. Woodbridge, UK: The Boydell Press, 1992.

Contamine, Philippe. *War in the Middle Ages*. Translated by M. Jones. Oxford: Basil Blackwell, 1984.

DeVries, Kelly. *A Cumulative Bibliography of Medieval Military History and Technology*. Leiden, The Netherlands: Brill, 2002; *Update*. Leiden, The Netherlands: Brill, 2005.

DeVries, Kelly. *Medieval Military Technology*. Peterborough, UK: Broadview Press, 1992.

DeVries, Kelly, Martin Dougherty, Iain Dickie, Phyllis G. Jestice, and Christer Jorgensen. *Battles of the Medieval World, 1000–1500: From Hastings to Constantinople*. New York: Barnes and Noble Books, 2006.

Haldon, John. *Warfare, State and Society in the Byzantine World, 565–1204*. London: UCL Press, 1999.

Hooper, Nicholas, and Matthew Bennett. *The Cambridge Illustrated Atlas of Warfare: The Middle Ages*. Cambridge: Cambridge University Press, 1996.

Keen, Maurice. *Chivalry*. New Haven, CT: Yale University Press, 1984.

Lot, Ferdinand. *L'art militaire et les armées au moyen-âge en Europe et dans le proche orient*. 2 vols. Paris: Payot, 1946.

Nicholson, Helen. *Medieval Warfare: Theory and Practice of War in Europe, 300–1500*. Houndmills, UK: Palgrave Macmillan, 2004.

Nicolle, David. *Medieval Warfare Source Book*. Vol. 1, *Warfare in Western Christendom*. Vol. 2, *Christian Europe and its Neighbors*. London: Brockhampton Press, 1995–1996.

Oman, Sir Charles W. C. *A History of the Art of War in the Middle Ages*. 2 vols. London: Methuen, 1924. Reprint, London: Greenhill Books, 1998.

Porter, Pamela. *Medieval Warfare in Manuscripts*. London: The British Library, 2000.

Prestwich, Michael. *Armies and Warfare in the Middle Ages: The English Experience*. New Haven, CT: Yale University Press, 1996.

Verbruggen J. F. *The Art of Warfare in Western Europe During the Middle Ages from the Eighth Century to 1340*. 2nd ed. Translated by S. Willard and R. W. Southern. Woodbridge, UK: The Boydell Press, 1997.

Arms and Armor

Alm, Josef. *European Crossbows: A Survey*. Translated by H. Bartlett Wells. Edited by G. M. Wilson. London: Trustees of the Royal Armouries, 1994.

Blair, Claude. *European Armour: circa 1066 to circa 1700*. London: B. T. Batsford, 1958.

Bradbury, Jim. *The Medieval Archer*. New York: St. Martin's Press, 1985.

Clark, John, ed. *The Medieval Horse and Its Equipment, c.1150–c.1450*. London: Her Majesty's Stationery Office, 1995.

Davis, R. H. C. *The Medieval Warhorse: Origin, Development and Redevelopment*. London: Thames and Hudson, 1989.

Dufty, A. R. *European Swords and Daggers in the Tower of London*. London: Her Majesty's Stationery Office, 1968.

Edge, David, and John Miles Paddock. *Arms and Armour of the Medieval Knight*. London: Saturn Books, 1996.

ffoulkes, Charles. *The Armourer and His Craft from the XIth to the XVth Century*. London: Methuen, 1912. Reprint, New York: Dover Publications, 1988.

Liebel, Jean. *Springalds and Great Crossbows*. Translated by Juliet Vale. Leeds, UK: Royal Armouries, 1998.

Mann, James. *European Arms and Armour*. 2 vols. London: Trustees of the Wallace Collection, 1962.

Norman, A. V. B. *The Medieval Soldier*. New York: Barnes and Noble Books, 1971.

Norman, A. V. B., and Don Pottinger. *English Weapons and Warfare, 449–1660*. Englewood Cliffs, NJ: Prentice-Hall, 1979.

Oakeshott, Ewart. *Records of the Medieval Sword*. Woodbridge, UK: Boydell Press, 1991.

Oakeshott, Ewart. *The Sword in the Age of Chivalry*. 1964. Reprint, Woodbridge, UK: The Boydell Press, 1994.

Peterson, Harold L. *Daggers and Fighting Knives of the Western World from the Stone Age till 1900*. London: Herbert Jenkins, 1968.

Reid, William. *The Lore of Arms: A Concise History of Weaponry*. New York: Facts on File Publications, 1976.

Strickland, Matthew, and Robert Hardy. *The Great Warbow: From Hastings to the* Mary Rose. Stroud, UK: Sutton Publishing, 2005.

Tarassuk, Leonid, and Claude Blair, eds. *The Complete Encyclopedia of Arms and Weapons*. New York: Bonanza Books, 1979.

Troso, Mario. *Le armi in asta: delle fanterie europee (1000–1500)*. Novara, Italy: Istituto Geographico de Agostini, 1988.

THE EARLY MIDDLE AGES

Military History

Bachrach, Bernard S. *The Anatomy of a Little War: A Diplomatic and Military History of the Gundovald Affair (568–586)*. Boulder, CO: Westview Press, 1994.

Bachrach, Bernard S. *Merovingian Military Organization, 481–751*. Minneapolis: University of Minnesota Press, 1972.

Collins, Roger. *The Arab Conquest of Spain, 710–797*. Oxford: Blackwell, 1989.

Elton, Hugh. *Warfare in Roman Europe, AD 350–425*. Oxford: Oxford University Press, 1996.

Ferrill, Arther. *The Fall of the Roman Empire: A Military Explanation*. London: Thames and Hudson, 1986.

Halsall, Guy. *Warfare and Society in the Barbarian West, 450–900*. Warfare and History. London: Routledge, 2003.

Heather, Peter. *The Fall of the Roman Empire: A New History of Rome and the Barbarians*. Oxford: Oxford University Press, 2006.

Ward-Perkins, Bryan. *The Fall of Rome and the End of Civilization*. Oxford: Oxford University Press, 2005.

Whitby, Michael. *Rome at War, AD 293–696*. Essential Histories. London: Osprey, 2002.

Arms and Armor

Bruce-Mitford, Rupert. *The Sutton-Hoo Ship-Burial*. Vol. 2, *Arms, Armour and Regalia*. London: British Museum Publications Ltd., 1978.

Davidson, Hilda Ellis. *The Sword in Anglo-Saxon England: Its Archaeology and Literature*. 1962. Reprint, Woodbridge, UK: The Boydell Press, 1994.

Dickinson, Tania, F. S. A. Härke, and Heinrich Härke. *Early Anglo-Saxon Shields*. London: The Society of Antiquaries of London, 1992.

Robinson, H. Russell. *The Armour of Imperial Rome*. London: Arms and Armour Press, 1975.

Siddorn, J. Kim. *Viking Weapons and Warfare*. Stroud, UK: Tempus Publishing, 2000.

Stephenson, I. P. *The Anglo-Saxon Shield*. Stroud, UK: Tempus Publishing, 2002.

Stephenson, I. P. *Roman Infantry Equipment: The Later Empire*. Stroud, UK: Tempus Publishing, 1999.

Swanton, M. J. *The Spearheads of the Anglo-Saxon Settlements*. London: The Royal Archaeological Institute, 1973.

Underwood, Richard. *Anglo-Saxon Weapons and Warfare*. Stroud, UK: Tempus Publishing, 1999.

THE CAROLINGIAN PERIOD

Military History

Bachrach, Bernard S. *Early Carolingian Warfare: Prelude to Empire*. Philadelphia: University of Pennsylvania Press, 2001.

Bowlus, Charles R. *The Battle of Lechfeld and its Aftermath, August 955: The End of the Age of Migrations in the Latin West*. Aldershot, UK: Ashgate, 2006.

Collins, Roger. *Charlemagne*. Toronto: University of Toronto Press, 1998.

Foote, Peter G., and David M. Wilson. *The Viking Achievement*. London: Sidgwick and Jackson, 1970.

Forte, Angelo, Richard Oram, and Frederick Pedersen. *Viking Empires*. Cambridge: Cambridge University Press, 2005.

Goldberg, Eric J. *Struggle for Empire: Kingship and Conflict Under Louis the German, 817–876*. Ithaca, NY: Cornell University Press, 2006.

Haywood, John. *The Penguin Atlas of the Vikings*. Harmondsworth, UK: Penguin, 1995.

Jones, Gwyn. *A History of the Vikings*. Oxford: Oxford University Press, 1968.

Sawyer, Peter. *Kings and Vikings: Scandinavia and Europe, AD 700–1100*. London: Methuen, 1982.

Sawyer, Peter, ed. *The Oxford History of the Vikings*. Oxford: Oxford University Press, 2001.

Arms and Armor

Coupland, Simon. "Carolingian Arms and Armor in the Ninth Century." *Viator* 21 (1990): 29–50.

Peirce, Ian. *Swords of the Viking Age.* Woodbridge, UK: The Boydell Press, 2002.

Tweddle, Dominic. *The Anglian Helmet from 16–22 Coppergate.* 2 vols. York, UK: York Archaeological Trust, 1992.

THE CRUSADES

Military History

Asbridge, Thomas. *The First Crusade: A New History.* Oxford: Oxford University Press, 2004.

Barber, Malcolm. *The New Knighthood: A History of the Order of the Temple.* Cambridge: Cambridge University Press, 1994.

Beeler, John. *Warfare in England, 1066–1189.* Ithaca, NY: Cornell University Press, 1966.

Bradbury, Jim. *The Battle of Hastings.* Stroud, UK: Sutton Publishing, 1998.

Bradbury, Jim. *Stephen and Mathilda: The Civil War of 1139–53.* Stroud, UK: Alan Sutton Publishing, 1996.

Christiansen, Eric. *The Northern Crusades.* 2nd ed. Harmondsworth, UK: Penguin Books, 1997.

Douglas, David C. *William the Conqueror.* Berkeley and Los Angeles: University of California Press, 1964.

Duby, Georges. *The Legend of Bouvines: War, Religion and Culture in the Middle Ages.* Translated by Catherine Tihanyi. Berkeley and Los Angeles: University of California Press, 1990.

France, John. *The Crusades and the Expansion of Catholic Christendom, 1000–1714.* London: Routledge, 2005.

France, John. *Victory in the East: A Military History of the First Crusade.* Cambridge: Cambridge University Press, 1994.

France, John. *Western Warfare in the Age of the Crusades, 1000–1300.* Ithaca, NY: Cornell University Press, 1999.

Gillingham, John. *Richard I.* New Haven, CT: Yale University Press, 1999.

Hillenbrand, Carole. *The Crusades: Islamic Perspectives.* New York: Routledge, 2000.

Holt, P. M. *The Age of the Crusades: The Near East from the Eleventh Century to 1517.* London: Longman, 1986.

Jordan, William Chester. *Louis IX and the Challenge of the Crusade: A Study in Rulership.* Princeton, NJ: Princeton University Press, 1979.

Loud, G. A. *The Age of Robert Guiscard: Southern Italy and the Norman Conquest.* Harlow, UK: Pearson Education, 2000.

Lyons, Malcolm Cameron, and D. E. P. Jackson. *Saladin: The Politics of the Holy War.* Cambridge: Cambridge University Press, 1982.

Madden, Thomas F. *A Concise History of the Crusades*. 2nd ed. Lanham, MD: Rowman and Littlefield, 2005.

Marshall, Christopher. *Warfare in the Latin East, 1192–1291*. Cambridge: Cambridge University Press, 1992.

Mayer, Hans Eberhard. *The Crusades*. Oxford: Oxford University Press, 1972.

Morillo, Stephen. *Warfare under the Anglo-Norman Kings, 1066–1135*. Woodbridge, UK: The Boydell Press, 1994.

Nicholson, Helen. *The Knights Hospitaller*. Woodbridge, UK: The Boydell Press, 2001.

O'Callaghan, Joseph F. *Reconquest and Crusade in Medieval Spain*. Philadelphia: University of Pennsylvania Press, 2003.

Powell, James M. *Anatomy of a Crusade, 1213–1221*. Philadelphia: University of Pennsylvania Press, 1990.

Queller, Donald E., and Thomas F. Madden. *The Fourth Crusade: The Conquest of Constantinople, 1201–1204*. 2nd ed. Philadelphia: University of Pennsylvania Press, 1997.

Richard, Jean. *The Crusades, c.1071–c.1291*. Cambridge: Cambridge University Press, 1999.

Riley-Smith, Jonathan. *The First Crusaders, 1095–1131*. Cambridge: Cambridge University Press, 1997.

Runciman, Steven. *A History of the Crusades*. 3 vols. New York: Harper and Row Publishers, 1964–1967.

Seward, Desmond. *The Monks of War: The Military Religious Orders*. London: Eyre Methuen, 1972.

Smail, R. C. *Crusading Warfare (1097–1193)*. Cambridge: Cambridge University Press, 1956.

Strayer, Joseph R. *The Albigensian Crusades*. Ann Arbor: The University of Michigan Press, 1971.

Strickland, Matthew. *War and Chivalry: The Conduct and Perception of War in England and Normandy, 1066–1217*. Cambridge: Cambridge University Press, 1996.

Urban, William H. *The Teutonic Knights: A Military History*. London: Greenhill Books, 2003.

Arms and Armor

Hoyland, Robert G., and Brian Gilmour, ed. *Medieval Islamic Swords and Swordmaking: Kindi's Treatise "On Swords and their Kinds" (Edition, Translation, and Commentary)*. Oxford: Gibb Memorial Trust, 2006.

Mann, James. "Arms and Armour." In *The Bayeux Tapestry: A Comprehensive Survey*, 2nd ed. Edited by F. Stenton, 56–69. London: Phaidon, 1957.

Nicolle, David C. *Arms and Armour of the Crusading Era, 1050–1350*. 2 vols. White Plains, NY: Kraus International Publications, 1988.

Rogers, R. *Latin Siege Warfare in the Twelfth Century*. Oxford: Clarendon Press, 1992.

THE LATE MIDDLE AGES

Military History

Allmand, Christopher. *Henry V*. Berkeley and Los Angeles: University of California Press, 1992.

Allmand, Christopher. *The Hundred Years War: England and France at War c. 1300–c. 1450*. Cambridge: Cambridge University Press, 1988.

Armstrong, Pete. *Bannockburn 1314: Robert Bruce's Great Victory*. London: Osprey, 2002.

Atiya, Aziz Suryal. *The Crusade of Nicopolis*. London: Methuen and Co., 1934.

Ayton, Andrew, and Philip Preston, eds. *The Battle of Crécy, 1346*. Woodbridge, UK: Boydell, 2005.

Babinger, Franz. *Mehmed the Conqueror and His Time*. Translated by Ralph Manheim. Edited by William C. Hickman. Princeton, NJ: Princeton University Press, 1978.

Barber, Richard. *Edward, Prince of Wales and Aquitaine: A Biography of the Black Prince*. 1978. Reprint, Woodbridge, UK: The Boydell Press, 1996.

Bartusis, Mark C. *The Late Byzantine Army: Arms and Society, 1204–1453*. Philadelphia: University of Pennsylvania Press, 1992.

Burne, Alfred H. *The Agincourt War: A Military History of the Latter Part of the Hundred Years War from 1369 to 1453*. London: Eyre and Spottiswoode, 1956.

Burne, Alfred H. *The Crecy War: A Military History of the Hundred Years War from 1337 to the Peace of Bretigny, 1360*. London: Eyre and Spottiswoode, 1955.

Contamine, Philippe. *Guerre, état et société à la fin du moyen âge: Études sur les armées des rois de France, 1337–1494*. Paris: Mouton, 1972.

Curry, Anne. *Agincourt: A New History*. Stroud, UK: Tempus Publishing, 2005.

DeVries, Kelly. *Infantry Warfare in the Early Fourteenth Century: Discipline, Tactics, and Technology*. Woodbridge, UK: The Boydell Press, 1996.

DeVries, Kelly. *Joan of Arc: A Military Leader*. Stroud, UK: Sutton Publishing, 1999.

Fowler, Kenneth. *The Age of the Plantagenet and the Valois: The Struggle for Supremacy 1328–1498*. New York: G. P. Putnam's Sons, 1967.

Goodman, Anthony. *The Wars of the Roses: Military Activity and English Society, 1452–97*. London: Routledge and Kegan Paul, 1981.

Goodman, Anthony. *The Wars of the Roses: The Soldiers' Experience.* Stroud: Tempus Publishing, 2005.

Green, David. *The Battle of Poitiers, 1356.* Stroud: Tempus Publishing, 2002.

Hewitt, H. J. *The Black Prince's Expedition of 1355–1357.* Manchester, UK: Manchester University Press, 1958. Reprint, London: Pen and Sword, 2004.

Hewitt, H. J. *The Organization of War Under Edward III, 1338–62.* New York: Manchester University Press, 1966. Reprint, London: Pen and Sword, 2004.

Housley, Norman. *The Later Crusades, 1274–1580: From Lyons to Alcazar.* Oxford: Oxford University Press, 1992.

Imber, Colin. *The Ottoman Empire, 1300–1650.* Houndmills, UK: Palgrave Macmillan, 2002.

Lucas, Henry Stephen. *The Low Countries and the Hundred Years' War, 1326–1347.* Ann Arbor: University of Michigan Press, 1929.

Mallett, Michael. *Mercenaries and their Masters: Warfare in Renaissance Italy.* Totowa, NJ: Rowman and Littlefield, 1974.

Nicholson, Ranald. *Edward III and the Scots: The Formative Years of a Military Career, 1327–1335.* Oxford: Oxford University Press, 1965.

Perroy, Edouard. *The Hundred Years War.* Translated by W. B. Wells. New York: Oxford University Press, 1951.

Rogers, Clifford J. *War Cruel and Sharp: English Strategy under Edward III, 1327–1360.* Woodbridge, UK: The Boydell Press, 2000.

Runciman, Steven. *The Fall of Constantinople, 1453.* Cambridge: Cambridge University Press, 1965.

Russell, P. E. *The English Intervention in Spain and Portugal in the Time of Edward III and Richard II.* Oxford: Clarendon Press, 1955.

Sumption, Jonathan. *The Hundred Years War: Trial by Battle.* Philadelphia: University of Pennsylvania Press, 1991.

Sumption, Jonathan. *The Hundred Years War: Trial by Fire.* London: Faber and Faber, 1999.

Vale, Malcolm. *War and Chivalry: Warfare and Aristocratic Culture in England, France and Burgundy at the End of the Middle Ages.* Athens: University of Georgia Press, 1981.

Arms and Armor

Gaier, Claude. *L'industrie et le commerce des armes dans les anciennes principautés belges du XIIIme à la fin du XVme siècle.* Paris: Société d'Edition "Les Belles Lettres," 1973.

Hall, Bert S. *Weapons and Warfare in Renaissance Europe: Gunpowder, Technology, and Tactics.* Baltimore, MD: The Johns Hopkins University Press, 1997.

Karcheski, Walter J., Jr., and Thom Richardson. *The Medieval Armour from Rhodes*. Leeds, UK: Royal Armouries and Higgins Armoury Museum, 2000.

Kelly, Jack. *Gunpowder: Alchemy, Bombards, and Pyrotechnics: The History of the Explosive that Changed the World*. New York: Basic Books, 2004.

Mann, James G. *A Further Account of the Armour Preserved in the Sanctuary of the Madonna della Grazie*. London: Society of Antiquaries of London, 1938.

Mann, James G. "The Sanctuary of the Madonna delle Grazie With Notes on the Evolution of Italian Armour During the Fifteenth Century." *Archaeologia* 80 (1930): 117–142.

Pfaffenbichler, Matthias. *Medieval Craftsmen: Armourers*. Toronto: University of Toronto Press, 1992.

Smith, Robert D., and Ruth Rhynas Brown. *Mons Meg and Her Sisters*. London: Trustees of the Royal Armouries, 1989.

Smith, Robert Douglas, and Kelly DeVries. *The Artillery of the Dukes of Burgundy, 1363–1477*. Woodbridge, UK: The Boydell Press, 2005.

Thordemann, Bengt. *Armour from the Battle of Wisby, 1361*. Stockholm: Almquist & Wiksells Boktryckeri, 1939. Reprint, Union City, CA: Chivalry Bookshelf, 2001.

Trapp, O., and M. Scalini. *The Armoury of the Castle of Churburg*. 2nd ed. Churburg: Magnus, 1995.

Waldman, John. *Hafted Weapons in Medieval and Renaissance Europe: The Evolution of European Staff Weapons between 1200 and 1650*. Leiden, The Netherlands: Brill, 2005.

Williams, Alan. *The Knight and the Blast Furnace: A History of the Metallurgy of Armour in the Middle Ages and the Early Modern Period*. Leiden, The Netherlands: Brill, 2003.

INDEX

ABOUT THE AUTHORS

KELLY DEVRIES is professor of history at Loyola College in Maryland and has most recently written *The Artillery of the Dukes of Burgundy, 1363–1477* (2006) with Robert Douglas Smith. His other books include: *Medieval Military Technology* (1992); *Infantry Warfare in the Early Fourteenth Century: Discipline, Tactics, and Technology* (1996); *The Norwegian Invasion of England in 1066* (1999); *Joan of Arc: A Military Leader* (1999); *A Cumulative Bibliography of Medieval Military History and Technology* (2002; update 2005); and *Guns and Men in Medieval Europe, 1200–1500: Studies in Military History and Technology* (2002). He also edited the English translation of J.F. Verbruggen's *De slag der guldensporen: Bijdrage tot de geschiedenis van Vlaanderens vrijheidsoorlog, 1297–1305*. In addition, he is the author of more than 50 articles on military history and the history of technology. He currently edits the *Journal of Medieval Military History* and is the Series Editor for the History of Warfare series of Brill Publishing.

ROBERT D. SMITH is an Independent Museum Consultant who formerly worked at the Royal Armouries Museum in Leeds, West Yorkshire, UK. His books include: *The Artillery of the Dukes of Burgundy, 1363–1477* (2006 with Kelly DeVries); *Bombards: Mons Meg and Her Sisters* (1989 with Ruth Rhynas Brown); *Heavy Metal: Europese harnassen in het vizier/Focus on European Armour* (2004); and *Boem!! 1000 jaar buskruit* (2006). He has also edited *British Naval Armaments* (1989) and *Make All Sure: The Conservation and Restoration of Arms and Armour* (2006). In addition he is the author of articles on conservation and the early history of artillery and gunpowder. He currently edits the *Journal of the Ordnance Society*.